God Hears Her

365 Devotions for Women by Women

Creative Journaling Edition

Our Daily Bread Publishing™

God Hears Her: 365 Devotions for Women by Women, Creative Journaling Edition

© 2017 by Discovery House
© 2021 Creative Journaling Edition by Our Daily Bread Publishing

All rights reserved.

Requests for permission to quote from this book should be directed to: Permissions Department, Our Daily Bread Publishing, PO Box 3566, Grand Rapids, MI 49501, or contact us by email at permissionsdept@odb.org.

Scripture quotations, unless otherwise indicated, are taken from the Holy Bible, New International Version®, NIV®. Copyright © 1973, 1978, 1984, 2011 by Biblica, Inc.™ Used by permission of Zondervan. All rights reserved worldwide. www.zondervan.com.

Scripture quotations marked ESV are taken from the ESV® Bible (The Holy Bible, English Standard Version®) copyright © 2001 by Crossway, a publishing ministry of Good News Publishers. Used by permission. All rights reserved.

Scripture quotations marked NASB are from the New American Standard Bible®, copyright © 1960, 1962, 1963, 1968, 1971, 1972, 1973, 1975, 1977, 1995 by The Lockman Foundation. Used by permission. (Lockman.org)

Scripture quotations marked NKJV are from the New King James Version®. Copyright © 1982 by Thomas Nelson. Used by permission. All rights reserved.

Scripture quotations marked NLT are taken from the Holy Bible, New Living Translation, copyright © 1996, 2004, 2015 by Tyndale House Foundation. Used by permission of Tyndale House Publishers, Inc., Carol Stream, Illinois 60188. All rights reserved.

Library of Congress Cataloging-in-Publication Data Available

ISBN: 978-1-64070-080-2

Printed in China
21 22 23 24 25 26 27 28 / 8 7 6 5 4 3 2 1

Foreword

*Because he turned his ear to me,
I will call on him as long as I live.*

Psalm 116:2

How do you know that God hears you when you call to Him? I mean, *really* hears you?

Over my lifetime, I can count on one hand the number of occasions when God specifically and personally revealed that He does, indeed, listen to my cries:

- my Hannah-like pleas for a child were answered, after nearly five years, through adoption;
- my late-night cries for a teenager missing curfew were answered when the child eventually arrived home;
- my prayers, with others', for a ministry's financial need were answered when a generous check arrived in the mail (and caused us to break out in praise);
- my begging howls that God would protect my husband from a health crisis and return me to his side from another continent were answered when I arrived to find him still alive.

In each moment, I sensed God coming near to reassure me that, yes, He is listening. And not just listening but also responding.

Despite these faith-bolstering memories, in much of my daily life, I can still feel unheard as I murmur and struggle and occasionally even whine. When God's silence descends, I turn beyond my own history to review how He has heard His people over generations.

Etched across the millennia are myriad instances of God's ear bending to listen:

- to Leah's and Rachel's prayers for a child (Genesis 30:17, 22);
- to Israel, groaning under slavery (Exodus 2:24);
- to Moses, interceding for his people on Mount Sinai (Deuteronomy 9:19);
- to Joshua, leading a battle at Gilgal (Joshua 10:14);
- to David, crying out for deliverance from Saul (2 Samuel 22:7).

And onward into the New Testament, where the Word, Jesus, walked this earth and listened in the flesh (JOHN 1:14). Today God's Spirit hears the groans of all of creation as we wait for our ultimate union with Him (ROMANS 8:26–27).

God hears.

In 1 John 5:14 we read, "If we ask anything according to his will, he hears us." The Greek word translated "hears," *akouo,* means to pay attention and to respond on the basis of having heard. Rather than suggesting a "formula" for ensuring God will grant our prayer requests, John urges us to pray in confidence because God's heart is for us. God hears in a way that is action oriented, and He wants to respond in love. *Akouo.* God hears.

The title and first entry of this book celebrate the fact that God hears her. Over and over in the Bible, God hears and responds to the needs of women, both named and unnamed. Jesus interacts with woman after woman, offering everlasting water to a disgraced woman at a well, restoring a demon-possessed son to his grief-stricken mother, receiving the spilled-out offering of Mary of Bethany, encouraging Mary Magdalene's broken heart in the first resurrection encounter.

As you read the words of each devotional in this volume—written by women just like you for women just like you—may you sense God bending His ear to your heart. God hears. God hears her. And because God hears and hears her, you can know that God hears you.

Elisa Morgan

January 1

GOD HEARS HER
1 SAMUEL 1:9-20

> Hannah was praying in her heart, and her lips were moving but her voice was not heard. Eli thought she was drunk.
>
> *1 Samuel 1:13*

One day I told my daughter I was going to read a grown-up book for a while, and then we would look at books together. When I started to read in silence, she looked at me and said, "Mommy, you aren't really reading." If I wasn't speaking, she assumed I wasn't processing words.

Like reading, prayer can be silent. The Old Testament character Hannah, who longed for a child, visited the temple and prayed "in her heart." Her lips were moving, but "her voice was not heard" (1 SAMUEL 1:13). She explained, "I was pouring out my soul to the Lord" (V. 15). God heard Hannah's silent prayer and gave her a son (V. 20).

Our all-knowing God searches our hearts and minds, and He hears every prayer—even silent ones. We can confidently pray—knowing He'll hear and answer (MATTHEW 6:8, 32). We can praise God, ask Him for help, and thank Him for blessings—even when no one else can hear us. If someone sees us talking to the Lord, he or she can say with confidence: "God hears her!"

Jennifer

The Lord is near to all who call on him.

PSALM 145:18

January 2

THE OLD AND THE NEW

GALATIANS 5:16–23

Therefore, if anyone is in Christ, the new creation has come: The old has gone, the new is here!

2 Corinthians 5:17

Typical January resolutions: lose weight, exercise more, stop chatting on the cell phone while driving.

We want to change things that we're unhappy about—even though most New Year's resolutions last no more than three weeks.

What if you were to ask God what He wants you to change, improve, or begin this year? He might prompt you to:

- Demonstrate more of the fruit of the Spirit in your life (GALATIANS 5:22–23).
- "Love your enemies and pray for those who persecute you" (MATTHEW 5:44).
- "Go into all the world and preach the gospel to all creation" (MARK 16:15).
- "Be content with what you have" (HEBREWS 13:5).

As believers and new creations, we can be free from old patterns and failures. As we ask God to help us live each day in the power of the Holy Spirit, He hears us, and He will help us shed the old and embrace the new (2 CORINTHIANS 5:17).

Cindy

January 3

NO APPETITE
NEHEMIAH 8:1–12

> Like newborn babies, crave pure spiritual milk, so that by it you may grow up in your salvation.
>
> *1 Peter 2:2*

When the people of Israel returned home after their seventy-year exile in faraway Babylon, their spiritual appetite was weak (NEHEMIAH 8:1-12). They had departed from God and His ways. To get the people back to spiritual health, Nehemiah organized a Bible seminar, and Ezra was the teacher.

Ezra read from the book of the law of Moses from morning until midday, feeding the people with the truth of God (NEHEMIAH 8:3). The people listened attentively. In fact, their appetite for God's Word was so stirred that the family leaders and the priests and Levites met with Ezra the following day to study the law in greater detail because they wanted to understand it (V. 13).

When we feel separated from God or spiritually weak, we too can find spiritual nourishment in God's Word. "Like newborn babes, crave pure spiritual milk, so that by it you may grow up in your salvation" (1 PETER 2:2). Ask the God who hears you to give you a renewed desire for relationship with Him. Then open your Bible and begin feeding your heart, soul, and mind with His Word.

Poh Fang

January 4

NOZOMI HOPE
2 CORINTHIANS 4:7–18

We have this treasure in jars of clay to show that this all-surpassing power is from God and not from us.
2 Corinthians 4:7

In 2011 a massive earthquake and tsunami took nearly 19,000 lives and destroyed 230,000 homes in northeastern Japan. In its aftermath, The Nozomi Project, named for the Japanese word for "hope," was created to provide sustainable income, community, and dignity—plus hope in a God who provides.

Nozomi women sift through the rubble to discover broken china shards that they turn into jewelry, which is sold around the world. This provides a livelihood for the women and shares symbols of their faith in Christ.

In New Testament times, people hid valuables in simple clay pots. Paul describes how the treasure of the gospel is contained in the human frailty of followers of Christ: jars of clay (2 CORINTHIANS 4:7). He suggests that the meager—and even broken—vessels of our lives can reveal God's power in contrast to our imperfections.

When God inhabits the imperfect and broken pieces in our lives, the healing hope of His power is often made visible. No, His repair work in our hearts doesn't hide our imperfections. But perhaps those etchings in our beings make His character more visible to others.

Elisa

January 5

TIME ALONE WITH GOD
MATTHEW 14:13-23

[Jesus] went up on a mountainside by himself to pray.

Matthew 14:23

Nearly a dozen little children were chattering and playing in the church room where I was helping. The room grew warm, so I propped the door open. One little guy saw this as his chance to escape, so he tiptoed out the door. Hot on his trail, I watched as he headed straight for his daddy's arms.

The little boy did what we need to do when life becomes overwhelming—he slipped away to be with his father. Jesus looked for opportunities to spend time with His heavenly Father in prayer. Some might say this was how He coped with the demands that depleted His human energy. In one instance, Jesus was headed to a solitary place when a crowd followed Him. Noticing their needs, Jesus miraculously healed and fed them. Then He "went up on a mountainside by himself to pray" (MATTHEW 14:23).

Jesus repeatedly helped hundreds of people, yet He didn't allow himself to become haggard and hurried. He nurtured His connection with God through prayer. How is it with you? Will you take time with God to experience His strength and fulfillment?

Jennifer

January 6

DRIVEN BY GOD
1 KINGS 8:54–63

"May he turn our hearts to him, to walk in obedience to him."

1 Kings 8:58

Recently I received an email inviting me to join a community of "driven people." When I looked up the word *driven*, I learned that a driven person is highly motivated to succeed and works hard to achieve her goals.

Is it good to be a driven person? Here's a fail-proof test: "Do it all for the glory of God" (1 CORINTHIANS 10:31). Think about what happened after Noah's flood. A group of people constructed a tower to "make a name" for themselves (GENESIS 11:4). They wanted to be famous and avoid being scattered all over the world. They were driven by the wrong motivation.

In contrast, as King Solomon dedicated the ark of the covenant and the new temple, he said, "I have built the temple for the Name of the LORD" (1 KINGS 8:20). Then he prayed, "May he turn our hearts to him" (V. 58). He was driven by God.

May our "hearts be fully committed to the LORD our God, to live by his decrees and obey his commands" (V. 61). Then we'll be the right kind of driven women.

Keila

January 7

THE KING COULD
MATTHEW 19:16–26

Jesus looked at them and said, "With man this is impossible, but with God all things are possible."
Matthew 19:26

As a child, I had a favorite book of nursery rhymes. Mine told me about Humpty Dumpty, a big, egg-shaped creature with a painted face and skinny arms and legs, perched happily on a wall. Then he fell and broke into countless pieces. I felt hopeless when I read that they "couldn't put Humpty Dumpty together again."

Since then, I've come to know Christ as my Savior and Lord. I've experienced His powerful and tender hands restoring the shattered pieces of my life and the lives of others. I've had the joy of seeing many seemingly hopeless drug addicts made new in Christ. So I've added a line to the Humpty Dumpty nursery rhyme: "What all the king's horses and all the king's men couldn't do, the King could!"

Are you or someone dear to you feeling broken today? Remember, no one is hopeless and beyond God's saving help. Jesus said, "With God all things are possible" (MATTHEW 19:26).

When the broken pieces of life seem beyond hope of repair, don't give up. We have a King who can put people back together again.

Joanie

January 8

PASSION UNLEASHED
ACTS 9:1–9

I press on to take hold of that for which Christ Jesus took hold of me.
Philippians 3:12

Emmett J. Scanlan, the actor who played Saul in the TV series *A.D. The Bible Continues*, portrayed Saul's efforts to eliminate believers in Jesus in a way that made me wince. I had trouble reconciling the fact that this man would become the beloved apostle Paul!

However, when Saul encountered Jesus while heading to Damascus, everything changed. And the minute his sight was restored and his calling was confirmed, the newly renamed Paul passionately dove into his work again. Only this time he was *for* Jesus and not against Him (ACTS 9:21).

Paul was a man of conviction and unbridled passion. Today people the world over read his letters for guidance and instruction in the Christian faith. His passion continues to resound through the ages (PHILIPPIANS 3:12).

What would the world look like if we lived for God with passion, conviction, and zeal? The world awaits that answer: "Creation waits in eager expectation for the children of God to be revealed" (ROMANS 8:19).

As with Paul, may passion for God flow from us as creation rejoices in the revelation of God's amazing handiwork!

Remi

January 9

I AM NOT FORGOTTEN
PSALM 13

> We wait in hope for the Lord; he is our help and our shield.
> **Psalm 33:20**

Waiting is hard at any time; but when time passes and our prayers seem to go unanswered, it's easy to feel that God has forgotten us. Worries loom large, and during the night the dark hours seem endless.

The psalmist grew weary as he waited (PSALM 13:1). He felt abandoned—as if his enemies were gaining the upper hand (v. 2). When we're waiting for God to resolve a difficult situation or to answer often-repeated prayers, it's easy to get discouraged.

Satan whispers that God has forgotten us and that things will never change. We may be tempted to give in to despair. Why bother to read the Bible, pray, or worship with fellow believers in Christ? But we need those spiritual lifelines the most when we're waiting. They help to hold us steady in the flow of God's love and to become sensitive to His Spirit.

The psalmist had a remedy. He focused on what he knew of God's love, reminding himself of past blessings and praising God. We can do the same, for we are never forgotten.

Marion

January 10

FAITH MIXED WITH DOUBT

MARK 9:14–27

Why, my soul, are you downcast? Why so disturbed within me? Put your hope in God, for I will yet praise him, my Savior and my God.

Psalm 42:11

When my close friend Sharon was killed in a car accident, my heart broke. I'm ashamed to admit it, but when life's circumstances hurt so much, my faith is often mixed with doubt. When Sharon died, I cried out to God with these questions:

Lord, I sure don't understand you. Why did you allow this death? "[The Lord's] understanding no one can fathom" (ISAIAH 40:28). "'My thoughts are not your thoughts, neither are your ways my ways,' declares the Lord" (ISAIAH 55:8).

Lord, *have you turned your back on the world?* "God is seated on his holy throne" (PSALM 47:8) and "rules forever by his power" (PSALM 66:7).

Lord, do you care about the pain? Have you forgotten to be good? I am "forgiving and good, abounding in love to all who call to [me]" (PSALM 86:5).

Yes, Lord, you have been good to me in countless ways, including listening to my doubts and questions about you.

The answers God gives us in His Word may not take away our sadness, but we can always rest in the truth that He is wise, sovereign, and good.

Anne

January 11

SOMEONE TO TRUST
JOHN 13:33–35

Many claim to have unfailing love, but a faithful person who can find?
Proverbs 20:6

"I just can't trust anyone," my friend said through tears. "Every time I do, they hurt me." Her story angered me. An ex-boyfriend she thought she could trust had spread rumors about her when they broke up. As she struggled to trust again after a pain-filled childhood, this betrayal proved it to her: people can't be trusted.

Her story was painfully familiar, reminding me of moments of unexpected betrayal in my own life. In fact, Scripture is candid about human nature. In Proverbs 20:6, the author voices the same lament as my friend.

What I could say to her is that betrayal is only part of the story. Although wounds from others are real, Jesus has made genuine love possible. In John 13:35, Jesus told His disciples that others would know they were His followers because of their love. Yes, people may hurt us, but because of Jesus there will also always be those who share His love unconditionally. Resting in Christ's unfailing love, may we find healing, community, and the courage to love others as He did.

Monica

January 12

FULL-CIRCLE COMPASSION
2 CORINTHIANS 1:3–7

> [God] comforts us in all our troubles, so that we can comfort those in any trouble with the comfort we ourselves receive from God.
>
> *2 Corinthians 1:4*

Following a tumultuous season in her life, Bethany Haley Williams battled shame and brokenness. The journey was difficult, but through Jesus she experienced healing that transformed her life.

Prompted by the grace and mercy she received, Bethany formed Exile International, a nonprofit that implements art/expressive therapy and long-term, rehabilitative care to restore and empower war-affected children in Africa. Of her efforts, Bethany said, "When your greatest heartache becomes your greatest ministry, grace comes full circle."

Bethany now devotes her life to living out the words of 2 Corinthians 1:3–4. Having received God's comfort, she is now able to give others "the same comfort God has given [her]" (V. 4 NLT).

God knows about our suffering and misfortunes, and He is with us in the pain. He is merciful, loving, and attentive to our needs; and He can use whatever we experience to lift up and help others who are in need.

No matter what we've done or what we're facing, God is there to shower us with His compassion and love—gifts we can then share with others.

Roxanne

January 13

THE NIGHT NO ONE CAME

MATTHEW 6:1-7

"Be careful not to practice your righteousness in front of others to be seen by them. If you do, you will have no reward from your Father in heaven."

Matthew 6:1

According to legend, one winter night composer Johann Sebastian Bach was scheduled to debut a new composition. He arrived at the church expecting it to be full. Instead, no one had come. Without missing a beat, Bach told his musicians that they would still perform as planned. They took their places, Bach raised his baton, and soon the empty church was filled with magnificent music.

This story made me do some soul-searching. Would I write if God were my only audience? How would my writing be different?

When I write devotionals; I try to keep readers in mind because I want to say something they will want to read and that will help them on their spiritual journey.

I doubt that the "devotional writer" David, whose psalms we turn to for comfort and encouragement, had "readers" in mind. The only audience he had in mind was God.

Whether our "deeds," mentioned in Matthew 6:1 (NKJV), are works of art or acts of service, they're really between God and us. He alone is our audience.

Julie

January 14

RINGS AND GRACE
HEBREWS 8:6–13

"I will remember their sins no more."

Hebrews 8:12 (ESV)

When I look at my hands, I'm reminded that I lost my wedding and engagement rings. I was multitasking as I packed for a trip, and I still have no idea where they ended up.

I dreaded telling my husband about my careless mistake—worried how the news would affect him. But he responded with great compassion and care for me. While there are times when I still want to earn his grace, he doesn't hold this episode against me.

So many times we think of our sins and feel we must do something to earn God's forgiveness. But God has said it is by grace, not by works, that we are saved (EPHESIANS 2:8–9). We have a God who forgives and no longer calls to mind the wrongs we have done.

We may still feel sad about our past, but we need to trust God's promise. The grace and forgiveness that come through faith in Jesus Christ are real. Praise God, when God forgives, He forgets.

Keila

January 15

MAKING PREPARATIONS

JOHN 14:1–6

"If I go and prepare a place for you, I will come back and take you to be with me that you also may be where I am."

John 14:3

As we viewed my father-in-law's body at the funeral home, one of his sons took his dad's hammer and tucked it alongside his folded hands. Years later, when my mother-in-law died, one of the children slipped a set of knitting needles under her fingers. Those sweet gestures brought comfort to us as we remembered how often they had used those tools during their lives.

Of course, we knew they wouldn't actually need those items in eternity. You can't take it with you (PSALM 49:16–17; 1 TIMOTHY 6:7)!

But some preparation for eternity had been necessary for them. That occurred when they trusted Jesus as their Savior. Planning for the life to come can't begin at death. Each of us must prepare our heart by accepting the gift of salvation made possible by Jesus's sacrifice on the cross.

God has made preparations as well: "If I go and prepare a place for you, I will come back and take you to be with me" (JOHN 14:3). He has promised to prepare a place for us to spend eternity with Him. Have you made your preparations for Him?

Cindy

January 16

DESTROYING THE DIVIDES

JOSHUA 7:1-12

"I will not be with you anymore unless you destroy whatever among you is devoted to destruction."

Joshua 7:12

A writing deadline loomed over me while a recent argument with my husband swirled through my mind. I stared at the blinking cursor, fingertips resting on the keyboard. *He was wrong too, Lord.*

When the computer screen went black, my reflection scowled. My unacknowledged wrongs were doing more than hindering my work. They were straining my relationship with my husband and my God. I grabbed my cell phone, swallowed my pride, and asked for forgiveness. Savoring the peace of reconciliation when my spouse apologized as well, I thanked God and finished my article on time.

The Israelites experienced the pain of personal sin and the joy of restoration. Joshua warned God's people not to enrich themselves in the battle for Jericho (JOSHUA 6:18), but Achan disobeyed (7:1). Only after his sin was exposed and dealt with (VV. 4-12) did the nation enjoy reconciliation with God.

Like Achan, we don't always consider how our sin turns our hearts from God and impacts others. Seeking forgiveness provides the foundation for healthy relationships with God and others. That's how we can enjoy His presence—together.

Xochitl

January 17

TAKING NOTICE
JOB 40:1-14

"Where were you when I laid the earth's foundation? Tell me, if you understand."

Job 38:4

When I clean my house for a special event, I become discouraged because I think guests won't notice what I clean—only what I don't clean. This brings to mind a larger philosophical and spiritual question: Why do humans more quickly see what's wrong than what's right?

But then I realize I am the same way with God. I tend to focus on what He hasn't done rather than on what He has, on what I don't have rather than on what I have, on the situations that He has not yet resolved rather than on the many He has.

The book of Job reminds me that the Lord doesn't like this situation any more than I do. After years of experiencing prosperity, Job suffered a series of disasters. Suddenly those became the focus of his life and conversations. Finally, God intervened and reminded Job of His sovereignty and of everything Job didn't know and hadn't seen (JOB 38-40).

Whenever we start focusing on the negative, let's stop, consider the life of Job, and notice all the wonders God has done and continues to do.

Julie

January 18

LOVING BEYOND BORDERS
3 JOHN 1-11

Dear friend, you are faithful in what you are doing for the brothers and sisters, even though they are strangers to you.

3 John 1:5

I first experienced the beauty of the global body of Christ when I traveled from South Africa to Malaysia as a teacher. In that country, with its varying religions and cultural beliefs, I found a spiritual home away from home. From the moment I stepped into the little church down the road, I was warmly welcomed and treated like family. Thousands of kilometers from where I grew up, I met people with the same spirit and the same love for Jesus.

God places great value on our favorable treatment of believers from outside our local church, and that brings us to Gaius in 3 John. John commended him for his faithfulness to the truth of the gospel as expressed by his generous care and welcome of traveling teachers (vv. 3–6) who went from city to city teaching the gospel (vv. 7–8).

There's nothing quite like traveling to a different city or country and meeting another believer in Jesus. God longs for us to simply focus on Him as we welcome each other with joy. *That's loving beyond borders!*

Ruth

January 19

PRAYER CIRCLES
LUKE 18:9-14

> "I tell you that this man, rather than the other, went home justified before God. For all those who exalt themselves will be humbled, and those who humble themselves will be exalted."
>
> Luke 18:14

Around the circle the sixth-grade girls went, taking turns praying for each other. "Father in heaven," Anna prayed, "please help Tonya not to be so boy crazy." Tonya added with a giggle, "And help Anna to stop acting so horrible in school." Then Talia prayed, "Lord, help Tonya to listen to her mother instead of always talking back."

Although the requests were real, the girls seemed to enjoy teasing their friends by pointing out their flaws in prayer. Their group leader reminded them about the seriousness of talking to almighty God and the importance of evaluating their own hearts.

If we use prayer to point out the faults of others while ignoring our own, we're like the Pharisee in Jesus's parable. He prayed, "God, I thank you that I am not like other people—robbers, evildoers, adulterers" (LUKE 18:11). Instead, we're to be like the man who asked God to be merciful to him, "a sinner" (V. 13).

The kind of prayer God desires from us flows out of a humble evaluation of our own sinful hearts.

Anne

Handwritten notes:

Missed a massage and prayers to God gave me relief from the anger. We all make mistakes. God had control. Very comforting to humble by with the help of God. Praise God from my heart.

January 20

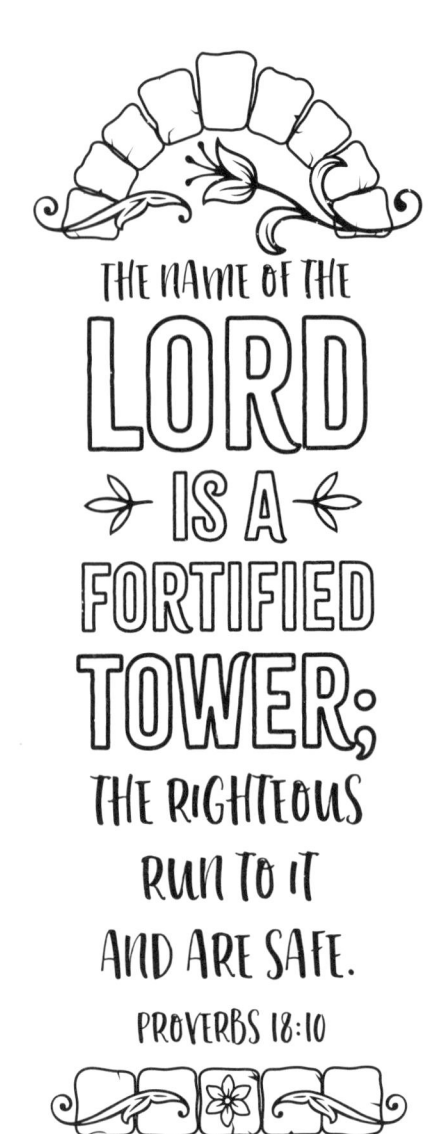

YOUR SAFE PLACE
PROVERBS 18:10-11

The name of the LORD is a fortified tower; the righteous run to it and are safe.
Proverbs 18:10

My daughter and I were arranging to attend an extended family gathering, and I offered to drive. "Okay. But I feel safer in my car. Can you drive it?" she asked. I assumed she preferred her more spacious vehicle to my compact one, so I responded, "Is my car too cramped?" "No, it's just that my car is my safe place. Somehow I feel protected there."

Her comment challenged me to think about my own personal "safe place." Immediately I thought of Proverbs 18:10, "The name of the LORD is a fortified tower; the righteous run to it and are safe." In Old Testament times, the walls and watchtower of a city provided warning of danger from without and shielding for its citizens within. The writer's point is that God's name provides true protection for His people.

What is your "safe place"? Wherever we seek safety, it is God's presence with us in that place that provides the strength and protection we really need.

Elisa

January 21

REAL FAITH
HEBREWS 11:6, 24–29

It is impossible to please God without faith. Anyone who wants to come to him must believe that God exists and that he rewards those who sincerely seek him.

Hebrews 11:6 (NLT)

I attended a boarding school in Nigeria where older students ruled over all of us younger students. Once, I misplaced a bowl belonging to a rather cranky older student. I received an ultimatum to find and return the bowl by the next morning, so I crawled into bed full of dread. I asked God for help before dropping into a troubled sleep. Imagine my awe the next day when the bowl mysteriously showed up in the student's drawer!

The Israelites experienced far greater awe when God parted the Red Sea for them to walk through before He defeated Pharaoh's army with the same waters (EXODUS 14:15–28; HEBREWS 11:29). Yet in a short while they were complaining about bitter water (EXODUS 15:24), and later they worshiped a golden calf instead of God (EXODUS 32:4).

True faith can be enhanced by mountaintop experiences. But the faith that pleases God is based on things that aren't visible (HEBREWS 11:1). Real faith helps us trust God no matter what.

Remi

January 22

A MYSTERIOUS FRAGRANCE
2 CORINTHIANS 2:12–3:6

For we are to God the pleasing aroma of Christ among those who are being saved and those who are perishing.
2 Corinthians 2:15

Most of us can think of someone—perhaps a relative or a friend—who is known for a particular perfume she wears. Even without seeing her, we know when she's nearby. Wordlessly, her fragrance welcomes us into her company.

Every Christian should also be known for wearing a particular perfume—the fragrance of Christ. But it can't be bought at a cosmetic counter. It can't even be bottled and sold by the church. This mysterious perfume rises only out of our intimate relationship with Christ, and it wafts a subtle yet noticeable influence toward others.

Someone said about a Christian in his small town, "That woman never crosses my pathway without my being better for it!" Most likely, this admired believer had given a verbal witness at some point. But without the aroma of Christ, her witness would not have been effective.

The apostle Paul asked, "Who is equal to such a task" as exuding an aroma that brings life? (2 CORINTHIANS 2:16). The answer? Our fragrance, our entire sufficiency, is from Christ alone. What fragrance will you be wearing today?

Joanie

January 23

CLEAN UP IN AISLE 9

EPHESIANS 4:11–32

> From him the whole body, joined and held together by every supporting ligament, grows and builds itself up in love, as each part does its work.
>
> *Ephesians 4:16*

My heart heavy, I was tempted to interrupt their conversation. Though I hadn't heard the entirety of their acidic discussion, I caught enough to know that the four shoppers were deeply dissatisfied with individuals at their local church. I didn't know them, but I grieved over this verbal ripping apart of the body of Christ in a public store aisle.

To verbally destroy one who has been created in God's image is not only inconsistent with the character of Christ, but it grieves the Holy Spirit as well (EPHESIANS 4:30). The words we speak about others are a direct window into our hearts (VV. 15, 29; LUKE 6:45).

The defining mark of Jesus's transformation in us is the way we address our differences within the body. Paul tells us to "get rid of all bitterness, rage and anger" (EPHESIANS 4:31). We're to be a distinctive people who value and respect others as we are "speaking the truth in love" (V. 15). And as we submit to the Holy Spirit, Christ-honoring words will flow from our hearts and mouths.

Regina

January 24

HOW LONG, GOD?
HABAKKUK 1:1-4

> How long, Lord, must I call for help, but you do not listen? Or cry out to you, "Violence!" but you do not save?
>
> *Habakkuk 1:2*

Not long ago I was certain God was moving my husband and me in a specific direction. We were encouraged and excited, for what we never thought would happen was coming together right before our very eyes. As we bathed the process in prayer, God seemed to be honoring our requests. Until the eleventh hour. That's when the door was slammed shut in our faces. We were shocked.

Why would you do this to us, God? Why lead us on? We felt like the prophet Habakkuk who complained to the Lord, "How long, Lord, must I call for help, but you do not listen?" (HABAKKUK 1:2). Like Habakkuk's two "complaints" found in chapters 1 and 2, it was good for us to be honest with God. He knew our questions and complaints.

Habakkuk, despite his questions, could state, "Yet I will rejoice in the Lord. . . . The Sovereign Lord is my strength" (HABAKKUK 3:18-19). God is still good, even when circumstances are not.

Marlena

January 25

STRANGERS AND FOREIGNERS

HEBREWS 11:8-16

He was looking forward to the city with foundations, whose architect and builder is God.

Hebrews 11:10

I parked my bicycle, fingering my map of Cambridge for reassurance. Directions not being my strength, I knew I could easily get lost in this maze of roads bursting with historic buildings.

Life should have felt idyllic, for I had just married my Englishman and moved to the United Kingdom. But I felt adrift. I didn't yet know what my role was as an American in Britain, and I realized that blending two stubborn people into one shared life was harder than I had anticipated.

I related to Abraham, who left everything to obey God and live as a stranger in a new land (GENESIS 12:1). He pressed through the cultural challenges while keeping faith in God (HEBREWS 11:9). Abraham lived by faith, longing for things promised, hoping and waiting for his heavenly home.

As Christ-followers we're all foreigners and strangers on this earth. By faith we press forward, knowing that God will lead and guide us, and by faith we believe He will never leave nor abandon us. By faith we long for home.

Amy

January 26

WHO'S AT THE CENTER?

PSALM 33:6–19

The plans of the Lord stand firm forever, the purposes of his heart through all generations.

Psalm 33:11

Recently, I had what for me was a "Copernican moment": I am not at the center of the universe. The world doesn't revolve around me. It doesn't move at my pace, in my terms, nor even in accord with my preferences.

Although we might wish it to be otherwise, life is not all about us. Everything revolves around the Lord. In Psalm 33, we read that all nature revolves around Him and His control (vv. 6–9). He assigned the sea its boundaries and locked the ocean in vast reservoirs. Everything in nature operates in accordance with the laws He has set.

Likewise, the lives of all humanity revolve around the Lord (vv. 13–19). God sees the whole human race. He made our hearts, and He understands everything we do. And He has the power to intervene in our lives and deliver us from situations spinning out of control.

Our life is created to be centered on God, not self. How thankful we can be to serve such a powerful God, who has every aspect of our lives under His control.

Poh Fang

January 27

FOLLOW THE INSTRUCTIONS

PSALM 119:129-136

> The unfolding of your words gives light;
> it gives understanding to the simple.
>
> *Psalm 119:130*

After a woman sued a fast-food restaurant for being burned by coffee, companies started changing their manuals and warning labels. Check out these instructions:

- On a frozen dinner: DEFROST BEFORE EATING
- On an iron: CAUTION! DO NOT IRON CLOTHES ON BODY
- On a peanut butter jar: MAY CONTAIN PEANUTS

If some people need these obvious guidelines on household items, think about how much more we need God's direction for life. Psalm 119 tells of the importance of His instruction manual—the Bible. On the pages of Scripture, we find what God wants us to believe, to be, and to do.

"Believe in the Lord Jesus, and you will be saved" (ACTS 16:31).

"Be kind and compassionate to one another, forgiving each other" (EPHESIANS 4:32).

Ask the Lord to teach you His statutes and to direct your steps according to His Word (PSALM 119:133, 135). Then read it often and follow the instructions.

Anne

January 28

MEET SHREK
EZEKIEL 34:11–16

"For this is what the Sovereign Lord says: I myself will search for my sheep and look after them."

Ezekiel 34:11

Shrek was a renegade sheep. For six years he was missing from his New Zealand flock. The person who found him in a cave on a mountain didn't recognize him as a sheep. "He looked like some biblical creature," he said. In a way, he was. Shrek was a picture of what happens to sheep that become separated from their shepherd.

Shrek had to be carried down the mountain because his fleece was so heavy (sixty pounds) he couldn't walk down on his own. To remove his fleece, the shearer had to turn Shrek upside down so he would remain still and not be harmed.

Shrek's story illustrates the metaphor Jesus used when He called himself the Good Shepherd (JOHN 10:11), and when God referred to His people as His flock (EZEKIEL 34:31). Like Shrek, we don't make good choices when we're on our own, and we become weighed down with consequences (EZEKIEL 33:10). To relieve us of the weight, we may have to be on our backs for a time. If so, it is good to remain still and trust the Good Shepherd to do His work.

Julie

January 29

LEAVING IT BEHIND
JOHN 4:9-14, 27-29

> Then, leaving her water jar, the woman went back to the town and said to the people, "Come, see a man who told me everything I ever did. Could this be the Messiah?"
>
> *John 4:28-29*

In the year or so after our teenage son got his driver's license and started carrying a wallet, we got several calls from people who had found it. We cautioned him to be more careful and not leave it behind.

Leaving things behind, though, is not always a bad thing. In John 4, we read about a woman who had come to draw water at a well. But after she encountered Jesus, her intent suddenly changed. Leaving her water jar behind, she hurried back to tell others what Jesus had said to her (vv. 28–29). Even her physical need for water faded in comparison to telling others about the Man she had just met.

Peter and Andrew did something that was similar when Jesus called them. They left their fishing nets (which was the way they earned their living) to follow Jesus (MATTHEW 4:18–20).

Our new life of following Jesus Christ may mean that we have to leave things behind, including those that don't bring lasting satisfaction. What we once craved cannot compare with the life and "living water" Jesus offers.

Cindy

January 30

AN ALTERNATIVE TO ANGER

PROVERBS 20:1–5

It is to one's honor to avoid strife.
Proverbs 20:3

One morning in Perth, Australia, Fionn Mulholland discovered his car was missing. He realized he had mistakenly parked in a restricted zone, and his car had been towed. Mulholland was frustrated—especially about the $600 fine he faced—but he decided not to be angry. Instead of venting his feelings, Mulholland wrote a humorous poem about the situation and read it to the worker at the tow yard. The worker liked the poem, and a possibly ugly confrontation never took place.

The book of Proverbs teaches, "It is to one's honor to avoid strife" (20:3). Strife is the friction that either simmers under the surface or explodes in the open between people who disagree about something.

God has given us the resources to live peacefully with others. His Word assures us it's possible to feel anger without letting it boil over (EPHESIANS 4:26). His Spirit enables us to override the sparks of fury that prompt us to strike out at people who upset us. And God has given us His example to follow when we feel provoked (1 PETER 2:23). There are alternatives to unnecessary anger.

Jennifer

Handwritten note:

Something I've been working on
accepting what I cannot change
No negativity
Only counting my blessing
God help me.

January 31

TASTE FOR YOURSELF
PSALM 34:1-8

> Taste and see that the Lord is good; blessed is the one who takes refuge in him.
>
> *Psalm 34:8*

A friend posted a Crock-Pot recipe on her Facebook page. The meal looked good, so I downloaded the recipe—intending to use it one day. Soon another friend was looking for similar meals, so I emailed her the recipe. She forwarded it to several friends, who passed it on as well.

Later I learned that the recipe had been forwarded far and wide though no one—not even the friend who posted it *originally*—had actually made the dish. We recommended it without having tasted it.

On occasion, we do something similar in matters of faith. While our motives to build "others up according to their needs" (EPHESIANS 4:29) are good and biblical, it's often easier to tell others' stories about trusting God than to exercise faith in Him ourselves.

God doesn't want me just to *talk* about Him; He wants me to *experience* Him.

Today may we taste for ourselves and see that God is good!

Roxanne

February 1

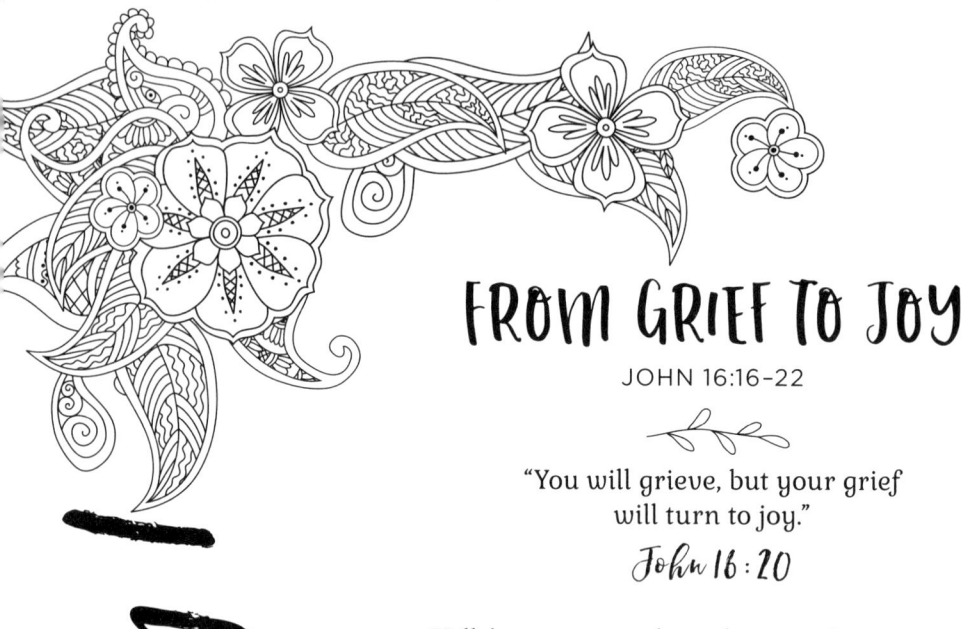

FROM GRIEF TO JOY

JOHN 16:16–22

"You will grieve, but your grief will turn to joy."
John 16:20

Kelly's pregnancy brought complications, and doctors were concerned. During her long labor, they decided to whisk her away for a Caesarean section. But despite the ordeal, Kelly quickly forgot her pain when she held her newborn son. Joy had replaced anguish.

Scripture affirms this truth: "A woman giving birth to a child has pain because her time has come; but when her baby is born she forgets the anguish because of her joy" (JOHN 16:21). Jesus used this illustration with His disciples to emphasize that though they would grieve His soon departure, that grief would turn to joy when they saw Him again (VV. 20–22).

Jesus was referring to His death and resurrection—and what followed. When Jesus ascended into heaven, He did not leave His friends grief-stricken. He sent the Holy Spirit, who would fill them with joy (JOHN 16:7–15; ACTS 13:52).

When someday we see Jesus face-to-face, the anguish we experience on this earth will be forgotten. But until then, the Lord has not left us without joy—He has given us His Spirit (ROMANS 15:13; 1 PETER 1:8–9).

Alyson

Your grief will turn to JOY

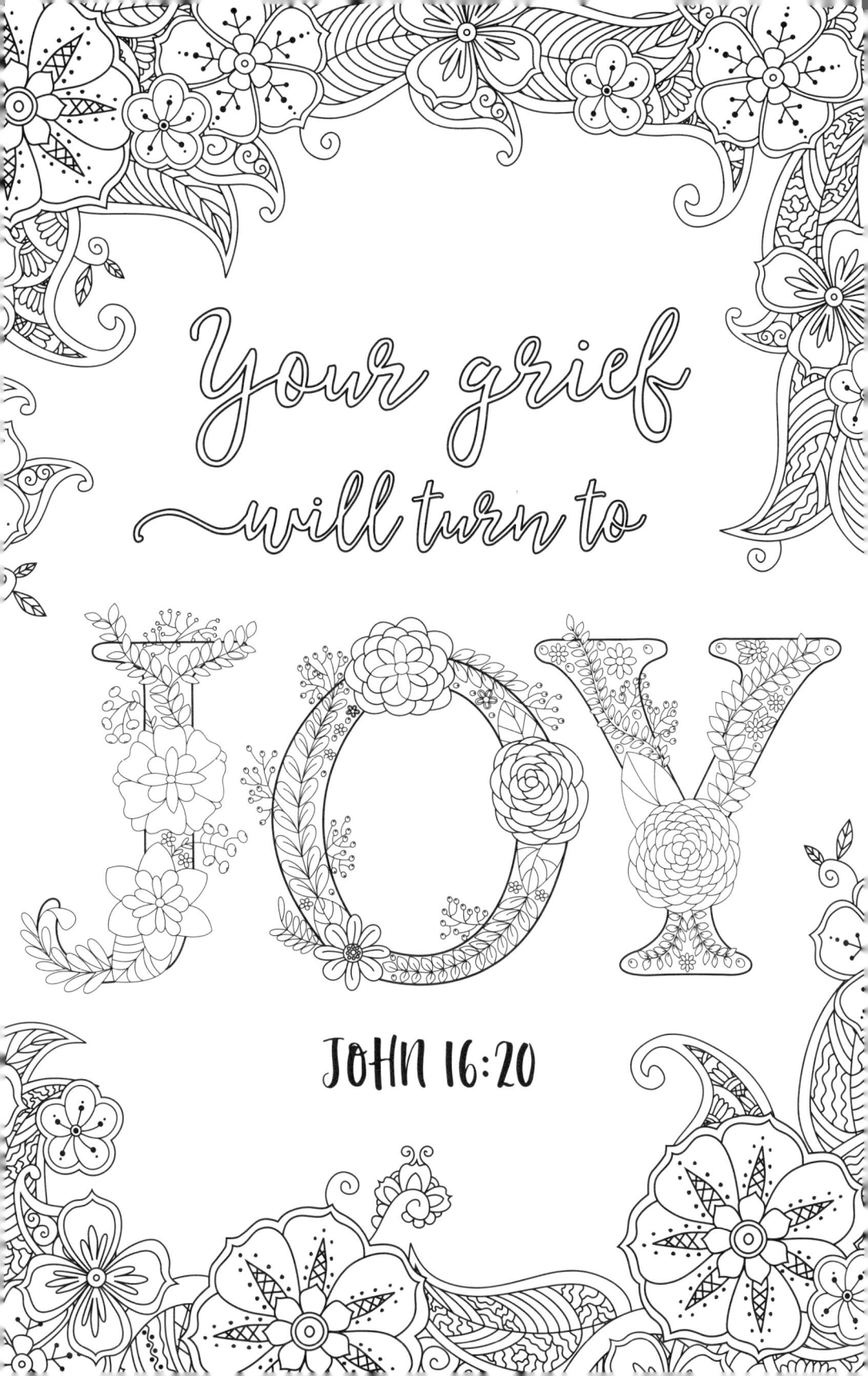

JOHN 16:20

February 2

LIVING IN TENTS

GENESIS 12:4-9

From there he went on toward the hills east of Bethel and pitched his tent.

Genesis 12:8

Growing up in Minnesota, I loved to go camping to enjoy the wonders of God's creation. But sleeping in a flimsy tent wasn't my favorite part of the experience—especially when a rainy night and a leaky tent resulted in a soggy sleeping bag.

I marvel to think that one of the heroes of our faith spent a hundred years in tents. When he was seventy-five years old, Abraham heard God's call to leave his country so the Lord could make him into a new nation (GENESIS 12:1-2). Abraham trusted God, obeyed Him, and lived the rest of his life—until he died at 175 (GENESIS 25:7)—in tents.

As we love and serve this world and the people in it, we may long for a deeper experience of home, of being rooted here on earth. Like Abraham, we can look with faith for the city to come, whose "architect and builder is God" (HEBREWS 11:10). And like Abraham, we can find hope that God is working to renew His creation, preparing a "better country—a heavenly one" to come (V. 16).

Amy

February 3

FOREVER FLOWERS

ISAIAH 40:1–8

The grass withers and the flowers fall, but the word of our God endures forever.

Isaiah 40:8

One day when he was little, my son Xavier gave me a beautiful bouquet of artificial flowers. He grinned as he arranged the silk white calla lily, yellow sunflower, and purple hydrangea in a glass vase. "Look, Mommy," he said. "They'll last forever. That's how much I love you."

Since then my boy has grown into a young man. Those silk petals have frayed. The colors have faded. Still, the Forever Flowers remind me of his adoration. And there is something else it brings to mind—one thing that truly stands forever—the limitless and lasting love of God, as revealed in His infallible and enduring Word (ISAIAH 40:8).

As the Israelites faced continual trials, Isaiah comforted them with confidence in God's enduring words. They trusted the prophet because his focus remained on God rather than their circumstances.

In a world filled with uncertainties and affliction, our feelings are ever shifting and as limited as our mortality (vv. 6–7). Still, we can trust God's unchanging love and character as revealed through His constant and eternally true Word.

Xochitl

February 4

THE ULTIMATE GOOD

PHILIPPIANS 3:1–11

I consider everything a loss because of the surpassing worth of knowing Christ Jesus my Lord.

Philippians 3:8

As I was growing up in Jamaica, my parents raised my sister and me to be "good people." In our home, good meant obeying our parents, telling the truth, being successful in school and work, and going to church—at least on Easter and Christmas. I imagine this definition of being a good person is familiar to many people, regardless of culture. In fact, the apostle Paul, in Philippians 3, used his culture's definition of being good to make a greater point.

Paul, devout first-century Jew, followed the letter of the moral law in his culture. He was the real deal in terms of being good according to Jewish custom. But Paul told his readers (and us) that there is something more than being good. He knew that being good was not the same as pleasing God.

Pleasing God, Paul writes, involves knowing Jesus (vv. 7–8). Paul considered his own goodness as "garbage" when compared to the "worth of knowing Christ Jesus." We are truly good—we please God—when our hope and faith are in Christ alone, not in our goodness.

Karen

February 5

SWEET COMPANY
JOHN 14:15–26

"The Spirit of truth ... lives with you and will be in you."

John 14:17

The elderly woman in the nursing home didn't speak to anyone or request anything. It seemed she merely existed, rocking in her creaky old chair. She didn't have many visitors, so one young nurse would often go into her room on her breaks. She didn't try to talk to the woman; she simply pulled up another chair and rocked with her. After several months, the elderly woman said to her, "Thank you for rocking with me." She was grateful for the companionship.

Before He went back to heaven, Jesus promised to send a constant companion to His disciples. He told them He would not leave them alone but would send the Holy Spirit (JOHN 14:17). That promise is still true for believers in Jesus today. Jesus said that the triune God makes His "home" in us (V. 23).

The Lord is our close and faithful companion throughout our entire life. He will guide us in our deepest struggles, forgive our sin, hear each silent prayer, and shoulder the burdens we cannot bear.

We can enjoy His sweet company today.

Anne

February 6

LISTENING TO GOD
GENESIS 3:8–17

The Lord God called . . . "Where are you?"
Genesis 3:9

My young son loves to hear my voice, except when I call his name loudly and sternly, followed by the question, "Where are you?" When I do that, I am usually calling for him because he has been into some mischief and is trying to hide from me.

Adam and Eve were used to hearing God's voice in the garden of Eden. However, after they disobeyed Him by eating the forbidden fruit, they hid from Him when they heard Him calling, "Where are you?" (GENESIS 3:9). They didn't want to face God (V. 11).

When God called for Adam and Eve and found them in the garden, His words did include correction and consequence (VV. 13–19). But God also showed them kindness and gave them hope for humankind in the promise of the Savior (V. 15).

God doesn't have to look for us. He knows where we are and what we are trying to hide. But as a loving Father, He wants to speak to our hearts and bring us forgiveness and restoration. He longs for us to hear His voice—and to listen.

Keila

February 7

LET DOWN YOUR HAIR

JOHN 12:1–8

> Then Mary took about a pint of pure nard, an expensive perfume; she poured it on Jesus' feet and wiped his feet with her hair. And the house was filled with the fragrance of the perfume.
>
> *John 12:3*

Shortly before Jesus was crucified, a woman named Mary poured a bottle of expensive perfume on His feet. Then, in an even more daring act, she wiped His feet with her hair (JOHN 12:3). Not only did Mary sacrifice what may have been her life's savings but she also sacrificed her reputation. In that culture, respectable women never let down their hair in public. But true worship is not concerned with what others think of us (2 SAMUEL 6:21–22). To worship Jesus, Mary was willing to be thought of as immodest, perhaps even immoral.

Some of us may feel pressured to be perfect when we go to church. But in a healthy church, we can let down our hair and not hide our flaws behind a façade of perfection. In church we should be able to reveal our weaknesses to find strength rather than conceal our faults to appear strong.

Worship isn't behaving as if nothing's wrong; it's making sure everything's right—right with God and with one another. When our greatest fear is letting down our hair, perhaps our greatest sin is keeping it up.

Julie

February 8

MY FRIENDS AND I

1 SAMUEL 18:1-4; 23:15-18

> Jonathan made a covenant with David because he loved him as himself.
>
> *1 Samuel 18:3*

"Such is friendship, for as . . . flowers drop their sweet leaves on the ground around them, so friends impart favor even to the places where they dwell," writes John Chrysostom (AD 347–407).

Jonathan and David illustrate the sweetness of a true friendship. Theirs was an immediate bond (1 SAMUEL 18:1), and they kept their friendship alive through loyalty (18:3; 20:16, 42; 23:18) and by nurturing it through expressions of concern. Jonathan gave gifts to David (18:4) and watched out for him in many difficulties (19:1–2; 20:12–13).

In 1 Samuel 23:16, we see the highest moment of their friendship. When David was a fugitive from Jonathan's father, "Jonathan, Saul's son, arose and went to David in the woods and strengthened his hand in God" (NKJV). Friends help you find strength in God during life's low points.

In a world where many relationships are about what we can get, let us be the type of friends who focus on what we can give. Remember, "greater love has no one than this: to lay down one's life for one's friends" (JOHN 15:13).

Poh Fang

February 9

HOPE AWAKENING
EZEKIEL 37:1–28

> [God] asked me, "Son of man, can these bones become living people again?"
> *Ezekiel 37:3*

In her blog, Gayla wrote about rescuing a nearly dead cactus. Under her care, the seemingly moribund plant thrived. She shared the transformation details to help those who thought their cacti were beyond hope.

When God asked whether the dry bones in the valley could live again, Ezekiel was surprised. It certainly didn't look like they could. So the prophet responded, "O Sovereign Lord, you alone know the answer to that" (EZEKIEL 37:3 NLT).

In the midst of their captivity, God's people likely felt that they would never be rescued. So God sent word through Ezekiel, likening Israel to the dry bones in the valley. Although hope seemed lost, God would bring deliverance from captivity. Instead of being cut off, they would stand again as a mighty army.

We can lose sight of hope during difficult situations. But with God, there's *always* hope. No matter what you're dealing with, hear these words that God shared with ancient Israel: "I am the Lord. I will put my Spirit in you, and you will live again" (EZEKIEL 37:13–14 NLT).

Hope and life spring from God!

Remi

February 10

LIVING WITH LIONS
DANIEL 6:19-28

"He is the living God, and he endures forever."
Daniel 6:26

At a Chicago museum, I saw one of the original Striding Lions of Babylon—a large, mural-type image of a ferocious winged lion. Symbolizing Ishtar, the Babylonian goddess of love and war, the lion was an example of 120 similar lions that lined a Babylonian pathway.

Historians say that after the Babylonians defeated Jerusalem, the Hebrew captives would have seen these lions during their time in Nebuchadnezzar's kingdom. It's likely that some of the Israelites would have believed Ishtar had defeated the God of Israel.

Daniel, one of the Hebrew captives, did not share the doubts that troubled some of his fellow Israelites. His commitment to God stayed steady. He prayed three times a day—with his windows open—even when he knew it would mean being tossed into a den of lions. After God rescued Daniel from the hungry animals, King Darius said, "[Daniel's God] is the living God. . . . He rescues and he saves" (DANIEL 6:26-27). Daniel's faithfulness influenced the Babylonian leaders.

Staying faithful to God despite pressure and discouragement can inspire other people to give Him glory.

Jennifer

February 11

PRIDE AND PREJUDICE

JOHN 1:43-51

"Nazareth! Can anything good come from there?" Nathanael asked. "Come and see," said Philip.

John 1:46

Sadly, even the best of us have prejudices. One day I was shocked to realize I had my own prejudice against a Christian denomination. I had been deeply hurt by people in it; and any time the denomination's name came up, words like "Pharisees" and "legalists" came to mind. I basically thought, Can anything good come from that denomination?

Nathanael once asked a similar question about Jesus's hometown. It all started when Philip told Nathanael that Jesus was the one Moses and the prophets wrote about (JOHN 1:45)—the promised Messiah. But Nathanael's response indicated that Nazareth had a bad rep. How was it possible the Messiah could come from such a place?

Nathanael was prejudiced against the Nazarene people. But Jesus gave him the surprise of his life. In his first conversation with Jesus, it was so evident that He was indeed the Messiah that Nathanael cried out: "Rabbi, you are the Son of God" (v. 49).

Yes, each of us has prejudices. But praise God, He does not! May we follow His loving ways.

Marlena

February 12

A WORK IN PROGRESS

JOHN 15:9–17

But grow in the grace and knowledge of our Lord and Savior Jesus Christ. To him be glory both now and forever! Amen.

2 Peter 3:18

Pablo Casals was considered the preeminent cellist of the first half of the twentieth century. One day a young reporter asked him: "Mr. Casals, you are ninety-five years old and the greatest cellist that ever lived. Why do you still practice six hours a day?"

Mr. Casals answered, "Because I think I'm making progress."

What a great attitude! As believers in Christ, we can learn from this. We should never be satisfied to think we have reached some self-proclaimed pinnacle of spiritual success, but rather we are to continue to "grow in the grace and knowledge of our Lord and Savior Jesus Christ" (2 PETER 3:18). The result of healthy growth is continuing to bear spiritual fruit throughout our lives. Our Lord promises: "I am the vine; you are the branches. If you remain in me and I in you, you will bear much fruit" (JOHN 15:5).

We can be confident that He who began "a good work" in us will continue it until it is finally finished on the day He returns (PHILIPPIANS 1:6).

Cindy

February 13

DRESSED UP
ROMANS 13:11–14

> Clothe yourselves with the Lord Jesus Christ.
> Romans 13:14

In her book *Wearing God*, author Lauren Winner says our clothes can silently communicate to others who we are. She writes, "The idea that, as with a garment, Christians might wordlessly speak something of Jesus—is appealing."

According to Paul, we too can wordlessly represent Christ. Romans 13:14 tells us to "clothe [ourselves] with the Lord Jesus Christ, and do not think about how to gratify the desires of the flesh." When we become Christians, we take on Christ's identity. We're "children of God through faith" (GALATIANS 3:26–27). That's our status. Yet each day we need to clothe ourselves in His character. We do this by striving to live for and to be more like Jesus, growing in godliness, love, and obedience and turning our back on the sins that once enslaved us.

This growth in Christ is a result of the Holy Spirit working in us and our desire to be closer to Him through study of the Word, prayer, and time spent in fellowship with other Christians (JOHN 14:26). When others look at our words and attitudes, what statement are we making about Christ?

Alyson

February 14

LOCKED INTO LOVE
ROMANS 8:31–39

Give thanks to the Lord, for he is good; his love endures forever.

Psalm 106:1

In 2015 the city of Paris removed forty-five tons of padlocks from the railings of the Pont des Arts pedestrian bridge. As a romantic gesture, couples would etch their initials onto a lock, attach it to the railing, click it shut, and throw the key into the River Seine.

After this ritual was repeated thousands of times, the bridge could no longer bear the weight of so much "love." Eventually the city, fearing for the integrity of the bridge, removed the "love locks."

The locks were meant to symbolize everlasting love, but human love does not always last. Human love can be fickle.

But there's one constant and enduring love—the love of God. "Give thanks to the Lord, . . . his love endures forever," proclaims Psalm 106:1. The promises of God's unfailing and everlasting love are found throughout Scripture. The greatest proof of this love is Jesus's death so those who put their faith in Him can live eternally. Nothing will ever separate us from His love (ROMANS 8:38–39).

Fellow believer, praise God! We are locked into His love forever.

Cindy

February 15

TIME TO GROW
GALATIANS 6:1–10

Let us not become weary in doing good, for at the proper time we will reap a harvest if we do not give up.

Galatians 6:9

In Debbie's new home, she discovered an abandoned plant—a moth orchard. She imagined how pretty it would look with new, bloom-bearing stems. She moved the pot into a spot by the window, cut off the dead leaves, and watered and fed it. Week after week she inspected the plant, but no new shoots appeared. "I'll give it another month," she told her husband, "and if nothing has happened by then, out it goes."

When decision day came, she could hardly believe her eyes. Two small stems were poking out from among the leaves! The plant was still alive.

Do you ever get discouraged by your apparent lack of spiritual growth? Perhaps you frequently lose your temper or enjoy a spicy piece of gossip. Or perhaps you neglect praying and reading your Bible for a while.

Why not tell a trusted friend about the areas of your life in which you want to grow spiritually, and ask that person to pray for and encourage you to be accountable? Be patient. You will grow as you allow the Holy Spirit to work in you.

Marion

February 16

WHOSE MESS?
MATTHEW 15:7-21

"For out of the heart come evil thoughts—murder, adultery, sexual immorality, theft, false testimony, slander. These are what defile a person."

Matthew 15:19-20

"Could they not carry their own garbage this far?" I grumbled to my husband, Jay, as I picked up empty bottles from the beach and tossed them into the trash bin less than twenty feet away. "I sure hope these people are tourists. I don't want to think any locals would treat our beach with such disrespect."

The next day I came across a prayer I had about judging others. It reminded me of how wrong I was to take pride in cleaning up other people's messes. The truth is, I have plenty of my own messes—especially in the spiritual sense.

I'm quick to conclude that the "garbage" stinking up my surroundings belongs to someone other than me. But that's not true. Nothing outside of me can condemn or contaminate me—only what's inside (MATTHEW 15:19-20). The real garbage is the attitude that causes me to turn up my nose at a tiny whiff of someone else's sin while ignoring the stench of my own.

Julie

February 17

THE LITTLE EVANGELIST
MARK 12:28–34

Love the Lord your God with all your heart and with all your soul and with all your mind and with all your strength.

Mark 12:30

My six-year-old neighbor, Michael, and I were talking in my front yard when two new neighbor kids stopped by. After I asked them their names, Michael's first question to them was, "Do you love God?" Sugar, a five-year-old boy, quickly responded, "No!" Michael gave him a look of disapproval and concern. When four-year-old Nana noticed he wasn't pleased with that answer, she said, "Yes!"

Michael's "witnessing strategy" may not be the most effective, but he does have an important question for the people he meets (and I've heard him ask it of several others as well).

Jesus was asked, "Of all of the commandments, which is the most important?" (MARK 12:28). He answered, "The Lord is one. Love the Lord your God with all your heart and with all your soul and with all your mind and with all your strength" (VV. 29–30).

Loving God is to be our top priority too. So, my young friend Michael wants to know, "Do you love God?"

Anne

February 18

DOING RIGHT IN GOD'S SIGHT

2 KINGS 12:1–15

> Joash did what was right in the eyes of the Lord all the years Jehoiada the priest instructed him.
>
> *2 Kings 12:2*

"Cowboy builders" is a term many British homeowners use for tradespeople who do shoddy construction work. The term is bandied about with fear or regret, often because of bad experiences.

No doubt there were rogue carpenters, masons, and stonecutters in biblical times, but tucked away in the story of King Joash repairing the temple is a line about the complete honesty of those who oversaw and did the work (2 KINGS 12:15).

However, King Joash "did what was right in the eyes of the Lord" (V. 2) only when Jehoiada the priest instructed him. As we see in 2 Chronicles 24:17–27, after Jehoiada died, Joash turned from the Lord and was persuaded to worship other gods.

The mixed legacy of a king who enjoyed a season of fruitfulness only while under the spiritual counsel of a godly priest makes me stop and think. What will our legacies be? Will we continue to grow and develop in our faith throughout our lives, producing good fruit? Or will we become distracted by the things of this world and turn to modern-day idols—such as comfort, materialism, and self-promotion?

Amy

February 19

SERVING WITHOUT DISTRACTION
LUKE 10:38–42

> Martha was distracted by all the preparations that had to be made. She came to him and asked, "Lord, don't you care that my sister has left me to do the work by myself? Tell her to help me!"
>
> *Luke 10:40*

While Martha served Jesus unsparingly, her sister Mary sat at His feet, listening and learning. Commenting on this situation, Charles H. Spurgeon (1834–92) wrote, "We should do much service and have much communion at the same time. For this we need great grace. It is easier to serve than to commune."

I once met a young mother who found the grace to do both. She hungered after God and His Word and was immersed deeply in family life each day. One day an idea came to her. In each room she placed paper and a pencil. As she served the Lord throughout the day in her home, she also kept herself open to God. Whenever a Scripture came to mind or something to confess or to pray about, she jotted it on the nearest pad of paper. In the evening after the children were asleep, she gathered her pieces of paper and pondered them prayerfully.

This woman found a way to be Martha and Mary at the same time. May we too discover ways to both serve God and commune with Him.

Joanie

February 20

HOW LONG?

HABAKKUK 1:2-11

How long, Lord, must I call for help?
Habakkuk 1:2

When I got married, I thought I would have children immediately. That did not happen, and the pain of infertility caused me to cry out to God, "How long?" I knew God could change my circumstance. Why didn't He?

Are you waiting on God? Are you asking, How long, Lord, before justice prevails in our world? Before there's a cure for cancer? Before I'm no longer in debt?

The prophet Habakkuk knew that feeling. In the seventh century BC, he cried out: "How long, Lord, must I call for help, but you do not listen? Or cry out to you, 'Violence!' but you do not save? . . . Why do you tolerate wrongdoing?" (1:2-3). He prayed, yet he struggled to reconcile how a just and powerful God could allow wickedness to continue in Judah. Why was God doing nothing?

There are days when we too feel as if God is doing nothing. Like Habakkuk, we ask God, "How long?"

We must continue to cast our burdens on the Lord because He cares for us. God hears us and will, in His time, give an answer.

Karen

February 21

NOT MINE
PROVERBS 3:1–26

> In all your ways submit to him, and he will make your paths straight.
> *Proverbs 3:6*

My husband and I believe that parents are the most influential people in a child's life. But we sometimes wonder if our parenting decisions are having the anticipated impact. Our kids are adolescents now, and they're having more and more experiences on their own. These days I find myself looking for more and more opportunities to pray for them.

Every parent faces the fear of failure. Those concerns are magnified when we recognize the influence we have over our children's spiritual development (PSALM 78:1-7). We are afraid they will wander from the truths we've tried to instill in them. That's why it's a comfort to know there's One who is always watching and who is always at work beyond what we can see (PSALM 33:18; PROVERBS 2:12, 16).

As parents, we can boldly pray God's wisdom over our children (PROVERBS 3:5-7, 13-18). And we must learn to "seek his will in all [we] do" (PROVERBS 3:6 NLT). Our greatest spiritual influence on our children is found in the way we live out our faith before them.

Regina

February 22

VICTORY OVER DEATH
DEUTERONOMY 31:1-8

But thanks be to God! He gives us the victory through our Lord Jesus Christ.
1 Corinthians 15:57

While in a coffee shop in Uganda, I met a young man who had witnessed and survived (by hiding in a frigid meat freezer) the September 21, 2013, terrorist attack at Westgate Mall in Nairobi, Kenya, which resulted in sixty-seven deaths. Although he was among those who were rescued, during the horrific ordeal the man saw the face of evil as innocent people were gunned down—some at point-blank range—if they failed to convince the radical militants that they shared the same religion.

As he watched people die, this young man had every reason to believe he wouldn't make it out alive. He told me, however, that because he was confident of having been saved by grace (EPHESIANS 2:8-9) and that Jesus is his Savior (1 TIMOTHY 1:1), he feared pain—but not death.

I consider it a gift from God to have met this man, for he's a living testimony that God and His Word can still our hearts and grant peace to our minds even during the most horrific situations on earth.

We can cling to that confidence, which is available through Christ alone.

Roxanne

February 23

A BOLD ENTRANCE
HEBREWS 4:14–16

> Let us then approach God's throne of grace with confidence, so that we may receive mercy and find grace to help us in our time of need.
> *Hebrews 4:16*

One morning, Scott Long and his wife had just awakened and were lying in bed when suddenly a young fellow entered their bedroom. He walked around the bed to Scott's side.

If the trespasser had been a total stranger, his entrance would've been criminal intrusion. If he had been a friend, his entrance would've been just plain obnoxious. But it was their toddler son who had entered their bedroom, jumped on the bed, and boldly said, "I want in the middle." Scott was struck with the beauty of a child's security in knowing he is wanted.

We are welcome in our heavenly Father's presence as well. Hebrews 4:16 tells us we can "approach God's throne of grace with confidence." We can approach Him confidently about anything—our needs and our desires—knowing that He cares for us (1 PETER 5:7).

Let's not be foolish and ignore the help we can find in prayer to our Father. Instead, let's approach Him with the boldness of a child who knows he is loved and wanted by his father.

Anne

February 24

STAYING TRUE

DANIEL 3:1-30

"We want to make it clear to you, Your Majesty, that we will never serve your gods or worship the gold statue you have set up."

Daniel 3:18 (NLT)

In the book of Daniel, Nebuchadnezzar had raised a golden image and decreed that everyone should bow to worship it. However, Shadrach, Meshach, and Abednego refused to bow down (3:12). Enraged, the king gave them one more chance to comply or face certain death.

The young men did not waver. They declined the king's offer, stating, "The God whom we serve is able to save us. . . . But even if he doesn't, we want to make it clear to you, Your Majesty, that we will never serve your gods or worship the gold statue you have set up" (vv. 17-18 NLT). Instead of focusing on whether God would deliver them, the three centered their lives and actions around who God is.

Our ability to stand in the midst of trials depends on our focus. If we're looking only for immediate deliverance, we may not endure. But if we're looking to Jesus, He'll help us to realize that whatever happens, we stand on who God is—not on what He does for us.

Remi

February 25

WHAT'S THAT TO YOU?

JOHN 21:15–22

> Jesus answered, "If I want him to remain alive until I return, what is that to you? You must follow me."
>
> *John 21:22*

We all struggle with being nosy at times. We can find ourselves checking out what's happening to other people, and we take our eyes off Jesus. We forget to be grateful for what He's done in our lives.

When Jesus reinstated Peter (JOHN 21:15–17) after his denial of the Lord earlier, the apostle immediately took his eyes off the Savior and asked Him if John would suffer the same way he would (V. 21). Considering Peter's query, Jesus basically replied, *Don't worry about him. Keep your focus on Me* (V. 22).

As we follow Him, our focus becomes Christ-centered and not centered on what's happening in the lives of others. This may mean, among other things, limiting social media. It also entails seeking God and His wisdom in dealing with the temptations and sins in our own lives. As we submit to the power of Christ, He frees us from being caught up in an unhealthy concern for the situation of others. When we keep our eyes on the Lord, He provides the view we need!

Marlena

February 26

GRANDMA'S RECIPE
PSALM 145:1–13

> Remember the days of old;
> consider the generations long
> past. Ask your father and he will
> tell you, your elders, and they
> will explain to you.
>
> *Deuteronomy 32:7*

Many families have a secret recipe, a special way of cooking a dish that makes it especially savory. For us Hakkas (my Chinese ethnic group), we have a traditional dish called abacus beads, named for its bead-like appearance. Really, you have to try it!

Grandma had the best recipe. But we never got around to asking Grandma for it. She is no longer with us, and her secret recipe is gone with her.

We miss Grandma, and it's sad to lose her recipe. But far more tragic would be failing to preserve the legacy of faith entrusted to us. God intends that the mighty acts of God be shared from one generation to the next (PSALM 145:5). Moses had earlier instructed the Israelites to "remember the days of old; . . . Ask your father and he will tell you, your elders, and they will explain to you" (DEUTERONOMY 32:7).

As we share our stories of how we received salvation and the ways the Lord has helped us face challenges, we honor Him and pass the faith along. That is much more important than passing recipes along.

Poh Fang

February 27

THE GREATEST LOVE STORY
SONG OF SOLOMON 2:4-16

My beloved is mine and I am his;
he browses among the lilies.

Song of Solomon 2:16

When John and Ann Betar celebrated their eighty-first wedding anniversary, they were considered the couple with the longest marriage in the United States. Their advice? "Don't hold a grudge. Forgive each other," John advises. And Ann adds, "It is unconditional love and understanding."

The Song of Songs captures this active commitment with two lovers delighting in and yearning for each other (1:15–16; 3:1–3). They love and are loved in return (2:16; 7:10) and are satisfied and content in each other's company (2:16; 4:9–11; 7:10). Surely this can be one of life's greatest joys.

The earthly love between husband and wife is an echo of the passionate love and fervent pursuit of Jesus for those who believe in Him. "This is how God loved the world: He gave his one and only Son, so that everyone who believes in him will not perish but have eternal life" (JOHN 3:16 NLT).

While it's beautiful to see the love a man and woman can share for decades, it pales compared to the amazing love God extends to us for eternity. *That's* the greatest love story!

Ruth

February 28

SPIRITUAL PLAGIARISM

JOHN 1:1–18

The Word became flesh and made his dwelling among us. We have seen his glory, the glory of the one and only Son, who came from the Father, full of grace and truth.

John 1:14

When I teach writing, I try to become familiar with each student's writing voice. That way I can tell if they "borrow" too heavily from another writer. Students are surprised to learn that their writing voice—what they say as well as how they say it—is as distinctive as their speaking voice. Just as the words we speak come from our hearts, so do the words we write. They reveal who we are.

We become familiar with God's voice in much the same way. By reading what He has written, we learn who He is and how He expresses himself. Satan, however, tries to make himself sound like God (2 CORINTHIANS 11:14). For example, by convincing people to do things that simulate godliness, such as trusting in an outward regimen of self-discipline rather than Christ's death for salvation (COLOSSIANS 2:23), Satan has led many astray.

God went to extremes to make sure we would recognize His voice. He not only gave us His Word but He also gave us the Word made flesh—Jesus (JOHN 1:14)—so we will not be easily deceived or misled.

Julie

February 29

I WILL
LEVITICUS 19:9–18

"Love your neighbor as yourself."
Leviticus 19:18

Shirley settled into her recliner after a long day. She looked out the window and noticed an older couple struggling to move a section of old fence left in a yard and labeled "free." Shirley grabbed her husband, and they headed out the door to help. The four of them wrestled the fence onto a dolly and pushed it up the city street and around the corner to the couple's home—laughing all the way at the spectacle they must be. As they returned to get a second section of fence, the woman asked Shirley, "You be my friend?" "Yes, I will," she replied. Shirley later learned that her new Vietnamese friend knew little English and was lonely because her grown children had moved hours away.

In Leviticus, God reminded the Israelites that they knew how it felt to be strangers (19:34) and how to treat others (VV. 9–18). God had set them apart to be His own nation, and in return they were to bless their "neighbors" by loving them as themselves. Jesus, the greatest blessing from God to the nations, later restated His Father's words and extended them to us all: "Love the Lord your God. . . . Love your neighbor as yourself" (MATTHEW 22:37–39).

Through Christ's Spirit living in us, we can love God and others because He loved us first (GALATIANS 5:22–23; 1 JOHN 4:19). Can we say with Shirley, "Yes, I will"?

Anne

March 1

BEING GLAD
PSALM 30

The Lord has done it this very day;
let us rejoice today and be glad.

Psalm 118:24

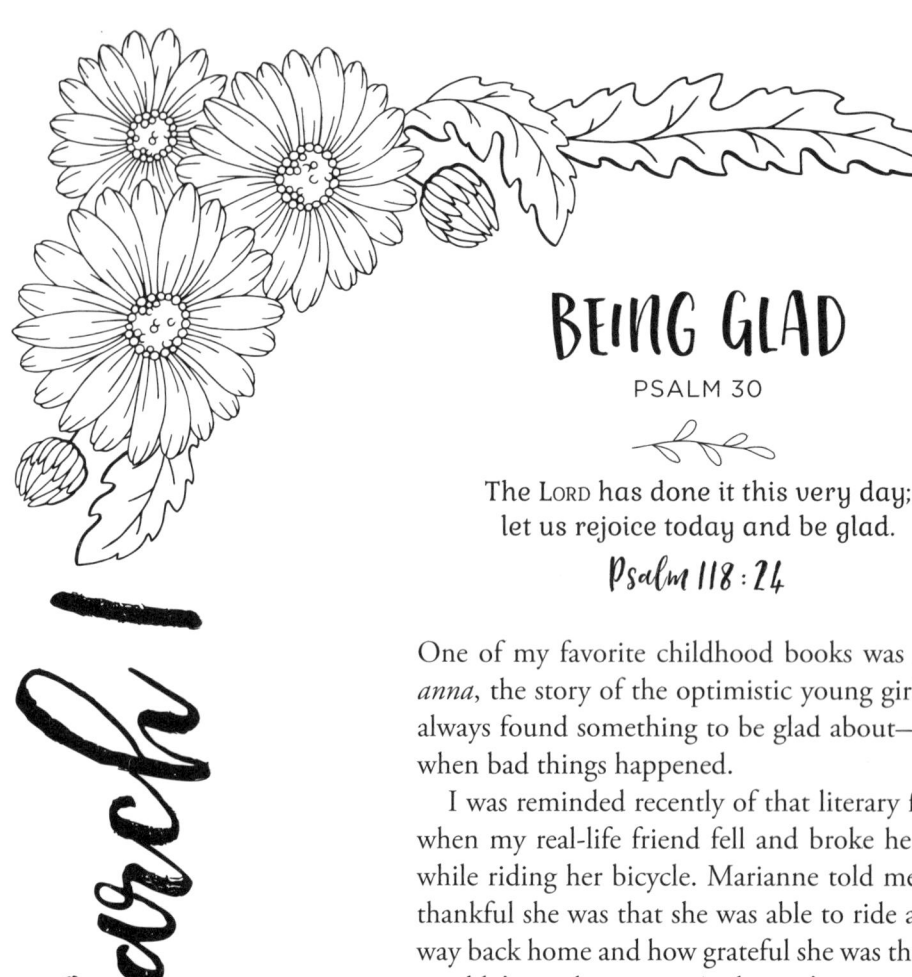

One of my favorite childhood books was *Pollyanna*, the story of the optimistic young girl who always found something to be glad about—even when bad things happened.

I was reminded recently of that literary friend when my real-life friend fell and broke her arm while riding her bicycle. Marianne told me how thankful she was that she was able to ride all the way back home and how grateful she was that she wouldn't need surgery. And wasn't it great, she marveled, that she has good bones, so her arm should heal fine!

Whew! Marianne is an example of someone who has learned to rejoice in spite of trouble. She has a confidence that God will care for her—no matter what.

Suffering eventually touches us all. And I think God looks at us with pleasure when we find reasons to be thankful (1 THESSALONIANS 5:16–18) despite the problem. As we do, we can be grateful that God is holding us close. It is when we trust in His goodness that we find gladness.

Cindy

LET US *rejoice* today

·AND·

BE GLAD.

♡ PSALM 118:24

March 2

TIME TO WAIT

GENESIS 8:1–12

After waiting another seven days, Noah released the dove again. This time the dove returned to him in the evening with a fresh olive leaf in its beak.

Genesis 8:10-11

More than a year had passed since the springs of the great deep had burst forth and the floodgates of heaven were unleashed on earth (GENESIS 7:11) in the flood of Noah's day. The world was completely submerged.

The deluge itself lasted only forty days, but drying out was another matter. God had been vocal when commissioning the ark—providing specific instructions. But now He was silent. Noah and his family waited and waited. Had God forgotten them?

No, He had not. He was working on their behalf to restore order. He sent a wind to recede the waters (GENESIS 8:1), and the ark came to rest on a mountain. And then the dove Noah sent out didn't return. Still, Noah waited until God spoke and told him to leave the ark (GENESIS 8:16). His patience and trust were rewarded with a renewed world.

Today's culture of instant gratification puts us in conflict with God's timing. When God seems silent, it's time for us to wait and trust him to sort things out in a way we never could. He's always worth the wait!

Remi

March 3

RIPE FOR THE HARVEST

JOHN 4:35–38

"Open your eyes and look at the fields! They are ripe for harvest."
~John 4:35~

In late summer, we went for a walk in the New Forest in England. We picked wild blackberries while watching horses frolic nearby. As I enjoyed the bounty of the sweet fruit planted by others many years before, I thought of Jesus's words to His disciples: "I sent you to reap what you have not worked for" (JOHN 4:38).

I love the generosity of God's kingdom reflected in those words. He lets us enjoy the fruits of someone else's labors, such as when we share our love for Jesus with a friend whose family—unbeknown to us—has been praying for her for years. I also love the implied limits of Jesus's words, for we may plant seeds that we will never harvest but someone else may. Therefore, we can rest in the tasks before us, knowing that we are not responsible for the outcomes.

What harvest fields lie before you? Before me? May we heed Jesus's loving instruction: "Open your eyes and look at the fields!" (V. 35).

Amy

March 4

LIFE TO THE FULL

MARK 10:28–31; JOHN 10:9–10

"I have come that they may have life, and have it to the full."

John 10:10

When I visited my sister's family, my nephews eagerly showed me their new chore system, a set of Choropoly boards. Each colorful electronic board keeps track of their chores—and rewards them accordingly. A job well done adds points to their "spending" account. A misdeed (like leaving the back door open) deducts from the total. A high-points total leads to exciting rewards, so my nephews are now motivated to do their work. And to keep the door closed!

I joked that I wished I had such an exciting motivational tool! But of course our Lord has given us motivation. Jesus didn't command obedience, He has promised that a life of following Him, while costly, is also a life of abundance, "life . . . to the full" (JOHN 10:10). Experiencing life in His kingdom is worth "one hundred times" the cost—now and eternally (MARK 10:29–30).

We serve a generous God—One who does not reward and punish as we deserve. He generously accepts our weakest efforts. Let us joyfully serve Him today.

Monica

March 5

QUESTIONS FOR GOD
JUDGES 6:11–16, 24

"Go in the strength you have.... I will be with you."
Judges 6:14, 16

Do you ever wonder why God has allowed suffering in your life? Old Testament hero Gideon did. One day "the angel of the Lord appeared to him and said, 'Mighty hero, the Lord is with you!'" Gideon responded, "If the Lord is with us, why has all this happened to us?" (JUDGES 6:12–13 NLT). Gideon wanted to know why it seemed as if God had abandoned His people.

God didn't answer that question. After Gideon had endured seven years of enemy attacks, starvation, and hiding in caves, God didn't explain why He never intervened. God could have revealed Israel's past sin as the reason, but instead He gave Gideon hope for the future. God said, "Go with the strength you have.... I will be with you" (VV. 14, 16 NLT).

When Gideon finally believed that God was with him and would help him, he built an altar and called it "the Lord is peace" (V. 24).

There is peace in knowing that whatever we do and wherever we go, we go with God who promised never to leave or forsake His followers.

Jennifer

March 6

HOLY DESPERATION
MARK 5:24-34

[Jesus] turned around in the crowd and asked, "Who touched my robe?"

Mark 5:30 (NLT)

When Jesus stood in the midst of the crowd and asked who had touched Him, the disciples must have thought He had lost it. So many people pressed in, yet He wanted to identify just one (MARK 5:31). Eventually, the woman trembled forward with a confession, stunning everyone (V. 5:33).

Jesus knew this woman needed Him. Doctors had drained her resources, and the nonstop bleeding condemned her to be unclean. To avoid contamination, family and friends had to keep away. She couldn't enter the temple. And this had been going on for twelve years! Jesus was her only hope (MARK 5:26-28). So she touched Him. And He knew it.

How do we "touch" Him? Do we approach God with the understanding that He's our only hope? Or do we come carelessly, browsing for blessings?

In Isaiah 29:13 and Matthew 15:8, the Scriptures address the problem of making a verbal show of faith without a true heart commitment. Jesus sees past the façade to what lies beneath. With true sincerity and in dire need, let's seek Him and His loving touch today.

Remi

March 7

STILL IN PROCESS
COLOSSIANS 3:10-19; 4:5-6

> Over all these virtues put on love, which binds them all together in perfect unity.
>
> *Colossians 3:14*

Transformation isn't always easy in our lives, especially when it involves our hearts. Relationships, whether with God, our spouse, or anyone else, are a journey—not a destination. Circumstances in life invariably bring stressors or adjustments that require us to submit humbly to God's continued work. God often uses our closest relationships to bring about the transformation that will be the witness of Jesus's love to an unbelieving world (JOHN 13:35; COLOSSIANS 4:5).

From hidden behaviors of the heart to our self-preservationist actions, God calls us to "put on the new self, which is being renewed in knowledge in the image of its Creator" (COLOSSIANS 3:10). True change, however, requires humility—a relinquishing of our rights that we might embrace His (PSALM 25:9; PROVERBS 10:12).

As our worth and purpose become more hidden with Jesus (COLOSSIANS 3:3), the less we need to prove we're right, the more we want His Word to come alive in us, and the more we truly love.

Regina

March 8

FIVE-FINGER PRAYERS
JAMES 5:13–18

Pray for each other.
James 5:16

Prayer is a conversation with God, not a formula. Yet sometimes we might need to use a "method" to freshen up our prayer time. I recently came across this "Five-Finger Prayer" to use as a guide when praying for others:

- When you fold your hands, the thumb is nearest you. So begin by praying for those closest to you—your loved ones (PHILIPPIANS 1:3–5).
- The index finger is the pointer. Pray for those who teach—Bible teachers and preachers, and those who teach children (1 THESSALONIANS 5:25).
- The next finger is the tallest. It reminds you to pray for those in authority over you—national and local leaders, and your supervisor at work (1 TIMOTHY 2:1–2).
- The fourth finger is usually the weakest. Pray for those who are in trouble or who are suffering (JAMES 5:13–16).
- Then comes your little finger. It reminds you of your smallness in relation to God's greatness. Ask Him to supply your needs (PHILIPPIANS 4:6, 19).

Whatever method you use, just talk with your Father. He wants to hear what's on your heart.

Anne

March 9

WHO WILL TELL THEM?
2 CORINTHIANS 4:1-6

It has now been revealed through the appearing of our Savior, Christ Jesus, who has destroyed death and has brought life and immortality to light through the gospel.

2 Timothy 1:10

World War II had ended. Peace had been declared. But Second Lieutenant Hiroo Onoda of the Japanese Imperial Army, stationed on Lubang Island in the Philippines, didn't know the war had ended. Attempts were made to track him down and tell him the war was over. But Onoda, whose last order in 1945 was to stay and fight, dismissed these attempts as propaganda from the enemy. He did not surrender until March 1974—nearly thirty years after the war had ended—when his former commanding officer traveled from Japan to the Philippines, rescinded his original order, and officially relieved Onoda of duty. Onoda finally believed the war was over.

When it comes to the good news about Jesus Christ, many still don't believe the truth: that He has "destroyed death and has brought life and immortality to light through the gospel" (2 TIMOTHY 1:10).

When others tell them the glorious news of salvation, they may respond with skepticism, but take heart. Imagine the freedom they'll find when they finally realize that the battle has been won!

Poh Fang

March 10

THE BLAME GAME
GENESIS 16:1-6; 21:8-13

> Then Sarai said to Abram, "You are responsible for the wrong I am suffering. I put my slave in your arms, and now that she knows she is pregnant, she despises me. May the LORD judge between you and me."
>
> *Genesis 16:5*

When Jenny's husband left her for another woman, she vowed never to meet his new wife. But when she realized that her bitterness was damaging her children's relationship with their father, she asked for God's help to take the first steps toward overcoming bitterness in an unchangeable situation.

In Genesis 16, we read the story of a couple to whom God later promised a baby. When Sarai suggested that her husband Abram have a child with their servant Hagar, she wasn't fully trusting God. When the baby was born, Hagar despised Sarai (16:3-4), and Sarai became bitter (vv. 5-6).

Hagar had been the slave with no rights, and suddenly she was special. How did Sarai react? By blaming others, including Abram (v. 5). God's promise was realized in the birth of Isaac fourteen years later. Even his weaning celebration was spoiled by Sarai's attitude.

It may have taken a miracle of grace to change Sarai's attitude, but through God's strength, she could have lived with it differently and given God the glory.

Marion

March 11

A GOOD INHERITANCE
2 TIMOTHY 1:1-5

I am reminded of your sincere faith, which first lived in your grandmother Lois and in your mother Eunice.

2 Timothy 1:5

Grandpa and Grandma Harris didn't have a lot of money, yet they made each Christmas memorable for my cousins and me. We always had plenty of food, fun, and love. And from an early age, we learned that it was Christ who made this celebration possible.

We want to leave the same legacy to our children. When we got together in a recent December to share Christmas with family, we realized that this wonderful tradition had started with Grandpa and Grandma. They were careful to plant the seeds of love, respect, and faith so we—their children's children—might imitate their example.

In the Bible we read about grandma Lois and mom Eunice, who shared with Timothy genuine faith (2 TIMOTHY 1:5). Their influence prepared this man to share the good news with many others.

We can prepare a spiritual inheritance for those we influence by living in close communion with God, giving them our attention, and sharing life with them. When our lives reflect the reality of God's love, we leave a lasting legacy for others.

Keila

March 12

A HINT OF HEAVEN
1 CORINTHIANS 14:6–12, 26

> So it is with you. Since you are eager for gifts of the Spirit, try to excel in those that build up the church.
>
> *1 Corinthians 14:12*

A world-class botanical garden was the setting for an all-church community gathering. As I walked around the gardens enjoying the beautiful surroundings cared for by folks who know and love plants, I realized that the evening was rich with symbols of how the church is supposed to function—a little hint of heaven on earth.

A garden is a place where each plant is placed in an environment where it will thrive. Gardeners prepare the soil, protect the plants, and make sure each one receives the nourishment it needs. The result is a beautiful, colorful, and fragrant place for people to enjoy.

Like a garden, church is meant to be a place where everyone works together for the good of all, a place where everyone flourishes because it's safe, a place where people are cared for according to their needs (1 CORINTHIANS 14:26).

Like well-cared-for plants, people growing in a healthy environment have a sweet fragrance that draws people to God by displaying the beauty of His love. The church is not perfect, but it really is a hint of heaven.

Julie

March 13

SINGING THROUGH SADNESS
LAMENTATIONS 3:19–24

> Because of the Lord's great love we are not consumed, for his compassions never fail.
>
> Lamentations 3:22

Our young daughter developed the habit of singing whenever I cut her toenails. This takes her mind off what is happening. Research shows that belting out your favorite tune has physiological, neurological, and emotional benefits.

According to the Bible, even a sad song can be beneficial. One example is a *lament*—a passionate expression of grief born out of regret or mourning. These can also bring hope and peace.

The weeping prophet Jeremiah admitted that his nation's disobedience led to the awful consequences faced by the people of Judah and Jerusalem (LAMENTATIONS 1:5). He frequently warned them of God's wrath, urging repentance (JEREMIAH 6:10–11; 18:11–12). But they refused to listen. Their city was destroyed and their families were taken into exile (1 CHRONICLES 9:1).

The prophet cries because his heart is broken as he sees the desperate plight of his people. Jeremiah experiences hope, however, as he remembers God's faithful love that never ends and His mercies that never cease (LAMENTATIONS 3:22–24).

Even a lament can remind you to put your hope in a faithful God.

Ruth

BECAUSE OF THE Lord's great love WE ARE NOT CONSUMED, FOR HIS COMPASSIONS NEVER FAIL.

LAMENTATIONS 3:22

March 14

TEACHING LINES
TITUS 2:1–15

In everything set them an example by doing what is good. In your teaching show integrity, seriousness and soundness of speech.

Titus 2:6-7

I overheard my eleven-year-old son telling his grandmother about one of his classes at school. "On our first day of studio art," he said, "our teacher told us to draw self-portraits. Everyone's was bad. The next day she taught us how to use lines, and everyone's self-portraits improved." In art and in life, it seems, using the appropriate tools helps us to line things up correctly and do what's best.

In the New Testament, the apostle Paul gave his protégé Titus a list of things he and other leaders should do and teach to other church members:

- "Teach the older men to exercise self-control, to be worthy of respect and to live wisely" (TITUS 2:2 NLT).
- "Teach the older women to live in a way that honors God" (2:3 NLT).
- "Train the younger women to love their husbands and their children, to live wisely and be pure" (2:4 NLT).
- "Encourage the young men to live wisely" (2:6 NLT).

Titus was to use these "lines" in guiding the people he was serving. They are good teaching tools for all who follow Jesus—the Master Teacher.

Roxanne

March 15

TRAINING FOR LIFE
1 CORINTHIANS 9:24–27

No, I strike a blow to my body and make it my slave so that after I have preached to others, I myself will not be disqualified for the prize.
1 Corinthians 9:27

I met a woman who has pushed her body and mind to the limit. She climbed mountains, faced death, and even broke a Guinness world record. Now she's engaged in a different challenge—raising her special-needs child. The courage and faith she employed while ascending the mountains she now pours into motherhood.

In 1 Corinthians, the apostle Paul speaks of a runner competing in a race. After urging a church full of people who were in love with their own rights to begin showing consideration for each other (chapter 8), he explains that he saw the challenges of love and self-sacrifice to be like a marathon of endurance (chapter 9). As followers of Jesus, they were to relinquish their rights in obedience to Him.

As athletes train their bodies to win, we can train our bodies and minds so our souls can flourish. As we ask the Holy Spirit to transform us, we leave our old selves behind. Empowered by God, we stop ourselves from actions that are not godly.

As we train ourselves in the Spirit of Christ, how might God want to mold us today?

Amy

March 16

THE VALLEY OF BLESSING

2 CHRONICLES 20:1, 13–22

> "If calamity comes... [we] will cry out to you in our distress, and you will hear us."
>
> *2 Chronicles 20:9*

French artist Henri Matisse felt his work in the last years of his life best represented him. During that time he experimented with a new style, creating colorful, large-scale pictures with which he decorated the walls of his room. This was important to him because he was ill and often confined to his bed.

Becoming ill, losing a job, or enduring heartbreak are examples of what some call "being in the valley," where dread overshadows everything else. The people of Judah experienced this when they heard an invading army was approaching (2 CHRONICLES 20:2–3). Their king prayed, "If calamity comes . . . [we] will cry out to you in our distress, and you will hear us" (V. 9). God responded, "Go out to face [your enemies] tomorrow, and the LORD will be with you" (V. 17).

When Judah's army arrived at the battlefield, their enemies had already destroyed each other. God's people praised God and named the place "The Valley of Berakah," which means "blessing."

God walks with us—making it possible to discover blessings in the valley.

Jennifer

March 17

VERY GOOD

GENESIS 1:24–31

> Then God looked over all he had made, and he saw that it was very good!
>
> *Genesis 1:31* (NLT)

Some days seem to have a theme running through them. Recently I had one of those days. Our pastor began his sermon on Genesis 1 with two minutes of breathtaking, time-lapse photography of blossoming flowers. Then, at home, a scroll through social media revealed numerous posts of flowers. Later, on a walk in the woods, the wildflowers of spring surrounded us—trilliums, marsh marigolds, and wild iris.

God created flowers and every other variety of vegetation (and dry ground to grow in), on the third day of creation. And twice on that day, God pronounced it "good" (GENESIS 1:10, 12). On only one other day of creation—the sixth—did God make that double pronouncement of "good" (VV. 25, 31).

In the creation story, we see a Creator God who delighted in His creation—and seemed to take joy in the very act of creating. Why else design a world with such colorful and amazing variety? And He saved the best for last when He "created mankind in his own image" (V. 27). As His image-bearers, we are blessed and inspired by His beautiful handiwork.

Alyson

March 18

DEFEATED ADVERSARY
EPHESIANS 6:10–18

Be alert and of sober mind. Your enemy the devil prowls around like a roaring lion looking for someone to devour.

1 Peter 5:8

The roaring lion may be the "king of the jungle," but the only lions many of us see are the lethargic felines that reside in zoos. Their days are filled with rest, and their dinner is served to them without the lions having to lift a single paw.

In their natural habitat, however, lions don't live such a laid-back life. Their hunger tells them to go hunting, so they seek the young, weak, sick, or injured. Crouching in tall grasses, they creep forward, and with a sudden pounce, they clamp their jaws on their latest victim.

Peter used "a roaring lion" as a metaphor for Satan—a confident predator, looking for easy prey to devour (1 PETER 5:8). In dealing with him, we must be vigilant to put "on the full armor of God" and be "strong in the Lord and in his mighty power" (EPHESIANS 6:10–11).

Satan may be a powerful foe, but people who are protected by salvation, prayer, and the Word of God need not be paralyzed in fear. James 4:7 assures us: "Resist the devil, and he will flee from you."

Cindy

March 19

BEWARE OF QUICK FIXES

PSALM 106:1–15

But they soon forgot what he had done and did not wait for his plan to unfold.

Psalm 106:13

The story is told of a young rich girl, accustomed to servants, who was afraid to climb a dark stairway alone. Her mother suggested that she overcome her fear by asking Jesus to go with her up the stairs. When the child reached the top, she was overheard saying, "Thank you, Jesus. You may go now."

We may smile at that story, but Psalm 106 contains a serious warning against dismissing God from our lives—as if that were possible. Israel took the Lord's mercies for granted, and God called that rebellion (v. 7). They developed malnourished souls because they chose to ignore Him (vv. 13-15). What a lesson for us!

Anticipate great things from God, but don't expect Him to come at your beck and call. Instead, be at His beck and call, eager to fulfill His will.

Like the little rich girl, ask God to accompany you through life's dark passageways. But instead of dismissing Him when your special needs are met, cling to Him as if your life depended on it. It does!

Joanie

March 20

WRITING LETTERS
2 CORINTHIANS 3:1-6

> You yourselves are our letter, written on our hearts, known and read by everyone.
> *2 Corinthians 3:2*

My mother and her sisters engage in what is becoming a lost art form—writing letters. Each week they pen personal words to each other with such consistency that one of their mail carriers worries when he doesn't have something to deliver!

As I reflect on this weekly exercise of the women in my family, it helps me appreciate even more the apostle Paul's words that those who follow Jesus are "a letter from Christ," who were "written not with ink but with the Spirit of the living God" (2 CORINTHIANS 3:3). Paul encouraged the church in Corinth to keep on following the true and living God as he had previously taught. In doing so, he memorably described the believers as Christ's letter. Their transformed lives were a more powerful witness to the Spirit's work than any written letter could be.

God's Spirit in us writes a story of grace and redemption! It is our lives that are the best witness to the truth of the gospel, for they speak volumes through our compassion, service, gratitude, and joy. What message might you send today?

Amy

March 21

THE GOOD, THE BAD, AND THE UGLY

1 SAMUEL 20:35–42

Never will I leave you; never will I forsake you.
Hebrews 13:5

A friend sent me this text message: "I'm so glad we can tell each other the good, the bad, and the ugly!" Friends for many years, we've learned to share our joys and our failures. We know we're far from perfect, so we share our struggles while also rejoicing in each other's successes.

David and Jonathan had a solid friendship too, beginning with the good days of David's victory over Goliath (1 SAMUEL 18:1–4). They shared their fears during the bad days of Jonathan's father's jealousy (18:6–11; 20:1–2). Finally, they suffered together during the ugly days of Saul's plans to kill David (20:42).

Good friends don't abandon each other when external circumstances change. They stay through the good and the bad days. Good friends also may point us to God in the ugly days, when we may feel tempted to walk away from Him.

Real friendships exemplify our perfect Friend, who remains loyal through the good, the bad, and the ugly days. As the Lord reminds us, "Never will I leave you; never will I forsake you" (HEBREWS 13:5).

Keila

Never will I leave you; never will I forsake you.

HEBREWS 13:5

March 22

WITH HOPE FULL
1 THESSALONIANS 4:13–5:11

> Brothers and sisters, we do not want you to be uninformed about those who sleep in death, so that you do not grieve like the rest of mankind, who have no hope.
>
> *1 Thessalonians 4:13*

Taking his dark, weathered hands in mine, we bowed to pray. As a custodian (him) and a teacher (me), our life experiences intersected in my tiny office. His mother had been sick for some time, and the disease had spread. Confident of God's ability to heal, we prayed for Him to restore her body—but we also asked for the miracle of comfort. As I write, he sits by her bedside and knows he will soon have to say good-bye. For now, anyway.

Death is never easy. We do all we can to hold on to those we love for just a little longer because, even for the believer, the separation brought on by death feels so permanent. We were designed for the eternal; we were not made for loss. Something inside us cries for everlasting life and *hope*.

How beautiful is hope for believers in Jesus: "[Christ] died for us so that, whether we are awake or asleep, we may live together with him" (1 THESSALONIANS 5:10). And we can comfort other believers with this truth: In Christ our hope is full!

Regina

March 23

WHAT'S IN THE BANK?
EPHESIANS 2:4–7

> Let us then approach God's throne of grace with confidence, so that we may receive mercy and find grace to help us in our time of need.
> ### Hebrews 4:16

In the winter of 2009, a large passenger plane made an emergency landing in New York's Hudson River. Captain Chesley Sullenberger, the pilot who landed the plane safely, was later asked about those moments in the air when he was faced with a life-or-death decision. "One way of looking at this," he said, "might be that for forty-two years I've been making small, regular deposits in this bank of experience, education, and training. And on [that day] the balance was sufficient so that I could make a very large withdrawal."

Most of us will face a crisis. It is in those times that we must dig down deep into the reserves of our spiritual bank account.

And what might we find there? If we have enjoyed a deepening relationship with God, we've been making regular "deposits" of faith. We have experienced His grace (2 CORINTHIANS 8:9; EPHESIANS 2:4–7). We trust the promise of Scripture that God is just and faithful (DEUTERONOMY 32:4; 2 THESSALONIANS 3:3).

God's love and grace are available when His children need to make a "withdrawal" (PSALM 9:10; HEBREWS 4:16).

Cindy

March 24

"BRING THE BOY TO ME"

MARK 9:14–27

"You unbelieving generation," Jesus replied, "how long shall I stay with you? How long shall I put up with you? Bring the boy to me."

Mark 9:19

"I don't believe in God and I won't go," Mark said.

Amy struggled to swallow the lump in her throat. Her son had changed from a happy boy to a surly, uncooperative young man. Life was a battleground, and Sunday had become a day to dread, as Mark refused to go to church with the family. Finally, his despairing parents consulted a counselor, who said, "Mark must make his own faith journey. You can't force him into the kingdom. Give God space to work. Keep praying, and wait."

Amy waited—and prayed. One morning the words of Jesus that she had read echoed through her mind. Jesus's disciples had failed to help a demon-possessed boy, but Jesus had the answer: "Bring the boy to me" (MARK 9:19). If Jesus could heal in such an extreme situation, surely He could also help her son. She mentally stepped back, leaving her son alone with the One who loved him even more than she did.

Every day Amy silently handed Mark to God, clinging to the assurance that He knew Mark's needs and would in His time and in His way work in his life.

Marion

March 25

WHAT'S IN A NAME?
JOHN 1:35-42

> "I tell you that you are Peter, and on this rock I will build my church, and the gates of Hades will not overcome it."
>
> *Matthew 16:18*

When Jesus renamed Simon to Peter/Cephas (JOHN 1:42), it wasn't a random choice. Peter means "the rock." But it took a while for him to live up to his new name. The account of his life reveals him as a fisherman known for his rash ways—a shifting-sand kind of guy. Peter disagreed with Jesus (MATTHEW 16:22-23), struck a man with a sword (JOHN 18:10-11), and even denied knowing Jesus (JOHN 18:15-27). But in Acts, we read that God worked in and through him as an amazing preacher to establish His church. Peter truly became a rock.

If you, like Peter, are a follower of Jesus, you have a new identity. In Acts 11:26, we read, "The disciples were called Christians first at Antioch." The name "Christians" means "Christ-ones." You now are one of the Christ-ones. This title lifts up who you are and calls you to become what you are not yet. God is faithful, and He will complete His good work in you (PHILIPPIANS 1:6).

Poh Fang

March 26

SOW WHAT?
MARK 4:1–20

A wicked person earns deceptive wages, but the one who sows righteousness reaps a sure reward.

Proverbs 11:18

On the clock tower of my alma mater is an Art Deco bas-relief sculpture titled *The Sower*. The inscription beneath it is from Galatians 6:7, "Whatsoever a man soweth." Michigan State University remains a leader in agricultural research, but this singular fact remains: Seeds of corn will not produce a crop of beans.

Jesus used many farming metaphors to explain the kingdom of God. In the parable of the sower (MARK 4), He compared the Word of God to seeds sown in different types of soil. As the parable indicates, the sower sows indiscriminately, knowing that some seed will fall in places where it will not grow.

Like Jesus, we are to sow good seed in all places at all times. God is responsible for where it lands and how it grows. The important thing is that we sow. We are to sow seeds that will reap eternal life (GALATIANS 6:8).

The answer to the question, "Sow what?" is "Sow what you want to reap." To reap a good harvest in your life, start sowing seeds of goodness.

Julie

March 27

SATISFIED IN JESUS
GENESIS 25:29–34

> But Jacob said, "Swear to me first." So he swore an oath to him, selling his birthright to Jacob.
> *Genesis 25:33*

The woman lost weight and began to feel attractive again. Soon she grew tired of her husband and their life—a life that included four small children. She threw away family stability—the love and devotion of her husband and the kids' well being—to satisfy her desires. When her marital vows became inconvenient, she violated them.

Much like Esau (GENESIS 25:32–33), she showed contempt for what was most important and sought fleeting gratification. The foundation of her family life was destroyed for relationships that were over about as fast as Esau's meal (V. 34). And like Esau, she wasn't thinking of the long-term consequences of her behavior (HEBREWS 12:16).

Sin can easily entangle us and trip us up when we start focusing solely on *ourselves* and not on Jesus (VV. 1–2). That's when destruction can creep into our lives.

Life's pleasures can't compare to the blessings of God. Jesus said, "I have come that [believers in Christ] may have life, and have it to the full" (JOHN 10:10). May we fix our eyes on Christ today and experience the fulfillment He alone provides!

Marlena

March 28

FIVE-MINUTE RULE
PSALM 102:1-17

He will respond to the prayer of the destitute; he will not despise their plea.
Psalm 102:17

I read about a five-minute rule that a mother had for her children. They had to be ready for school five minutes before it was time to leave each day.

They would gather around Mom, and she would pray for each one by name, asking for the Lord's blessing on their day. Then she'd give them a kiss, and off they'd run. Even neighborhood kids would be included in the prayer circle if they happened to stop by. One of the children said many years later that she learned from this experience how crucial prayer is to her day.

The writer of Psalm 102 taught the importance of prayer. He cried out, "Hear my prayer, Lord; . . . when I call, answer me quickly" (vv. 1–2). God looks down "from his sanctuary on high, from heaven he [views] the earth" (v. 19).

God wants to hear from you. Whether you follow the five-minute rule or need to spend more time crying out to Him in deep distress, talk to the Lord each day. Your example may have a big impact on someone close to you—and on you!

Anne

March 29

OVERFLOWING FRUIT

GALATIANS 5:16–25

"I chose you and appointed you so that you might go and bear fruit—fruit that will last."

John 15:16

During the spring and summer, I admire the fruit growing in our neighbors' yard. Their cultivated vines climb a shared fence to produce large bunches of grapes. Branches dotted with purple plums and plump oranges dangle just within our reach.

Although we don't till the soil, plant the seeds, or water and weed the garden, the couple next door share their bounty with us. They take responsibility for nurturing their crops and allow us to delight in a portion of their harvest.

This reminds me of another harvest—the harvest of the fruit of the Spirit.

Christ-followers are commissioned to claim the benefits of living by the power of the Holy Spirit (GALATIANS 5:16–21). As God's seeds of truth flourish in our hearts, the Spirit produces an increase in our ability to express "love, joy, peace, forbearance, kindness, goodness, faithfulness, gentleness and self-control" (VV. 22–23).

Over time, the Holy Spirit can change our thinking, our attitudes, and our actions. As we grow and mature in Christ, we can have the added joy of loving our neighbors by sharing the benefits of His generous harvest.

Xochitl

March 30

HE IS THERE
PSALM 139:1–12

"Be strong and courageous. Do not be afraid . . . because of them, for the Lord your God goes with you; he will never leave you nor forsake you."

Deuteronomy 31:6

Tanya's fiancé, David, was lying in the intensive care unit after a delicate procedure to repair a brain aneurysm. David's eyes focused on Tanya, who had hardly left his side in several days. In wonder, he said, "Every time I look up, you're here. I love that. Every time I think of you, I open my eyes and you are there."

That young man's appreciation for the woman he loves reminds me of the way we should feel about God's presence in our lives.

In Psalm 139, we read what King David thought of God's precious presence. He wrote, "You have searched me, Lord, and you know me. You know when I sit and when I rise; . . . you are familiar with all my ways. . . . If I go up to the heavens, you are there" (vv. 1–3, 8).

No matter what happens to us, we have this assurance: "God is our refuge and strength, an ever-present help in trouble" (PSALM 46:1). Open your eyes and your heart. He is there.

Cindy

March 31

OUR NEW NAME
REVELATION 2:12–17

> "Whoever has ears, let them hear what the Spirit says to the churches. To the one who is victorious, I will give some of the hidden manna. I will also give that person a white stone with a new name written on it, known only to the one who receives it."
>
> *Revelation 2:17*

She called herself a worrier, but when her child was hurt in an accident, she learned to escape that restricting label. As her child was recovering, she met with friends to talk and pray, asking God for help and healing. As she turned her fears and concerns into prayer, she realized that she was changing from being a *worrier* to a prayer *warrior* and that the Lord was giving her a new name.

In Jesus's letter to the church at Pergamum, the Lord promises to give the faithful a white stone with a new name on it (REVELATION 2:17). Biblical commentators debate the meaning, but most agree that this white stone points to our freedom in Christ. In biblical times, juries in a court of law used a white stone for a not-guilty verdict and a black stone for guilty. A white stone also gained the bearer entrance into such events as banquets; likewise, those who receive God's white stone are welcomed to the heavenly feast. Jesus's death brings us freedom and new life—and a new name.

What new name might God give you?

Amy

April 1

RECIPE FOR SUCCESS
JOSHUA 1:1-9

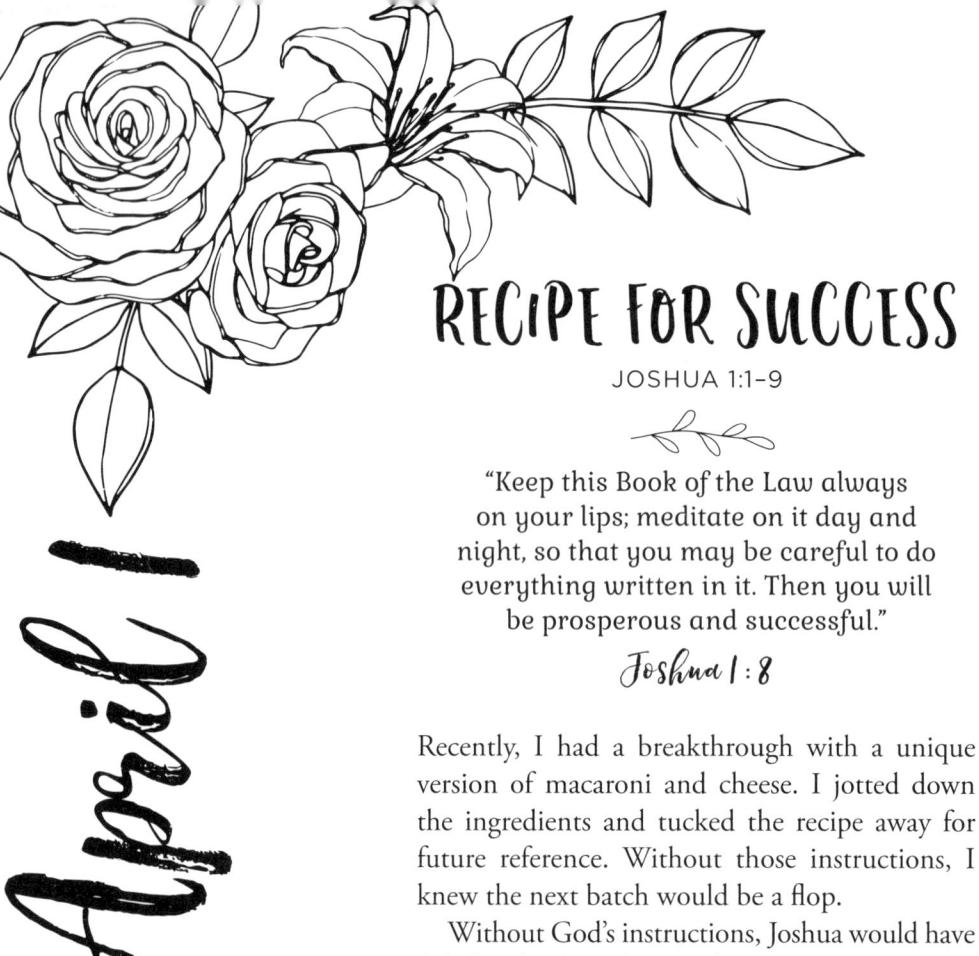

"Keep this Book of the Law always on your lips; meditate on it day and night, so that you may be careful to do everything written in it. Then you will be prosperous and successful."

Joshua 1:8

Recently, I had a breakthrough with a unique version of macaroni and cheese. I jotted down the ingredients and tucked the recipe away for future reference. Without those instructions, I knew the next batch would be a flop.

Without God's instructions, Joshua would have failed at leading the Israelites into the Promised Land. The first step was to "be strong and courageous" (JOSHUA 1:6). Next, he was to continually meditate on the book of the law, and finally, he was to do everything it said. As long as Joshua followed the directions, God promised him that he would be "successful" (V. 8).

God's "recipe for success" can work for us too. In the original Hebrew, "you will be . . . successful" means "then you will act wisely." Just as God called Joshua to walk in wisdom, He wants us to "live, not as unwise but as wise" (EPHESIANS 5:15).

As we take courage in the Lord, feast on His Word, and obey Him, we have a recipe for godly success that's better than anything we could cook up on our own.

Jennifer

Live, not as unwise but as wise.

EPHESIANS 5:15

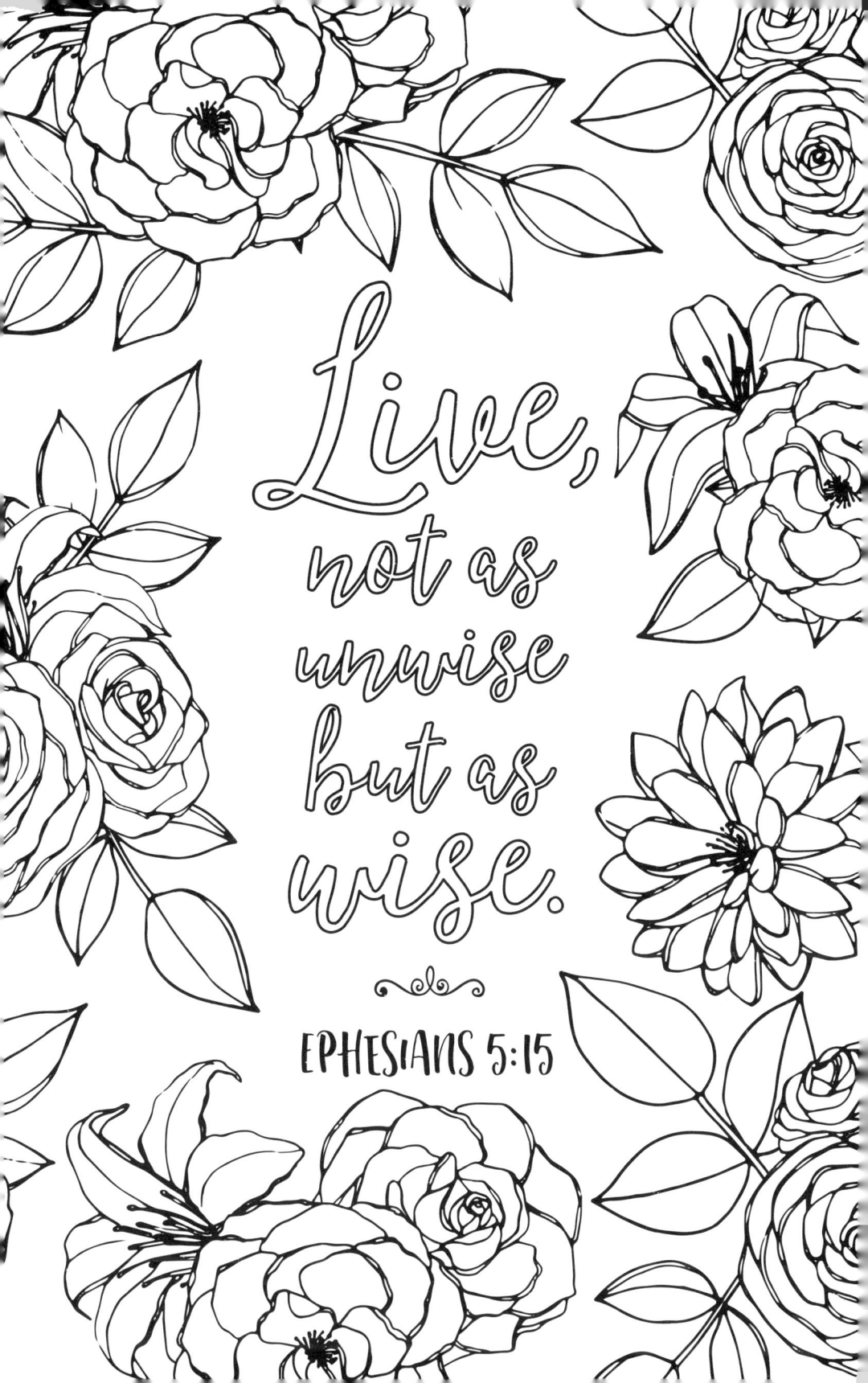

April 2

PREMATURE

ISAIAH 51:1–16

"I have put my words in your mouth and covered you with the shadow of my hand—I who set the heavens in place, who laid the foundations of the earth."

Isaiah 51:16

Born at thirty-four weeks, he was three pounds of miracle. Tubes and wires extended from his diminutive body to monitor his progress. He often became frustrated with the equipment restricting his movement. But when his dad reached through the small opening in the incubator to gently cup his tiny head in his large hand, he grew still and drifted off to sleep.

Scripture tells us, "Humans plan their course, but the Lord establishes their steps" and "the plans of the Lord stand firm forever" (PROVERBS 16:9; PSALM 33:11). But in a world where options seem to extend infinitely, we become convinced of our own infallibility. We forget God's sovereignty—until a crisis arises that reminds us of our frailty (ISAIAH 51:6). *We are not in control.*

Like a premature infant, we bear the image of what we *will* one day become. While we wait in hope, God reaches out to us in our deepest moments of need and cups us in His hand (VV. 12, 16). Here we learn to rest in hope in the Lord "who set the heavens in place" (V. 16).

Regina

April 3

LEARN THE COST
1 PETER 1:17–21

You were bought at a price. Therefore honor God with your bodies.

1 Corinthians 6:20

When we gave our two-year-old son a pair of new boots, he was so happy he didn't take them off until bedtime. But the next day he forgot all about the boots and put on his old sneakers. My husband said, "I wish he knew how much things cost."

A child receives gifts with open arms, but we know he can't be expected to fully appreciate the sacrifices his parents make to give him new things.

Sometimes I behave like a child. With open arms I receive God's gifts through His many mercies, but am I thankful? Do I consider the price that was paid so I can live a full life?

The cost was expensive—more than "perishable things such as silver or gold" (1 PETER 1:18). Peter goes on to say it required "the precious blood of Christ, a lamb without blemish and defect" (V. 19). Jesus gave His life, a high price to pay, to make us part of His family. And God raised Him from the dead (V. 21).

When we understand the cost of our salvation, we learn to be truly thankful.

Keila

April 4

THE LAST FEW POUNDS

LUKE 14:25–35

"In the same way, those of you who do not give up everything you have cannot be my disciples."

Luke 14:33

Whatever weight-loss plan you choose, you're bound to lose pounds—at least for a while. But most dieters reach a plateau before they reach their goal, and many get discouraged when the thrill leaves before all the weight does. Many give up.

Something similar happens in our Christian lives. When we begin our walk with Jesus, we easily shed many of the sins that have weighed us down. Then we discover that "little" sins like jealousy, resentment, and anger don't drop away as readily as the "big" ones. Some of us get so discouraged that we lose sight of our commitment to Christ and go back to some of our old ways of living.

When Jesus talked about the cost of being His disciple (LUKE 14:25-35), He wanted those who heard Him to realize that believing in Him and following Him involve more than simply starting something. It also means sticking with it—even if it's hard.

So whether we're talking about weight loss or spiritual gain, the message is the same: What matters most is not how we start but how we finish.

Julie

April 5

REMEMBERING . . .

PSALM 119:17–19, 130–134

> I have hidden your word in my heart that I might not sin against you.
>
> Psalm 119:11

One difficult part of growing older is the fear of short-term memory loss. But Dr. Benjamin Mast, an expert on Alzheimer's, offers encouragement. He says that patients' brains are often so "well worn" and "habitual" that they can hear an old hymn and sing along to every word. He suggests that spiritual disciplines such as reading Scripture, praying, and singing hymns cause truth to become "embedded" in our brains, ready to be accessed when prompted.

In Psalm 119 we read how the power of hiding God's words in our heart can strengthen us, teach us obedience, and direct our footsteps (vv. 28, 67, 133). This in turn gives us hope and understanding (vv. 49, 130). Even when we begin to notice memory slips in ourselves or in the life of a loved one, God's Word, memorized years earlier, is still there, "stored up" or "treasured" in the heart (v. 11 ESV, NASB). God's words will continue to speak to us.

Nothing—not even a failing memory—can separate us from His love and care. We have His word on it.

Cindy

April 6

SOAKING UP GOD'S WORD

DEUTERONOMY 6:1–9

"These commandments that I give to you today are to be on your hearts. Impress them on your children."

Deuteronomy 6:6-7

When our son Xavier was a toddler, we took a family trip to the Monterey Bay Aquarium. As we entered the building, I pointed to a large sculpture suspended from the ceiling. "Look. A humpback whale."

"Enormous," Xavier said.

My husband turned to me. "How does he know that word?"

"He must have heard us say it." I shrugged, amazed that our toddler had soaked up vocabulary we'd never intentionally taught him.

In Deuteronomy 6, God encouraged His people to be intentional about teaching younger generations to know and obey the Scriptures. As the Israelites increased their knowledge of God, they and their children would be more likely to grow in reverence of Him (vv. 2–5).

By intentionally saturating our hearts and our minds with Scripture (v. 6), we will be better prepared to share God's love and truth with children during our everyday activities (v. 7). Leading by example, we can equip and encourage young people to recognize and respect the authority and relevance of God's unchanging truth (vv. 8–9).

Xochitl

April 7

MULTIPLY IT
REVELATION 22:1-5

No longer will there be any curse. The throne of God and of the Lamb will be in the city, and his servants will serve him.

Revelation 22:3

After Amy had battled cancer for five years, her doctor told her the treatments were failing. She had just a few weeks to live.

Seeking assurance about eternity, Amy asked her pastor, "What will heaven be like?"

He asked her what she liked most about her life on earth. She talked about walks and caring friends and the laughter of children. "So, then, are you saying I will have all of that there?" she asked longingly.

He replied, "I believe that your life there will be far more beautiful and amazing than anything you ever loved or experienced here. Think about what's best here for you and multiply it over and over and over. That's what I think heaven will be."

The Bible doesn't describe in detail life in eternity, but it does tell us that being with Christ in heaven is "better by far" than our present circumstance (PHILIPPIANS 1:23).

Most important, we will see the Lord Jesus face-to-face. Our deepest yearnings will be fully satisfied in Him.

Anne

April 8

AT THE CAR WASH

ISAIAH 43:1–13

"When you pass through the waters, I will be with you; and when you pass through the rivers, they will not sweep over you. When you walk through the fire, you will not be burned; the flames will not set you ablaze."

Isaiah 43:2

I'll never forget the first time I used an automatic car wash. I pushed the money into the slot, nervously checked and rechecked my windows, eased the car up to the line, and waited. Powers beyond my control moved my car forward. There I was, cocooned inside, when a thunderous rush of water, soap, and brushes hit my car from all directions. *What if I get stuck in here?* I thought irrationally. Suddenly the waters ceased and my car was propelled into the outside world again, clean and polished.

I've had many stormy times in my life when it seemed I was a victim of forces beyond my control. "Car wash experiences," I call them. But my assurance in these times is that when I passed through deep waters my Redeemer had been with me, sheltering me against the rising tide (ISAIAH 43:2). On the other side, I could say with confidence, "He is a faithful God!"

Are you enduring a car wash experience? Trust God to bring you through to the other side. Then you'll be a shining testimony of His keeping power.

Joanie

When you pass through *the waters,* I WILL BE WITH YOU; and when you pass through the *rivers,* THEY WILL NOT SWEEP OVER YOU. When you walk through the FIRE, YOU WILL NOT BE BURNED; the flames will not set you ablaze.

ISAIAH 43:2

April 9

LOVING A PRODIGAL
LUKE 15:11–32

"We had to celebrate and be glad, because this brother of yours was dead and is alive again; he was lost and is found."

Luke 15:32

I have a special friend who has impressed me with the profound and sacrificial love she and her husband have lavished on their children, particularly a former prodigal son.

"[My son] took us on a twelve-year journey into this world of prodigaldom," she says. She founded a worldwide day of prayer for prodigals, which began as an effort by this mom to pray for her son—who has returned to his faith.

The biblical prodigal son said callously to his father, "I want my share of your estate now before you die" (LUKE 15:12 NLT). After receiving his inheritance early, he moved away and squandered his inheritance. Not until he lost everything did he return home and confess his sins to his father, who welcomed him with open arms.

"You don't give up," my friend says, "because you do love that wayward one." She says we learn that from God, "who keeps on loving, keeps on believing, keeps on forgiving."

Praise God for His love for all of us . . . even the prodigals. He patiently calls, "Come back to life!" (LUKE 15:32 NLT).

Roxanne

April 10

UNDESERVED PRAISE
LUKE 5:27-32

"I have not come to call the righteous, but sinners to repentance."
Luke 5:32

Even before I could afford a self-cleaning oven, I managed to keep my oven clean. Guests even commented on it. "Wow, your oven is so clean! It looks like new." I accepted the praise even though I knew I didn't deserve it. The answer was not my meticulous scrubbing—it was clean because I seldom used it.

How often, I wonder, am I guilty of accepting undeserved admiration for my "clean" life? It's easy to appear virtuous; simply do nothing difficult, controversial, or upsetting to people. But Jesus said we are to love people who don't agree with us. Love requires that we get involved in the messy situations of people's lives. Jesus was frequently in trouble with religious leaders who were more concerned about keeping their own reputations clean than they were about the spiritual condition of those they were supposed to care for. They considered Jesus and His disciples unclean for mingling with sinners, but Jesus was just trying to rescue them (LUKE 5:30–31).

True disciples of Jesus are willing to risk their own reputations to help others out of the mire of sin.

Julie

April 11

HEART MATTERS

PROVERBS 4:20-27

Above all else, guard your heart, for everything you do flows from it.

Proverbs 4:23

The human heart pumps at a rate of seventy to seventy-five beats per minute—and it circulates about two thousand gallons of blood each day. Every day, the heart creates enough energy to drive a truck twenty miles. In a lifetime, that's equivalent to driving to the moon and back. A healthy heart can do amazing things, but if the heart malfunctions, the whole body shuts down.

The same could be said of our "spiritual heart." In Scripture, the word *heart* represents the center of our emotions, thinking, and reasoning. It is the "command center" of our life.

So when we read, "Guard your heart" (PROVERBS 4:23), it makes a lot of sense. But it's difficult advice to keep. Life will always make demands on our time and energy, and taking time to hear God's Word and do what it says may not seem a priority. We won't notice the consequences of neglect right away, but over time it may give way to a spiritual heart attack.

We need God's help not to neglect His Word, but to use it to align our hearts with His every day.

Poh Fang

April 12

DIDN'T GET CREDIT?
COLOSSIANS 4:7–18

"Let your light shine before others, that they may see your good deeds and glorify your Father in heaven."
Matthew 5:16

During the wildly popular Hollywood musicals of the 1950s and 1960s, Audrey Hepburn, Natalie Wood, and Deborah Kerr thrilled viewers with their compelling performances. But did you know that it was Marni Nixon whose voice was often dubbed in for singing instead of the voices of those leading ladies?

In the body of Christ there are often people who faithfully support those with a more public role. The apostle Paul depended on exactly that kind of person in his ministry. Tertius's work as a scribe gave Paul his powerful written voice (ROMANS 16:22). Epaphras's consistent behind-the-scene prayers laid an essential foundation for Paul and the early church (COLOSSIANS 4:12–13). Paul's work would not have been possible without support from these fellow and other servants (VV. 7–18).

We may not have highly visible roles, yet we know that God is pleased when we fulfill our essential part in His plan. When we "give [ourselves] fully to the work of the Lord" (1 CORINTHIANS 15:58), we will find value and meaning in our service as it brings glory to God and draws others to Him.

Cindy

April 13

KNEE-DEEP IN DAFFODILS

LUKE 24:13–34

"It is true! The Lord has risen and has appeared to Simon."

Luke 24:34

When the first flowers of spring bloomed in our yard, my five-year-old son waded into a patch of daffodils and noticed some debris from plants that had expired months before. "Mommy," he said, "when I see something dead, it reminds me of Easter because Jesus died on the cross." I replied, "When I see something alive—like the daffodils—it reminds me that Jesus came back to life!"

One reason we know Jesus rose from the grave is this: He approached two travelers headed to Emmaus three days after His crucifixion. Jesus walked with them, ate dinner with them, and gave them a lesson in Old Testament prophecy (LUKE 24:15–27). Clearly, Jesus was alive! The pair returned to Jerusalem and told the disciples, "It is true! The Lord has risen" (V. 34).

If Jesus had not come back to life, our faith would be pointless. We would still be under the penalty of our sin (1 CORINTHIANS 15:17). However, Jesus "was raised to life for our justification" (ROMANS 4:25). Today we can be right with God because Jesus is alive!

Jennifer

April 14

GOD'S CLOCKS KEEP PERFECT TIME

LUKE 2:36-40

> Coming up to them at that very moment, she gave thanks to God and spoke about the child to all who were looking forward to the redemption of Jerusalem.
>
> Luke 2:38

I visit two elderly women from time to time. One has no financial worries, is fit for her age, and lives in her own home—but always has something negative to say. The other is crippled with arthritis, lives in simple accommodations, and is very forgetful. But to every visitor, her first comment is always the same: "God is so good to me." On my last visit, I noticed that she had written on her reminder pad: "Out to lunch tomorrow! Wonderful! Another happy day."

Anna was a prophetess at the time of Jesus's birth, and her circumstances were hard (LUKE 2:36-37). Widowed early and possibly childless, she may have felt purposeless and destitute. But her focus was on serving God. She yearned for the Messiah, but she kept busy about God's business—praying, fasting, and teaching others all that she had learned from Him.

Finally, the day arrived when she—now in her eighties—saw the infant Messiah in Mary's arms. Her patient waiting was worthwhile. Her heart sang with joy as she praised God and passed the glad news on to others.

Marion

April 15

THE ARLINGTON LADIES

MATTHEW 26:6-13

"Truly I tell you, wherever this gospel is preached throughout the world, what she has done will also be told, in memory of her."

Matthew 26:13

In 1948 the US Air Force Chief of Staff noticed that no one attended the funeral of an airman at Arlington National Cemetery, and that deeply disturbed him. He talked with his wife about his concern that each soldier be honored at burial, and she began a group called the Arlington Ladies.

Someone from the group honors each deceased soldier by attending his or her funeral. The ladies also write personal notes of sympathy and speak words of gratitude to family members. If possible, a representative keeps in contact with the family for months afterward. Margaret Mensch, an Arlington Lady, says, "It's an honor to . . . pay tribute to the everyday heroes that make up the armed forces."

Jesus showed the importance of paying tribute. After a woman poured a costly, fragrant oil on His head, He said that she would be honored for years to come (MATTHEW 26:13). The disciples thought her act was wasteful, but Jesus called it "a beautiful thing" (V. 10) for which she would be remembered.

It's our privilege to honor all who have done "a beautiful thing" in Jesus's name.

Anne

April 16

DANGEROUS SHORTCUTS
MATTHEW 4:1–10

Jesus answered, "It is written: 'Man shall not live on bread alone, but on every word that comes from the mouth of God.'"
Matthew 4:4

During recent elections in my country, one struggling mom exchanged her vote for a bag of diapers. Her choice disappointed me. "What about your convictions?" I asked. She remained silent. Six months after her candidate won, taxes went even higher. Everything is now more expensive . . . even diapers!

Political corruption is not new. Neither is spiritual corruption. Satan tried to lure Jesus into "selling" His convictions (MATTHEW 4:1–10). The tempter came to Him when He was tired and hungry, offering Him immediate satisfaction, fresh bread in seconds, a miraculous delivery, and the kingdoms of the world.

But Jesus knew better. He knew that shortcuts were dangerous. They may offer a road free from suffering, but in the end the pain they carry is much worse than anything we can imagine. "It is written," Jesus said three times during His temptation (VV. 4, 7, 10). He held firm to God and His Word.

When we are tempted, God can help us too. We can depend on Him and the truth of His Word to help us avoid dangerous shortcuts.

Keila

April 17

TIME TOGETHER
PSALM 147:1–11

The Lord delights in those who fear him, who put their hope in his unfailing love.

Psalm 147:11

My mom has Alzheimer's, a disease that progressively destroys the memory, can adversely affect behavior, and eventually leads to the loss of speech—and more.

I grieve because of my mom's disease but am thankful she is still here and we can spend time together—and even converse. It thrills me that whenever I go to see her she lights up with joy and exclaims, "Alyson, what a pleasant surprise!" We enjoy each other's company; and even in the silences when words escape her, we commune together.

This perhaps is a small picture of our relationship with God. Scripture tells us, "The Lord delights in those who fear him, who put their hope in his unfailing love" (PSALM 147:11). God calls those who believe in Jesus as their Savior His children (JOHN 1:12). And although we may make the same requests over and over again or lack for words, He is patient with us because He has a loving relationship with us. He is happy when we converse with Him in prayer—even when the words escape us.

Alyson

April 18

NOT FEAR BUT FAITH

NUMBERS 13:25–14:9

"The Lord is with us. Do not be afraid of them."

Numbers 14:9

"My husband was offered a promotion in another country, but I feared leaving our home, so he declined the offer," my friend shared with me. She explained later that she sometimes wonders what they missed in not moving.

The Israelites let their anxieties paralyze them when they were called to inhabit a rich and fertile land that flowed "with milk and honey" (EXODUS 33:3). When they heard the reports of the powerful people in large cities (NUMBERS 13:28), fear caused many of the Israelites to reject the call to enter the land.

But Joshua and Caleb urged them not to be afraid, saying the "Lord is with us" (14:9). Although the people there appeared large, the Israelites could trust God's presence.

My friend wasn't commanded to move to another country like the Israelites were, yet she regretted letting fear close off the opportunity. What about you—do you face a fearful situation? If so, know that the Lord is with you and will guide you. With His never-failing love, we can move forward in faith.

Amy

April 19

FEELING COMPASSION
LUKE 10:25–37

> But he wanted to justify himself, so he asked Jesus, "And who is my neighbor?"
>
> Luke 10:29

Stephen Crane's story "The Open Boat" tells the tale of four men attempting to survive in a lifeboat at sea. One of the men ironically reflected on a poem he had read as a schoolboy about a soldier fighting in Algiers. He realized "he had never considered it his affair that a soldier of the Legion lay dying in Algiers, nor had it appeared to him as a matter for sorrow." He hadn't felt compassion for the soldier—until now.

The word *compassion* literally means "to suffer with someone." Our ability to feel others' pain may be lacking until we find ourselves suffering through our own pain. Like the expert in religious law who tested Jesus, we justify our own apathetic response when it comes to fulfilling the latter part of what Jesus said was the greatest commandment (LUKE 10:27).

Saving us from our sharpest place of desperation, Jesus showed great compassion as He gave His life for us. Through the power of the Holy Spirit, may we do no less for others.

Regina

A TIME FOR EVERYTHING

ECCLESIASTES 3:1-14

> There is a time for everything, and a season for every activity under the heavens.
>
> *Ecclesiastes 3:1*

While flying recently, I watched a mother and her children a few rows ahead of me. While the toddler played contentedly, the mother gazed into the eyes of her newborn, smiling at him and stroking his cheek. I enjoyed the moment with a touch of wistfulness, thinking of my own children at that age and the season that has passed me by.

I reflected, however, on King Solomon's words in the book of Ecclesiastes about "every activity under the heavens" (V. 1). He describes "a time to be born and a time to die" (V. 2). Perhaps King Solomon in these verses despairs at what he sees as a meaningless cycle of life. But he also acknowledges the role of God in each season, that our work is a "gift of God" (V. 13), and that "everything God does will endure forever" (V. 14).

We may remember times in our lives with longing. We know, however, that God promises to be with us in every season of life (ISAIAH 41:10). We can count on His presence and continue walking with Him.

Amy

April 20

April 21

THE TREASURE CHEST
HEBREWS 11:32–40

We do not want you to become lazy, but to imitate those who through faith and patience inherit what has been promised.
Hebrews 6:12

When I was young, my mother let me rummage through her button box as I recovered from an illness. It cheered me to come across old, familiar buttons and remember the garments they once adorned. I especially liked it when she picked out an old, overlooked button and used it again.

Similarly, I often leaf through my Bible during distressing times and recall familiar promises that have strengthened me. I'm always encouraged to find help from promises I've never noticed before.

I remember one dark morning during my husband's terminal illness when I was looking for a word from God to sustain me. In Hebrews 11, I noted that God had rescued His suffering people in some dramatic ways. Yet I couldn't always identify. Then I read about someone "whose weakness was turned to strength" (V. 34). I realized that even in my weakness I could find His strength. My faith was renewed.

Are you being tested? Remember, there are many promises in the Bible. Generations have proven them true, and so can you.

Joanie

April 22

JUST THE RIGHT TIME

HEBREWS 9:11-22

> But Jesus answered, "No more of this!" And he touched the man's ear and healed him.
>
> Luke 22:51

Early in his career, jazz player Herbie Hancock was invited to play in the quintet of legendary Miles Davis. Later Hancock admitted being nervous but described it as a wonderful experience because Davis was so nurturing. During one performance, when Davis was near the high point of his solo, Hancock played the wrong chord. He was mortified, but Davis continued as if nothing had happened. "He played some notes that made my chord right," Hancock said.

What an example of loving leadership! Davis simply adjusted his plan and turned a potentially disastrous mistake into something beautiful.

What Davis did for Hancock, Jesus did for Peter. When Peter cut off the ear of a soldier who had come to arrest Jesus, Jesus reattached the ear (LUKE 22:51), indicating that His kingdom was about healing, not hurting. Time after time Jesus used the disciples' mistakes to show a better way.

What Jesus did for His disciples, He also does for us. What He does for us, we can do for others. Instead of magnifying every mistake, we can turn them into beautiful acts of forgiveness, healing, and redemption.

Julie

April 23

HOW CAN I HELP YOU?

MARK 10:43–52

"What do you want me to do for you?" Jesus asked him. The blind man said, "Rabbi, I want to see."

Mark 10:51

Seminary president Haddon Robinson met with a wealthy donor to seek a sizable contribution. When Robinson asked for a specific amount, the donor replied: "I was prepared to give you much more if you had asked."

This story reminds us to "approach God's throne of grace with confidence, so that we may receive mercy and find grace to help us in our time of need" (HEBREWS 4:16).

It's vital for us to bring our requests to God, because He delights to give His children good gifts (MATTHEW 7:11). We can freely share our requests with Him, remembering that they should reflect our seeking after His kingdom above all else. Then God in His wisdom will give us what we truly *need*—not just what we *want* (6:33).

Let's continue to seek after God and to fulfill our mission within His kingdom, and as we do, let's bring our requests to Him. He may be prepared to provide even more than we ask for (EPHESIANS 3:20).

Marlena

April 24

HOPE FOR A MUDDER

JAMES 1:2-4

> Not only so, but we also glory in our sufferings, because we know that suffering produces perseverance; perseverance, character; and character, hope.
>
> Romans 5:3-4

When my husband built a covered porch on the front of our house, he built the top of the corner post on a slant to thwart any possible bird's nest activity. At first it worked. But after two days of steady rain, we saw that a nest did indeed appear in the spot we thought was impossible. Because of the rain, Mrs. Robin was able to mix up a batch of mud mortar. Weaving it with twigs and grass, our determined feathered friend had built herself a new nest. She had persevered.

Perseverance is inspiring! Trying to live a Christ-honoring life while experiencing hardship can leave us frustrated and discouraged. But when we depend on God to help us through our difficulties, we are empowered to keep going even when we can't always see the resolution of our problems. Galatians 6:9 reminds us not to grow "weary in doing good" and encourages us not to give up.

Is God using a seemingly insurmountable challenge in your life to produce perseverance? Let Him produce in you character, and through character, hope (ROMANS 5:3-4).

Cindy

April 25

SMILE
PSALM 29:1-11

The Lord gives strength to his people; the Lord blesses his people with peace.

Psalm 29:11

I once met a beautiful girl named Mercy, a patient at a Kampala, Uganda, hospital. During one visit, her brother explained that their parents had died and he, at age fourteen, was Mercy's sole caregiver. "I have learned you . . . gave pillows to the patients last week," he said. "My sister has never slept on a pillow before. Would you please bring her one?"

Mercy had the most beautiful smile I've ever seen. As I looked into her eyes, I knew I was witnessing someone experiencing God's peace—the inexplicable peace of Philippians 4:7.

The next day I brought Mercy a pillow. Her huge smile grew even wider. I sat and held her hand a long time. When I returned the following day, her bed was empty; she had died. The hospital let me view her body to say goodbye. Her head was resting on the pillow on which she had slept for just one night, and her mouth was closed . . . but *smiling*.

Dear Lord, help us grasp more profoundly what Mercy knew—that you will never abandon your children.

Roxanne

April 26

THE SMALL THINGS
PSALM 116:1-9

Every good and perfect gift is from above.
James 1:17

My friend Gloria, who had not been able to leave her house except for doctors' appointments, called with excitement in her voice. "My son just attached new speakers to my computer, so now I can go to my church!" She could now hear the live broadcast of her church's worship service. She raved about God's goodness.

Gloria teaches me about having a thankful heart. Despite her many limitations, she's thankful for the smallest of things. She's had a lifetime of seeing God provide for her, and she talks about Him to anyone who visits or calls.

We don't know what difficulties the author of Psalm 116 was encountering. Some Bible commentaries say it was probably sickness because he said, "The cords of death entangled me" (v. 3). But he gave thanks to the Lord for being gracious and full of compassion when he was "brought low" (vv. 5–6).

When we're low, it can be hard to look up. Yet if we do, we see that God is the giver of all good gifts in our life—great and small—and we learn to give Him thanks.

Anne

April 27

SHARING A CUP OF COMFORT
2 CORINTHIANS 1:3-11

Our hope for you is firm, because we know that just as you share in our sufferings, so also you share in our comfort.
2 Corinthians 1:7

A friend mailed me some of her homemade pottery, but some of it was damaged during the journey. After my husband glued the broken mess back together, I displayed the beautifully blemished cup on a shelf.

Like that pieced-together pottery, I have scars that prove I can still stand strong after the difficult times God has brought me through. Sharing how the Lord has worked in and through my life can help others during their times of suffering.

The apostle Paul praises God because He is the "Father of compassion and the God of all comfort" (2 CORINTHIANS 1:3). The Lord uses our trials and sufferings to make us more like Him. His comfort in our troubles equips us to encourage others as we share what He did for us during our time of need (V. 4).

Like Paul, we can be comforted in knowing that the Lord redeems our trials for His glory. We can share His cups of comfort and bring reassuring hope to the hurting.

Xochitl

THE SHRINKING PIANO

PHILIPPIANS 1:1–11

He who began a good work in you will carry it on to completion until the day of Christ Jesus.

Philippians 1:6

For three consecutive years, my son participated in a piano recital. The last year he played, I watched him mount the steps and set up his music. He played two songs, sat down next to me, and whispered, "Mom, this year the piano was smaller." I said, "No, it's the same piano you played last year. You're bigger!"

Spiritual growth, like physical growth, often happens slowly over time. It is an ongoing process that involves becoming more like Jesus, and it happens as we are transformed through the renewing of our minds (ROMANS 12:2).

Spiritual growth involves the Holy Spirit, our willingness to change, and time. At certain points in our lives, we may look back and see that we have grown spiritually. May God give us the faith to continue to believe that "He who began a good work in [us] will carry it on to completion until the day of Christ Jesus" (PHILIPPIANS 1:6).

Jennifer

April 29

NOT AGAIN
2 THESSALONIANS 2:13–17

But we ought always to thank God for you, brothers and sisters loved by the Lord, because God chose you as firstfruits to be saved through the sanctifying work of the Spirit and through belief in the truth.

2 Thessalonians 2:13

As I was reading the text message on my mobile phone, my temperature started to rise and my blood began to boil. I was on the verge of shooting back a nasty message when an inner voice told me to cool down and reply tomorrow. The next morning after a good night's sleep, the issue that had upset me so greatly seemed trivial. I had blown it out of proportion. I was unwilling to inconvenience myself so I could help someone.

Regretfully, I am tempted to respond in anger more often than I would like to admit. I constantly find myself having to put into practice familiar Bible truths, such as "In your anger do not sin" (EPHESIANS 4:26) and "Let each of you look out not only for his own interests, but also for the interests of others" (PHILIPPIANS 2:4 NKJV).

Thankfully, God has given us His Spirit, who will assist us in our battle with our sin. Paul and Peter both called it the "sanctifying work of the Spirit" (2 THESSALONIANS 2:13; 1 PETER 1:2). With His help, we can have victory.

Poh Fang

April 30

FREE FROM FEAR

PSALM 34:1-10

I sought the LORD, and he answered me; he delivered me from all my fears.

Psalm 34:4

Fear sneaks into my heart without permission. It paints a picture of hopelessness and steals my peace. What am I fearful about? Safety of my family or the health of loved ones. The loss of a job or a broken relationship. Fear turns my focus inward and reveals an untrusting heart.

When these fears and worries strike, how good it is to read David's prayer in Psalm 34: "I sought the LORD, and he answered me; he delivered me from all my fears" (v. 4). And how does God deliver us from our fears? When we "look to him" (v. 5), we trust Him to be in control. Then David mentions a different type of fear—a deep respect and awe of the One who surrounds us and delivers us (v. 7). We can take refuge in Him because He is good (v. 8).

This awe of His goodness helps put our fears into perspective. When we remember who God is and how much He loves us, we can relax into His peace. In seeking the Lord we can be delivered from our fears.

Keila

MAY DAY

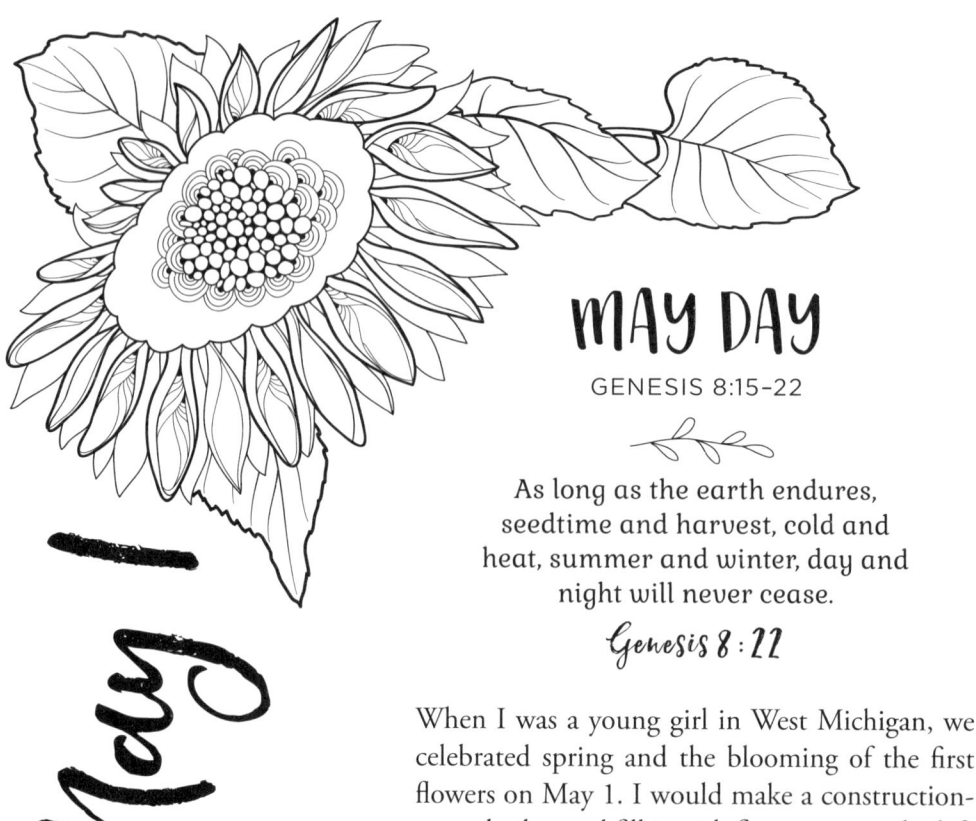

GENESIS 8:15-22

> As long as the earth endures, seedtime and harvest, cold and heat, summer and winter, day and night will never cease.
>
> *Genesis 8:22*

When I was a young girl in West Michigan, we celebrated spring and the blooming of the first flowers on May 1. I would make a construction-paper basket and fill it with flowers—mostly daffodils and violets. Then I would place the basket on my neighbor's doorstep, knock on her door, and hide behind a bush. I'd peek out to watch her as she opened the door and picked up her surprise.

The beauty of springtime flowers and the regular changing of the seasons remind us of God's faithfulness. When Noah and his family and the animals came out of the ark after the floodwaters receded, God gave them this promise: "As long as the earth endures, seedtime and harvest, cold and heat, summer and winter, day and night will never cease" (GENESIS 8:22). And He's been faithful to keep that promise ever since. God "made the universe," and He continues to uphold "all things by his powerful word" (HEBREWS 1:2-3).

Let's thank God today for His beautiful creation and for His faithfulness in sustaining His world and us.

Anne

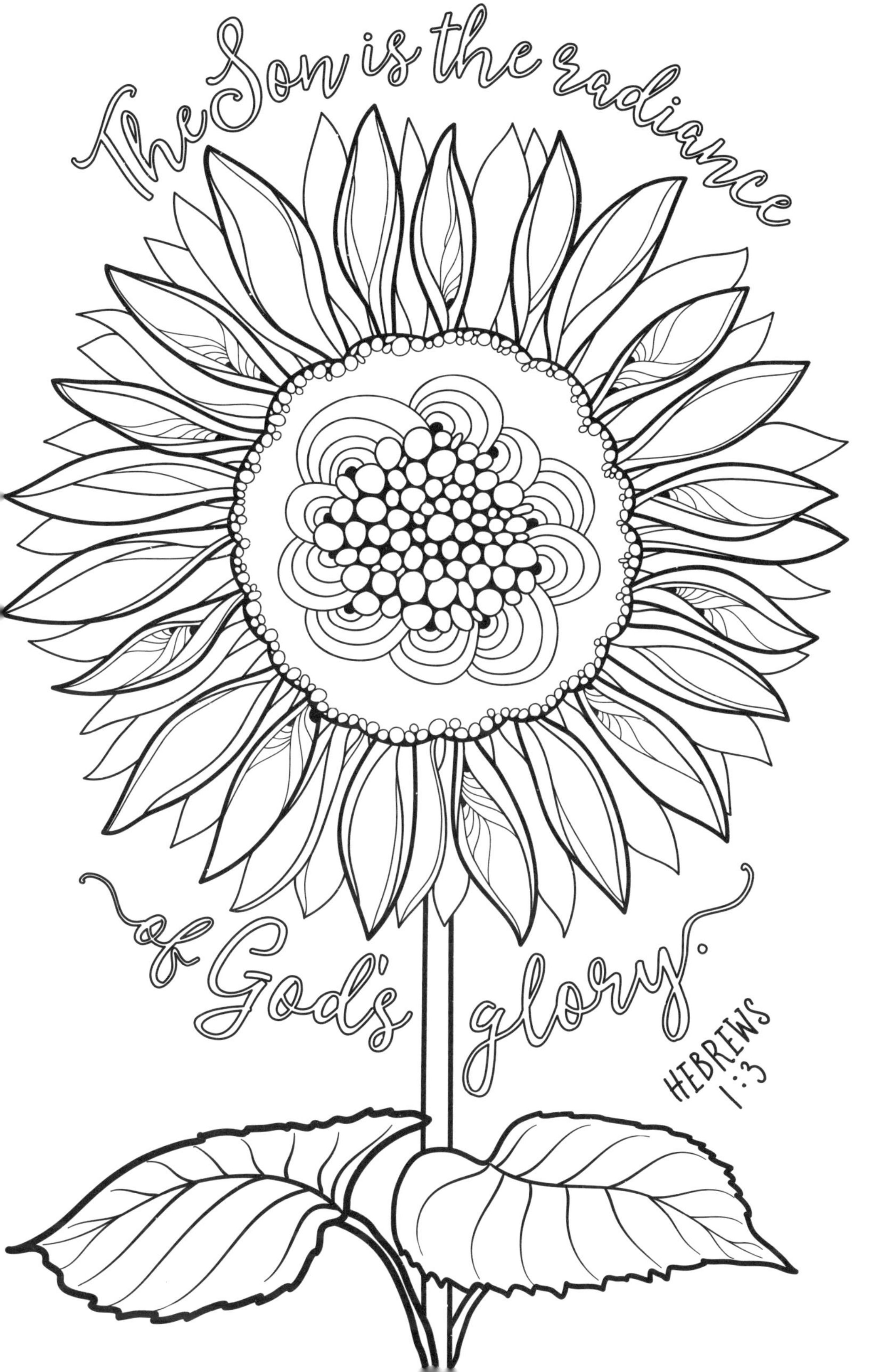
The Son is the radiance
of God's glory.
HEBREWS 1:3

May 2

SEEING OURSELVES
1 CORINTHIANS 11:23-24

Everyone ought to examine themselves before they eat of the bread and drink from the cup.

1 Corinthians 11:28

Long ago, before the invention of mirrors or polished surfaces, people rarely saw themselves. Puddles of water, streams, and rivers were among the few ways they could see their own reflection.

But mirrors changed that. And the invention of cameras took fascination with our looks to a whole new level. We now have lasting images of ourselves from any given time throughout our life. This is good for keeping memories alive, but it can be detrimental to our spiritual well-being. We can tend to become focused on outward appearance—with little interest in examining our inner selves.

Self-examination is crucial for a healthy spiritual life. It is so important that Scripture says we are not to participate in the Lord's Supper without first examining ourselves (1 CORINTHIANS 11:28). The point of this self-examination is not only to make things right with God but also to make sure we are right with one another. We can't celebrate communion properly if we're not living in harmony with other believers.

Self-examination promotes unity with others and a healthy relationship with God.

Julie

May 3

UNPLANNED CHANGE

PSALM 37:1–24

The Lord makes firm the steps of the one who delights in him

Psalm 37:23

A few years ago, our county's board of education decided not to renew our church's lease of the school building where we met every Sunday.

Shocked, we considered other venues but couldn't find anything suitable for a while. When we planted the church, we understood the unpredictability of using a shared facility. But we hadn't planned on *this*.

Plans are doors of hope to what we believe God would have us do. David knew the importance of giving our plans to God: "Commit your way to the Lord; trust in him and he will do this" (PSALM 37:5). Instead of being overwhelmed by the coming change, it was important for my husband and me to "be still before the Lord and wait patiently for him" (V. 7).

Surrendering our plans to God doesn't mean He will fulfill them the way we would like, but He does direct the "steps of the one who delights in him" (V. 23). When we trust Him in the midst of the unplanned, He takes unexpected changes and transforms them into opportunities for us to grow our faith.

Regina

May 4

BUILDING A LIFE
JOHN 20:11–18

For to me, to live is Christ and to die is gain.
Philippians 1:21

The day after my husband, Bill, died in 1982, I went alone to his grave. As with Mary Magdalene who visited Jesus's tomb, the risen Lord was waiting for me. Although I was still numbed by Bill's untimely death from cancer, I felt the Lord impressing the words of Philippians 1:21 on my mind.

I wove a prayer around the words of that verse: "Lord, how often I've heard Bill testify, 'For to me, to live is Christ, and to die is gain.' Well, your servant has now died—an untold loss for us, an unspeakable gain for him. I know I must not live in the past, precious as it is. For to me, to live is you!'"

As I turned to leave, I knew I had prayed a foundational prayer. Much recovery and rebuilding lay before me, but beneath me was the firm foundation of Jesus Christ.

Has a loved one's death tested your foundation? Let Paul's words, written in the face of death, encourage you to offer a foundational prayer of your own. Then begin to rebuild your life on the risen Christ!

Joanie

May 5

LIE DOWN
EXODUS 20:8–11

He makes me lie down in green pastures, he leads me beside quiet waters, he refreshes my soul. He guides me along the right paths for his name's sake.

Psalm 23:2-3

Our golden retriever can get so overly excited that he'll go into a seizure. To prevent that from happening, we try to calm him with a soothing voice. When he hears "lie down," he avoids eye contact with us and starts complaining. Finally, with a dramatic sigh of resignation, he gives in and plops to the floor.

Sometimes we too need to be reminded to lie down. In Psalm 23, we learn that our Good Shepherd makes us "lie down in green pastures." He knows we need the calmness that rest provides.

Our bodies are designed to rest. God himself rested on the seventh day after His work of creation (GENESIS 2:2–3; EXODUS 20:9–11). Jesus knew there was a time to minister to the crowds and a time to rest. He instructed His disciples to go with Him "to a quiet place and get some rest" (MARK 6:31).

Rest is a gift—a good gift from our Creator who knows exactly what we need. Praise Him that He sometimes makes us "lie down in green pastures."

Cindy

May 6

KNOWN BY GOD
GALATIANS 4:8–12

Formerly, when you did not know God, you were slaves to those who by nature are not gods.
Galatians 4:8

In 1996 I was a press manager for the Olympic Village, home to all the athletes who were competing in the Atlanta Games.

One night as I was taking some people into the village, all was going well until one couple began to shout, "Why aren't the cameras on us? Don't you people know who we are?" I sure didn't. But eventually they landed a reality TV show and became famous, as they wanted.

Many people today have that view—that it's important to be known by others. They don't know that it's best to be known by our Creator. Jesus corrected that thinking: "Now this is eternal life: that they know you, the only true God, and Jesus Christ, whom you have sent" (JOHN 17:3).

In Galatians 4, Paul said, "Now that you know God—or rather are known by God," he said, "how is it that you are turning back . . . ? Do you wish to be enslaved by them all over again?" (V. 9).

There's something far greater than fame. May we turn to God today and experience the joy and life found in His presence.

Roxanne

REMEMBER THE CROSS

MARK 15:19–20, 33–39

"Surely this man was the Son of God!"
Mark 15:39

In my church, a large cross stands at the front of the sanctuary. It represents the original cross where Jesus died. There God allowed His perfect Son to die for the sake of every wrong thing we have ever done. On the cross, Jesus finished the work required to save us from the death we deserve (ROMANS 6:23).

The sight of a cross causes me to consider what Jesus endured for us. He was flogged and spit on. The soldiers hit Him in the head with sticks. They mocked him. They tried to make Him carry His own cross. At Golgotha, they hammered nails through His flesh to keep Him on the cross. Those wounds bore the weight of His body as He hung there. Six hours later, Jesus took His final breath (MARK 15:37). A centurion who witnessed Jesus's death declared, "Surely this man was the Son of God!" (V. 39).

The next time you see the symbol of the cross, consider what it means. God's Son suffered and died there and then rose again to make eternal life possible. For me. For you.

Jennifer

May 7

May 8

A PLEASANT DIVERSION?

ROMANS 11:33–12:2

> Do not conform to the pattern of this world, but be transformed by the renewing of your mind. Then you will be able to test and approve what God's will is—his good, pleasing and perfect will.
>
> *Romans 12:2*

A friend who was looking for a church to attend told me she had found just what she was looking for: "I like this church because I don't have to change my lifestyle of partying. It doesn't make me feel guilty or require anything of me. I feel good about myself when I'm there."

But is this what Jesus calls us to? Author W. Waldo Beach says, "No amount of air-conditioning and pew-cushioning in the suburban church can cover over the hard truth that . . . discipleship is costly. . . . No one can understand Christianity to its depths who comes to it to enjoy it as a pleasant weekend diversion."

Being a Christian means we know Jesus personally because we have received Him by faith as our Savior from sin. We deny our will and choose His instead. He transforms our thinking, our values, and our priorities to reflect what is acceptable to God (ROMANS 12:1–2).

True faith is not a pleasant weekend diversion—it is a vibrant relationship with Jesus!

Anne

May 9

PAINFUL PRUNING
JOHN 15:1-5

"He cuts off every branch in me that bears no fruit, while every branch that does bear fruit he prunes so that it will be even more fruitful."

John 15:2

Last summer we planted rosebushes in the backyard in honor of my *abuelita*, my grandmother. Wild and sweet-smelling roses had grown around her house. The roses we planted would be a beautiful reminder of her.

I was joyful as I watched the roses bloom all summer. Then came the first frost. I knew it was time to lop off the roses and prune the branches.

Just as I had to prune the rosebushes to foster annual renewal, sometimes God needs to do some pruning in us. Even though it's painful and we don't welcome it, He prunes us so we "will be even more fruitful" (JOHN 15:2). His aim isn't to hurt us, but to conform us into the image of Jesus (ROMANS 8:29) for our blessing and growth (JOB 5:17).

Maybe you're going through a difficult time. You're struggling and wish the hurt and discomfort would go away. That's understandable. Yet, if you're being pruned, you can look to the future with great expectation. God is making sure you bear even more fruit. He'll never waste your pain and suffering.

Marlena

May 10

HE WILL REPLY
PSALM 91

He will call on me, and I will answer him; I will be with him in trouble, I will deliver him and honor him.

Psalm 91:15

When I came upon the Twitter page of my favorite Korean movie star, I decided to drop her a note. I sent my message and waited. But she never replied.

Thankfully, that's not the way it is with God.

We know He responds to us. He is the "Most High," the "Almighty" (PSALM 91:1). Yet He is accessible to us. God invites: "Call upon Me, and I will answer" (V. 15 NKJV).

An ancient legend tells of a monarch who hired weavers to make tapestries and garments. The king gave instructions to seek his aid if they had any difficulties. One young weaver was successful work while the others experienced trouble. When the boy was asked why he was successful, he said, "Didn't you notice how often I called for the king?" They replied, "But he's busy. We thought you were wrong in disturbing him." He replied, "I just took him at his word, and he was always happy to help me!"

Our God is like that king—only so much greater. He is loving and kind enough to care about our smallest concern and faintest whisper.

Poh Fang

May 11

NOTHING IS USELESS
1 CORINTHIANS 15:42–58

Nothing you do for the Lord is ever useless.

1 Corinthians 15:58 (NLT)

In my third year battling discouragement and depression caused by limited mobility and chronic pain, I confided to a friend, "My body's falling apart. I feel like I have nothing of value to offer God or anyone else."

"Would you say it doesn't make a difference when I greet you with a smile or listen to you?" she asked. "Would you tell me it's worthless when I pray for you?"

"Of course not."

"Then why are you telling yourself those lies? You do all those things for me and for others."

I thanked God for reminding me that nothing we do for Him is useless.

Because God promises we'll be resurrected through Christ (1 CORINTHIANS 15:43), we can trust Him to use every small effort done for Him to make a difference in His kingdom (V. 58).

Even when we're physically limited, a smile, a word of encouragement, a prayer, or a display of faith during our trial can be used to minister to others. When we serve the Lord, no job or act of love is too menial to matter.

Xochitl

May 12

THE REMEDY FOR JEALOUSY
1 SAMUEL 18:5–15

So from that time on Saul kept a jealous eye on David.
1 Samuel 18:9 (NLT)

While babysitting my grandsons, I asked them what they had done the previous weekend. Bridger, age three, recounted breathlessly that he got to stay overnight with his aunt and uncle—and he had ice cream and rode a carousel and watched a movie! Next it was five-year-old Samuel's turn. He simply said, "Camping." "Did you have fun?" I asked. "Not so much," he answered forlornly.

Samuel forgot how much fun he had camping with his dad when he heard Bridger excitedly tell about his weekend.

All of us can fall prey to jealousy. King Saul gave in to the green-eyed monster when the praise David received exceeded his: "Saul has killed his thousands, and David his ten thousands!" (1 SAMUEL 18:7 NLT). Saul was outraged and "from that time on . . . kept a jealous eye on David" (V. 9 NLT). He was so incensed he tried to kill David!

God has given us many blessings, including both abundant life here and the promise of eternal life to come. Depending on His help and focusing on Him in thankfulness can help us overcome jealousy.

Alyson

May 13

FACE-TO-FACE

EXODUS 33:7–14

> The LORD would speak to Moses face to face, as one speaks to a friend.
>
> Exodus 33:11

Although we're all connected electronically like never before, nothing beats time together in person. Those who love each other, whether family or friends, like to share with each other face-to-face.

We see this face-to-face relationship between the Lord and Moses, the man God chose to lead His people. Moses grew in confidence over the years of following God, and he continued to follow Him despite the people's rebelliousness and idolatry. After the people worshiped a golden calf instead of the Lord (SEE EXODUS 32), Moses set up a tent outside of the camp in which to meet God, while they had to watch from a distance (33:7–11). As the pillar of cloud signifying God's presence descended to the tent, Moses spoke on their behalf. The Lord promised that His presence would go with them (V. 14).

We no longer need someone like Moses to speak with God for us. Instead, just as Jesus offered His disciples, we can have friendship with God through Christ (JOHN 15:15). We too can meet with Him, with the Lord speaking to us as one speaks to a friend.

Amy

May 14

EYES TO SEE
JOSHUA 3:1–11

I spread out my hands to you; I thirst for you like a parched land.
Psalm 143:6

My first glimpse of the Promised Land from the hills of Moab was disappointing. "Did this look a lot different when the Israelites got here?" I asked our guide as we looked toward Jericho. "No," she answered. "It has looked the same for thousands of years."

I rephrased the question. "What did the Israelites see when they got here?" "The biggest oasis on the face of the whole earth," she replied.

Then I understood. I had ridden across the barren desert in the luxury of an air-conditioned bus stocked with cold bottled water. To me, an oasis was nothing spectacular. The Israelites had spent years wandering in a hot, dry desert. To them, the sprawling patch of pale green in the hazy distance meant refreshing, life-sustaining water.

Like an oasis, God's goodness is found in dry and difficult places. How often, I wonder, do we fail to see His goodness because our spiritual senses have been dulled by comfort. Sometimes God's gifts are seen more clearly when we are tired and thirsty. May we always thirst for Him (PSALM 143:6).

Julie

May 15

A LESSON LEARNED

PHILIPPIANS 4:10–19

> I am not saying this because I am in need, for I have learned to be content whatever the circumstances.
>
> *Philippians 4:11*

Mary was widowed and facing serious health challenges, so her daughter invited her to move into the new "granny apartment" attached to her home. Although it would involve leaving friends and the rest of her family many miles away, Mary rejoiced in God's provision.

Six months into her new life, her contentment slipped away. She missed her Christian friends, and her new church was too far away to get to independently.

Then she read something nineteenth-century preacher Charles Spurgeon had written. "Now contentment is one of the flowers of heaven, and it must be cultivated," he pointed out. "Paul says, 'I have learned to be content,' as if he didn't know how at one time."

Mary concluded that if an ardent evangelist like Paul, confined to prison, abandoned by friends, and facing execution could learn contentment, then so could she.

Mary said, "I confessed my inward grumbling and asked for God's forgiveness. Soon after that a newly retired lady asked if I would be her prayer partner, and others offered me a ride to church. My needs were wonderfully met."

Marion

May 16

PENCIL BATTLES
JUDGES 2:11-22

> But when the judge died, the people returned to ways even more corrupt than those of their ancestors, following other gods and serving and worshiping them. They refused to give up their evil practices and stubborn ways.
>
> *Judges 2:19*

As I learned to write my letters, my first-grade teacher insisted that I hold my pencil in a specific way. As she watched me, I held it the way she wanted me to. But when she turned away, I obstinately reverted to holding the pencil the way I found more comfortable.

Decades later, I realize that my wise teacher knew that my stubborn habit would grow into a bad writing practice that would result in my hand tiring more quickly.

Children rarely understand what is good for them. They operate almost entirely on what they want at the moment. Perhaps the "children of Israel" were aptly named as generation after generation stubbornly insisted on worshiping the gods of the nations around them rather than the one true God. Their actions greatly angered the Lord because He knew what was best, and He removed His blessing from them (JUDGES 2:20–22).

If a rebellious spirit is keeping us from obeying God, it's time for a change of heart. Return to the Lord; He is gracious and merciful.

Cindy

May 17

ISN'T HE BEAUTIFUL

ISAIAH 9:1–7

> For to us a child is born, to us a son is given, and the government will be on his shoulders. And he will be called Wonderful Counselor, Mighty God, Everlasting Father, Prince of Peace.
>
> *Isaiah 9:6*

A group of children from our city was in a worship service, and we started to sing. Ariel, age seven, leaned close to me and softly said, "I love this song; it makes me cry."

The music and words about Jesus, her Savior, touched her heart as we sang the John Wimber song "Isn't He Beautiful."

Yes, the Lord Jesus is beautiful. We don't find a specific reference in the Bible describing Him that way, but His personal character is strong yet gentle, holy yet forgiving, majestic yet humble—all combined. Simply beautiful!

In his prophecy, Isaiah described Jesus and His coming in this way: "To us a Child is born, to us a Son is given, and the government will be on his shoulders. And he will be called Wonderful Counselor, Mighty God, Everlasting Father, Prince of Peace" (ISAIAH 9:6).

Jesus is the Wonderful Counselor—giving us comfort and wisdom. The Everlasting Father—providing for all our needs and protecting us. And the Prince of Peace—offering reconciliation with God and others.

Isn't Jesus beautiful! Worship Him.

Anne

Wonderful Counselor, MIGHTY GOD, Everlasting Father, PRINCE of PEACE.

ISAIAH 9:6

May 18

ONE WHO SERVES
LUKE 22:24-27

"For who is greater, the one who is at the table or the one who serves? Is it not the one who is at the table? But I am among you as one who serves."

Luke 22:27

"I'm nobody's servant!" I cried out. That morning the demands of my family seemed too much as I frantically helped find my husband's blue tie while feeding the crying baby and recovering the lost toy from under the bed for our two-year-old.

Later that day, I came across something Jesus said, "For who is greater, the one who is at the table or the one who serves? Is it not the one who is at the table? But I am among you as one who serves" (LUKE 22:27).

Today's society insists that we should aim to "be somebody." We want the best-paying job, the highest position in the company, an important role at church. Yet whatever position we are in, we can learn about service from our Savior.

We all hold different roles, but here's the question: Do we carry out those roles with an attitude of service? Even though my everyday routine is sometimes tiring, I'm thankful the Master helps me, because I want to follow His steps and willingly serve others.

May God help each of us be one who serves.

Keila

May 19

WORRIER OR WARRIOR?

EPHESIANS 3:14–21

Now to him who is able to do immeasurably more than all we ask or imagine, according to his power that is at work within us.

Ephesians 3:20

A missionary wrote a newsletter to thank his supporters for being "prayer warriors." Because of a typing error, though, he called them "prayer worriers." For some of us, that might be a good description.

In his book *Growing Your Soul*, Neil Wiseman writes, "Prayer must be more than a kind of restatement of fretting worries or a mulling over of problems. Our petitions must move beyond gloomy desperation, which deals mostly with calamity and despair."

During an anxious time in my life, I became a "prayer worrier." I would beg, "Lord, please keep my neighbor from causing me problems tomorrow." Or, "Father, don't let that ornery person spread gossip about me."

But then the Lord taught me to pray for people, rather than against them. Paul was no "prayer worrier." He prayed for God's people that they might know the strength, love, and fullness of God, who is able to do far more than we can ask or even think (EPHESIANS 3:14–21). Such confidence made Paul a true "prayer warrior." Isn't that what we all want to be?

Joanie

May 20

THE BARKING LION

PROVERBS 22:1–5

A good name is more desirable than great riches; to be esteemed is better than silver or gold.

Proverbs 22:1

Visitors to a zoo were outraged when the "African lion" started barking. Zoo staff said they had disguised a Tibetan mastiff—a very large dog—as a lion because they could not afford the real thing. That zoo's reputation was severely damaged.

Reputation is fragile; once it's called into question, it's hard to restore. Scripture encourages us: "A good name is more desirable than great riches" (PROVERB 22:1). True value must be placed not in what we have but in who we are.

Ancient Greek philosopher Socrates said, "The way to gain a good reputation is to endeavor to be what you desire to appear." As followers of Jesus, we bear His name. Because of His love for us, we strive to walk worthy of Him, reflecting His likeness in our words and deeds.

When we fail, He picks us up again by His love. By our example, others around us will be led to praise the God who has redeemed and transformed us (MATTHEW 5:16)—for the name of the Lord is worthy of glory, honor, and all praise.

Poh Fang

May 21

TRIED AND PURIFIED
JOB 23:1-12

When he has tested me, I will come forth as gold.
Job 23:10

During an interview, singer and songwriter Meredith Andrews spoke about being overwhelmed as she tried to balance outreach, creative work, marital issues, and motherhood. Reflecting on her distress, she said, "I felt like God was taking me through a refining season—almost through a crushing process."

The Old Testament character Job was overwhelmed after losing so much. And although Job had been a daily worshiper of God, he felt that the Lord was ignoring his pleas for help. Job claimed he could not see God whether he looked to the north, south, east, or west (JOB 23:2–9).

In the middle of his despair, Job had a moment of clarity. He said, "[God] knows the way that I take; when he has tested me, I will come forth as gold" (V. 10). Sometimes God uses difficulty to burn away our self-reliance, pride, and earthly wisdom.

Pain and problems can produce the shining, rock-solid character that comes from trusting God when life is hard.

Jennifer

May 22

EXPECT AND EXTEND MERCY

LUKE 18:9-14

"God, have mercy on me, a sinner."
Luke 18:13

When one friend's choices were leading her deeper into sin, I complained to another friend who responded gently. "Aren't you the one who always says Jesus sets our standard of holiness, so we shouldn't compare our sins to the sins of others? And by talking about your friend, we're gossiping. So—"

"We're sinning." I lowered my head. "Please, pray for both of us."

In Luke 18, Jesus shared a parable about two men approaching the temple to pray in very different ways (vv. 9-14). Like the Pharisee, we can become trapped in a circle of comparing ourselves to other people. We can boast about ourselves (vv. 11-12) and live as though we have the right to judge and the responsibility or the power to change others.

But when we look to Jesus as our example of holy living and encounter His goodness firsthand, like the tax collector, our desperate need for God's grace is magnified (v. 13). As we experience the Lord's loving compassion and forgiveness personally, we'll be forever changed and empowered to expect and extend mercy, not condemnation, to others.

Xochitl

May 23

CAMPING PSALMS

PSALM 8:1-9

> L ORD, our Lord, how majestic is your name in all the earth!
> *Psalm 8:1*

When my husband and I go for nature walks, one of our favorite subjects to photograph are the fungi that spring up overnight and dot the woods with splashes of bright orange, red, and yellow!

These snapshots of nature inspire me to lift my eyes to the Maker—who created not only mushrooms but also the stars in the heavens. He designed a world of infinite scope and variety. And He placed us in the very middle of this beauty to enjoy and to rule over it (GENESIS 1:27–28; PSALM 8:6–8).

My thoughts turn to one of our family's "camping psalms"—psalms we read as we sit around the fire. "L ORD, our Lord, how majestic is your name in all the earth! . . . When I consider your heavens, the work of your fingers, the moon and the stars, which you have set in place, what is mankind that you are mindful of them, human beings that you care for them?" (PSALM 8:1–4).

How amazing that the great God who created the world in all its splendor cares for you and me!

Alyson

Lord, our Lord, HOW MAJESTIC IS YOUR NAME IN ALL THE EARTH.

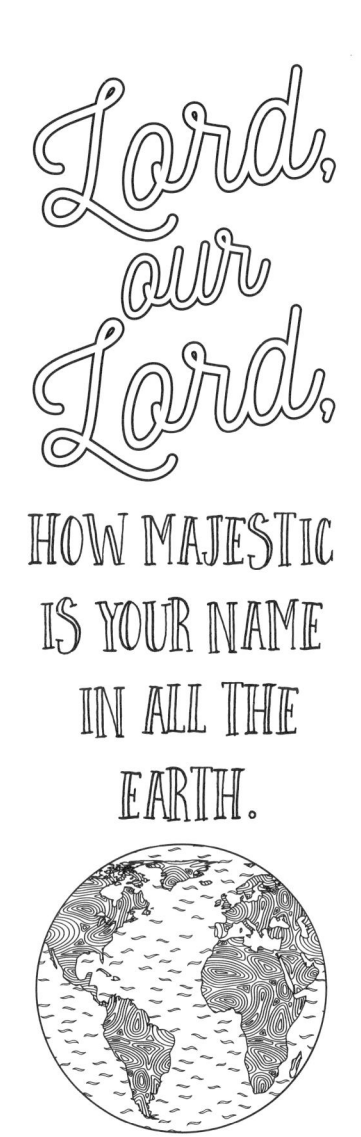

PSALM 8:1

May 24

DOWN THE UP STAIRCASE

2 CHRONICLES 12:1–8

"If my people, who are called by my name, will humble themselves and pray and seek my face and turn from their wicked ways, then I will hear from heaven, and I will forgive their sin and will heal their land."

2 Chronicles 7:14

The video starts with a puppy at the top of the stairs—afraid to go down. Despite encouragement from people cheering at the bottom, Daisy can't figure it out. She wants to join them, but fear keeps her at the top. Then a bigger dog comes to help. Simon runs up the steps and then back down, showing Daisy how easy it is. After a few furtive attempts, Daisy finally dares to let her back legs follow the front ones. Simon stays beside her. She makes it. Everyone celebrates!

What a beautiful picture of discipleship. We spend much of our time trying to teach others to climb up, but the more important, and more difficult, thing to learn is how to "go down." Throughout Scripture we read that God desires humility of us. Because the people of Judah humbled themselves, the Lord said, "I will not destroy them" (2 CHRONICLES 12:7).

On numerous occasions, God demonstrated humility by coming down (EXODUS 3:7–8, 19:10–12; MICAH 1:3). Finally, God sent Jesus, who spent His life teaching the technique we are to follow (PHILIPPIANS 2:5–11).

Julie

May 25

Bound by Love
GENESIS 15:1–20

> On that day the Lord made a covenant with Abram and said, "To your descendants I give this land, from the Wadi of Egypt to the great river, the Euphrates."
>
> *Genesis 15:18*

"How are you?" I asked my friend. She immediately began to wipe away tears. She had watched as countless younger friends had married over the years while she had not. As each year slips by, her fears of growing old alone intensify.

I knew—as she does—that God is faithful and more than sufficient. Although singleness is—like marriage—a gift from God, my friend wanted to marry. So I assured her of my love and God's love—something she truly needed to hear.

Genesis 15 records a similar ache. Carrying a God-given desire to have a child, Abraham had God's promise of provision (GENESIS 12:2; 13:14-16), but as time passed, he asked, "Sovereign Lord, how can I know that I will gain possession of it?" (15:8). God responded with a sacred oath (HEBREWS 6:13-17). Creating an unbreakable covenant, He promised to fulfill what had been promised to Abraham.

Each of us has unmet longings (11:8-19)—it's the reality we face in an imperfect world. Yet this truth remains: *God keeps His promises and answers our greatest longings with himself.*

Regina

May 26

AN EASY YOKE
MATTHEW 11:25-30

> "Take my yoke upon you and learn from me, for I am gentle and humble in heart, and you will find rest for your souls."
>
> Matthew 11:29

A Sunday school teacher read Matthew 11:30 to her class and then asked, "Jesus said, 'My yoke is easy.' Who can tell me what a yoke is?" A boy raised his hand and replied, "A yoke is something they put on the necks of animals so they can help each other."

Then the teacher asked, "What is the yoke Jesus puts on us?" A quiet little girl raised her hand and said, "It is God putting His arm around us."

When Jesus came, He offered an "easy" and "light" yoke compared to the yoke of the religious leaders (MATTHEW 11:30). They had placed "heavy burdens" on the people (MATTHEW 23:4 NKJV), which no one could possibly keep.

As we recognize our need for forgiveness, Jesus comes alongside us. He places His yoke on us, freeing us from guilt and helping us live a life that's pleasing to God.

Do you need Jesus's help? He says, "Come to me. . . . Take my yoke upon you and learn from me" (MATTHEW 11:28–29). He longs to put His arm around you.

Anne

May 27

CARELESS WORDS
JAMES 3:1–12

Likewise, the tongue is a small part of the body, but it makes great boasts. Consider what a great forest is set on fire by a small spark.
James 3:5

When my daughter suffered ill health, her husband was wonderfully caring and supportive. "You have a real treasure there!" I said.

"You didn't think that when I first knew him," she said with a grin.

She was right. When Icilda and Philip got engaged, I was concerned. They were such different personalities. I had shared my misgivings about Philip quite bluntly.

I was horrified to realize that the critical things I said so casually fifteen years earlier had stayed in her memory. It reminded me how much we need to guard what we say. We are quick to point out what we consider to be weaknesses in family, friends, or work colleagues, or to focus on their mistakes rather than their successes. "The tongue is a small part of the body," says James (3:5), yet the words it shapes can destroy relationships.

Perhaps we should make David's prayer our own as we start each day: "Set a guard over my mouth, Lord; keep watch over the door of my lips" (PSALM 141:3).

Marion

May 28

A DAY TO REST

EXODUS 23:10–13

"Six days do your work, but on the seventh day do not work."

Exodus 23:12

One Sunday I stood by the gurgling stream that wends its way through our North London community, delighting in the beauty it brings to our otherwise built-up area. I felt myself relax as I watched the cascading water and listened to the birds chirping. I paused to give the Lord thanks for how He helps us to find rest for our souls.

The Lord instituted a Sabbath—a time for rest and renewal—for His people in the ancient Near East because He wanted them to thrive. As we see in the book of Exodus, He tells them to sow their fields for six years and rest on the seventh. So too with working six days and resting on the seventh.

We can approach our day of rest with expectancy and creativity, welcoming the chance to worship and do something that feeds our souls, which will vary according to our preferences.

How can we rediscover the beauty and richness of setting apart a day to rest if that's missing from our lives?

Amy

May 29

VISIBLE VULNERABILITY
EPHESIANS 4:2-6

Be completely humble and gentle; be patient, bearing with one another in love.

Ephesians 4:2

As I ventured out several weeks after shoulder surgery, I was fearful. I had become comfortable using my arm sling, but my physical therapist told me to stop wearing it. That's when I saw this statement: "At this stage, sling wear is discouraged except as a visible sign of vulnerability in an uncontrolled environment."

Ah, that was it! I feared the enthusiastic person who might give me a bear hug or the unaware friend who might bump me accidentally. I was hiding behind my flimsy baby-blue sling because I feared being hurt.

Allowing ourselves to be vulnerable can be scary. We want to be accepted for who we are, but we fear that if people truly knew us, they might reject us.

But as members of God's family, we have a responsibility to help each other grow in faith. We're told to "encourage one another," to "build each other up" (1 THESSALONIANS 5:11), and to "be patient, bearing with one another in love" (EPHESIANS 4:2).

When we are vulnerable with other believers, we will share the wonder of God's gift of grace in our lives.

Cindy

May 30

ENJOYING HIS MEAL

1 CORINTHIANS 11:23-34

When he had given thanks, he broke it and said, "This is my body, which is for you; do this in remembrance of me."

1 Corinthians 11:24

It's not about the table. It's not about the chairs. It's not about the food, although it helps if it has been cooked with love. A good meal is enjoyed when we concentrate on those we're with.

I love gathering around the table, enjoying a good chat with friends and family. However, instant technology has made it difficult. Sometimes we are more concerned about what others—sometimes miles away—have to say than what the person just across the table is saying.

We have been invited to another meal at the table when we come together in one place to celebrate the Lord's Supper. It's not about the church, if it's big or small. It's not about the type of bread. It's about turning off our thoughts from our worries and concerns and focusing on Jesus.

When was the last time we enjoyed communion? Do we enjoy His presence, or are we more concerned with what's going on somewhere else? This is important because "whenever you eat this bread and drink this cup, you proclaim the Lord's death until he comes" (1 CORINTHIANS 11:26).

Keila

May 31

WORLD'S FASTEST WALKERS

LUKE 10:38–42

> She had a sister called Mary, who sat at the Lord's feet listening to what he said.
>
> Luke 10:39

According to a study measuring the pace of city life, people in the biggest hurry live right here in Singapore. We walk sixty feet in 10.55 seconds, compared to 12 seconds for New Yorkers and 31.6 seconds for people in Blantyre, Malawi, Africa.

The study also revealed that walking speeds have increased by 10 percent in the past twenty years. Perhaps we need to slow down.

Are you caught up in the frenzy of a busy life? Pause and consider Jesus's words to Martha: "You are worried and upset about many things, but few things are needed—or indeed only one. Mary has chosen what is better, and it will not be taken away from her" (LUKE 10:41–42).

Notice Jesus's gentle words. He didn't rebuke Martha for wanting to be a good host but rather reminded her about her priorities. Martha had allowed the necessary to get out of proportion. She was so busy doing good that she didn't take time to sit at Jesus's feet.

In our drive to be productive, let's remember the one thing worth being concerned about—enjoying time with our Savior.

Poh Fang

June 1

IT'S BEAUTIFUL
MARK 14:3-9

"Leave her alone," said Jesus. "Why are you bothering her? She has done a beautiful thing to me."

Mark 14:6

After being away on business, Terry wanted to pick up some small gifts for his children. The clerk at the airport gift shop recommended a number of costly items. When Terry said he didn't have much money to spend, the clerk tried to make him feel cheap. But Terry knew his children would be happy with whatever he gave them because it came from a heart of love. And he was right—they loved the gifts he bought.

During Jesus's last visit to the town of Bethany, Mary wanted to show her love for Him (MARK 14:3-9). So she brought "an alabaster jar of very expensive perfume" and anointed Him (V. 3). Jesus said, "She has done a beautiful thing for me" (MARK 14:6). Jesus delighted in her gift, for it came from a heart of love. Even anointing Him for burial was beautiful!

What can you give Jesus to show your love? Your time? Your talent? Your treasure? It doesn't matter if it's costly or inexpensive, whether others understand or criticize. Whatever is given from a heart of love is beautiful to Him.

Anne

She has done a beautiful thing to me. —Jesus

MARK 14:6

June 2

WHAT GOD OWES US
COLOSSIANS 1:9–14

Live a life worthy of the Lord and please him in every way: bearing fruit in every good work, growing in the knowledge of God.

Colossians 1:10

A story is told about a vendor who sold bagels for fifty cents each at a street corner food stand. A jogger ran past and threw a couple of quarters into the bucket but didn't take a bagel. This went on for months. One day as he was jogging by, the vendor stopped him. The runner asked, "You probably want to know why I put money in but never take a bagel, don't you?" "No," said the vendor. "I just wanted to tell you that the bagels have gone up to sixty cents."

Too often we treat God similarly. Not only are we ungrateful for what He's given us—but we also want more. Somehow we feel that God owes us good health, a comfortable life, material blessings. God doesn't owe us anything, yet He gives us everything.

The psalmist said, "This is the day the Lord has made; we will rejoice and be glad in it" (PSALM 118:24 NKJV). That should be enough.

Each day, whether good or bad, is one more gift from our God. Our grateful response should be to live to please Him.

Cindy

June 3

STANDING ON THE EDGE

JOSHUA 3:9-17

So when the people broke camp to cross the Jordan, the priests carrying the ark of the covenant went ahead of them.

Joshua 3:14

My little girl, a nonswimmer, stood apprehensively at the pool's edge. Her instructor waited in the pool with outstretched arms. As my daughter hesitated, I saw the questions in her eyes: *Will you catch me? What will happen if my head goes under?*

The Israelites probably had some big questions as they prepared to cross the Jordan River. Could they trust God to make dry ground appear in the riverbed? Was God guiding their new leader, Joshua, as He had led Moses? Would God help them defeat the threatening Canaanites on the other side?

To get answers to these questions, the Israelites had to act. In faith, they "broke camp to cross the Jordan" (v. 14). Exercising their faith allowed them to see that God was with them, was still directing Joshua, and would help them settle in Canaan (vv. 7, 10, 17).

Are you facing a test of faith? Move forward based on God's character and His unfailing promises. Rely on Him to help you move from where you are to where He wants you to be.

Jennifer

June 4

SHOULD I FORGIVE?
MATTHEW 18:23–25

Forgive as the Lord forgave you.
Colossians 3:13

I arrived early at church to help set up for an event. A woman stood crying at the opposite end of the sanctuary. She had gossiped about me in the past, so I drowned out her sobs with a vacuum cleaner. Why should I care about someone who didn't like me?

But then the Holy Spirit reminded me that God had forgiven me, and I crossed the room. The woman said her baby had been in the hospital for months. We cried, embraced, and prayed for her daughter. After working through our differences, we became good friends.

In Matthew 18, Jesus spoke of a king who decided to settle his accounts. A servant who owed a staggering amount of money pleaded for mercy. After the king canceled his debt, that servant tracked down and condemned a man who owed him far less than what he had owed the king. The king imprisoned the wicked servant because of his unforgiving spirit (vv. 23–34).

Offering forgiveness frees us to enjoy God's undeserved gift of mercy as we invite Him to accomplish beautiful works of peace-restoring grace in all of our relationships.

Xochitl

June 5

THE PROMISED SPIRIT

2 KINGS 2:5-12

When they had crossed, Elijah said to Elisha, "Tell me, what can I do for you before I am taken from you?" "Let me inherit a double portion of your spirit," Elisha replied.

2 Kings 2:9

Tenacity and audacity—Elisha had heaps of both. Having spent time with Elijah, he witnessed the Lord working through the prophet by performing miracles and by speaking truth in an age of lies. Second Kings 2:1 tells us that Elijah was about to be taken "up to heaven," and Elisha didn't want him to leave.

The time came for the dreaded separation, and Elisha knew he needed what Elijah had if he was going to successfully continue the ministry. So he made a daring demand: "Let me inherit a double portion of your spirit" (2 KINGS 2:9). His bold request was a reference to the double portion given the firstborn son or heir under the law (DEUTERONOMY 21:17). Elisha wanted to be recognized as the heir of Elijah. And God said yes.

Recently one of my mentors—a woman who spread the good news of Jesus—died. We grieved the loss of her love and example. Yet despite her departure, she did not leave us alone. We too had God's presence through the Holy Spirit. Praise God for that!

Amy

June 6

LIGHTEN THE LOAD
PHILIPPIANS 4:10-20

I can do all this through him who gives me strength.
Philippians 4:13

I once read about a distraught Christian woman who was upset because her children had become unruly. She phoned her husband at work one day and tearfully described the visit of a friend who had pinned this verse above the kitchen sink: "I can do all things through Christ who strengthens me" (PHILIPPIANS 4:13 NKJV). The friend had meant well. She was trying to be helpful, but her action just made the mom feel even more like a failure.

Sometimes it's not helpful merely to quote a Scripture verse to someone. Philippians 4:13 was Paul's personal testimony that he had learned to be content in all situations, in plenty and in want (VV. 11–12). His secret of contentment was that he could "do all things through Christ" who strengthened him (V. 13 NKJV).

We too can live by Paul's secret. We can be victorious through Christ's strength, but we shouldn't force this truth on people who are feeling overwhelmed. We need each other; we all have burdens to bear. Let's use the strength Christ gives us to minister to others and find ways to lighten their loads.

Joanie

June 7

GOOD INFLUENCE

NUMBERS 16:1-33

The earth opened its mouth and swallowed them and their households, and all those associated with Korah.

Numbers 16:32

We have two five-month-old puppies that love to explore. Azusa is the one filled with true wanderlust. Seymour simply becomes her partner in crime. Seymour's affinity to follow his sister out the door shows that misplaced loyalty can lead one astray.

Despite the miracles God had performed, the influence of ten spies caused the Israelites to cower in fear (NUMBERS 13). And it was the voice of others that brought distraction and, for some, rebellion (16:1-3, 19). Rather than offering wise counsel, Korah, Dathan, and Abiram used their influence destructively.

The freedom of believers in Jesus is a powerful gift. Our salvation, however, doesn't fail-proof our decisions, and the temptation to falter often appears in the context of relationships (2 CORINTHIANS 11:3-4; 2 PETER 3:17). We gain much in our relationships with others: comfort, inspiration, instruction, and more. We weren't made to live in isolation. It's critical that we develop the ability to discern between a life-giving, good influence and relationships that can atrophy our walk with God.

Regina

June 8

REFRAMING THE PICTURE

DEUTERONOMY 32:7–12

> Like an eagle that stirs up its nest and hovers over its young, that spreads its wings to catch them and carries them aloft. The Lord alone led him; no foreign god was with him.
>
> Deuteronomy 32:11-12

For three months I had a ringside seat—or should I say a bird's-eye view—of God's amazing handiwork. Ninety feet above the floor of Norfolk Botanical Garden, workers installed a webcam focused on the nest of a family of bald eagles, and online viewers were allowed to watch.

When the eggs hatched, Mama and Papa Eagle were attentive to their offspring, taking turns hunting for food and guarding the nest. But one day when the eaglets still looked like fuzzballs with beaks, both parents disappeared. I worried that harm had come to them.

My concern was unfounded. The webcam operator enlarged the camera angle, and there was Mama Eagle perched on a nearby branch.

Moses used eagle imagery to describe God. As eagles care for their young, God cares for His people (DEUTERONOMY 32:11-12). Despite how it may seem, the Lord "is not far from any one of us" (ACTS 17:27). This is true even when we feel abandoned.

Julie

No Wonder!

SONG OF SOLOMON 1:1-4

We love because he first loved us.
1 John 4:19

"He's perfect for you," my friend told me. She was talking about a guy she had just met. She described his kind eyes, his kind smile, and his kind heart. When I met him I had to agree. Today he's my husband, and no wonder I love him!

In the Song of Solomon, the bride describes her lover. His love is better than wine and more fragrant than ointments. His name is sweeter than anything in this world. So she concludes that it's no wonder he is loved.

But there is Someone far greater than any earthly loved one. His love satisfies our every need. His sacrifice became a sweet-smelling aroma to God (EPHESIANS 5:2). And His name is above every name (PHILIPPIANS 2:9). No wonder we love Him!

It is a privilege to love Jesus. It is the best experience in life! Do we take the time to tell Him so? Do we express with words the beauty of our Savior? If we show His beauty with our lives, others will say, "No wonder you love Him!"

Keila

June 9

June 10

A LARGE PORTION
LUKE 22:7-30

He took bread, gave thanks and broke it, and gave it to them, saying, "This is my body given for you; do this in remembrance of me."

Luke 22:19

As I was putting my eleven-year-old son to bed one night, we talked about what had happened at church that morning. When we went forward to take communion, he broke off the bread and ended up with an exceptionally large piece—causing both the administering elder and me to break into smiles.

After reflecting a minute on what had happened, he said, "Mom, do you think God wants me to partake (yes, he said 'partake'!) in a big portion of the body? Maybe that's why that happened."

When Jesus gathered His disciples for the Last Supper, "he took bread, gave thanks and broke it, and gave it to them, saying, 'This is my body given for you; do this in remembrance of me'" (LUKE 22:19).

Earlier in His ministry, Jesus had proclaimed, "I am the living bread. . . . Whoever eats this bread will live forever" (JOHN 6:51).

As we take the bread, let's reflect on what Christ has done for us. Our relationship with God is healed by means of His body being broken.

Roxanne

June 11

TINY ISLAND
TITUS 3:1–7

> Remind the people . . . to slander no one, to be peaceable and considerate, and always to be gentle toward everyone.
>
> *Titus 3:1-2*

Singapore is a tiny island. It's so small that one can hardly spot it on the world map. Because it is densely populated, consideration of others is especially important. A man wrote to his fiancée who was coming to Singapore for the first time: "Space is limited. Therefore . . . you must always have that sense of space around you. You should always step aside to ensure you are not blocking anyone. The key is to be considerate."

The apostle Paul wrote to Titus, a young pastor, "Remind the people . . . to be obedient, to be ready to do whatever is good, to slander no one, to be peaceable and considerate, and always to be gentle toward everyone" (TITUS 3:1–2). The world knows that Christians are supposed to be different. If we are cantankerous, self-absorbed, and rude, what will others think about Christ and the gospel we share?

Being considerate, which is a good motto to live by, is possible as we depend on the Lord. It is one way to model Christ and demonstrate to the world that Jesus saves and transforms lives.

Poh Fang

June 12

EAGER FOR HEAVEN

2 TIMOTHY 4:6–18

> The twelve gates were twelve pearls, each gate made of a single pearl. The great street of the city was of gold, as pure as transparent glass.
>
> Revelation 21:21

My nine-year-old neighbor Jasmine was sitting on the porch with me one summer evening. Out of the blue she started talking about her bad choices and how she needed God's forgiveness. We talked and prayed together, and she asked Jesus to be her Savior.

Questions about heaven poured out of her: "Are the streets really gold? Will my mom be there? What if she isn't? Will I sleep on a cloud? What will I eat?" I assured her that heaven would be a perfect home and that she would be with Jesus. She replied with excitement, "Well, then let's go right now!"

Paul had a heavenly perspective too (PHILIPPIANS 1:23). His testimony was, "To me, to live is Christ and to die is gain" (V. 21). He knew that this life was about knowing, trusting, and serving God. But he also knew that life in heaven would be "better by far" because he would "be with Christ" (V. 23). Paul wanted to stay but was ready to go.

Jasmine is ready to go now. Are we as eager for heaven as she is?

Anne

June 13

A Wonderful Explosion

JOHN 13:31–35

"A new command I give you: Love one another. As I have loved you, so you must love one another."

John 13:34

In the book *Kisses from Katie*, Katie Davis recounts the joy of moving to Uganda and adopting several Ugandan girls. One day one of her daughters asked, "Mommy, if I let Jesus come into my heart, will I explode?" At first Katie said no.

However, after she thought more about the question, Katie explained that when we decide to give our lives and hearts to Jesus, "we will explode with love, with compassion, with hurt for those who are hurting, and with joy for those who rejoice." In essence, knowing Christ results in deep concern for the people in our world.

We can consistently display this loving response because of the Holy Spirit's work in our hearts. When we receive Christ, the Holy Spirit comes to live inside us. The apostle Paul said, "When you believed, you were marked . . . [with] the promised Holy Spirit" (EPHESIANS 1:13).

Caring for others—with God's supernatural assistance—shows the world we are His followers (JOHN 13:35). This also reminds us of His love for us. Jesus said, "As I have loved you, so you must love one another" (V. 34).

Jennifer

June 14

IF ONLY . . .
JOHN 11:21–35

"Lord, if you had been here, my brother would not have died."

John 11:32

As we exited the parking lot, my husband slowed to wait for a young woman riding her bike. When Tom nodded to indicate she could go first, she smiled, waved, and rode on. Moments later, the driver of a parked SUV threw open his door, knocking the young bicyclist to the pavement. Her legs bleeding, she cried as she examined her bent-up bike.

Later we reflected on the accident: If only we had made her wait. If only the driver had looked before opening his door. If only . . . Difficulties catch us in a cycle of second-guessing ourselves.

When unexpected trouble comes, we sometimes question the goodness of God. We may even feel the despair Martha and Mary experienced when their brother died. Oh, if Jesus had come when He first found out Lazarus was sick (JOHN 11:21, 32)!

Like Martha and Mary, we don't always understand why hard things happen. But we can rest in the assurance that God is working out His purposes for a greater good. In every circumstance, we can trust the wisdom of our faithful and loving God.

Cindy

June 15

NEW BIRTH
PSALM 139:7–16

You formed my inward parts; You covered me in my mother's womb.
Psalm 139:13 (NKJV)

What is it about babies that makes us smile? Many people will stop everything at the sight of a baby and will flock to gaze at the little one. I noticed this when I visited my dad at a nursing home. Though most of the residents were wheelchair-bound and suffered from dementia, the visit of a family with a baby almost unfailingly brought a spark of joy to their eyes that became a smile. It was amazing to watch.

Perhaps babies bring a smile because of the wonder of a new life—so precious, tiny, and full of promise. Seeing a baby can remind us of our awesome God who loved us so much that He gave us life. "You formed my inward parts," the psalmist says. "You covered me in my mother's womb" (PSALM 139:13 NKJV).

Not only does He give us physical life, but He also offers us spiritual rebirth through Jesus (JOHN 3:3–8). God promises believers new bodies and life eternal when Jesus returns (1 CORINTHIANS 15:50–52).

Physical life and spiritual rebirth—gifts to celebrate from our Father's hand.

Alyson

June 16

PARENTS WHO PRAY

MATTHEW 19:13–15

Then people brought little children to Jesus for him to place his hands on them and pray for them. But the disciples rebuked them.

Matthew 19:13

A young mother sent these lines to a magazine: "I wish I could wrap my children in bubble wrap to protect them from the big, bad world outside."

Author Stormie Omartian understands how that mother feels. In her book *The Power of a Praying Parent*, she writes, "One day I cried out to God, saying, 'Lord, this is too much for me. I can't keep a twenty-four-hours-a-day, moment-by-moment watch on my son. How can I ever have peace?'"

God responded by leading Stormie and her husband to become praying parents. They began to intercede for their son daily, mentioning the details of his life in prayer.

Wrapping our children in prayer, as Jesus did (MATTHEW 19:13–15), is a powerful alternative to bubble wrap. He cares more about our children than we do, so we can release them into His hands by praying for them. As we pray, He will give us the peace we long for (PHILIPPIANS 4:6–7).

This challenge is for all parents—even those whose children have grown up: Don't ever stop wrapping your children in prayer!

Joanie

CLOTHED BY GOD
ZECHARIAH 3

"See, I have taken away your sin, and I will put fine garments on you."

Zechariah 3:4

When my kids were toddlers, they would play outside in our sodden English garden and become covered in mud and dirt. I would remove their clothes at the door and wrap them in towels before sticking them in the bath. They'd soon move from dirty to clean with the addition of soap, water, and hugs.

In a vision given to Zechariah, we see Joshua, a high priest, covered in rags that represent sin and wrongdoing (ZECHARIAH 3:3). But the Lord makes him clean, removing his filthy clothes and covering him in rich garments (3:5). The new turban and robe signify that the Lord has taken his sins from him.

We too can receive God's cleansing as we become free of our wrongdoing through the saving work of Jesus. As a result of His death on the cross, we can have the mud and sins that cling to us washed away as we receive the robes of God's sons and daughters.

Ask God to remove any filthy rags you're wearing so you too can put on the wardrobe He has reserved for you.

Amy

June 17

June 18

OUT OF CONTEXT
LUKE 4:1–13

"Sanctify them by the truth; your word is truth."
John 17:17

When a friend started making random despairing statements, people were concerned for him and started giving advice and offering encouragement. As it turned out, he was simply having fun by quoting song lyrics out of context to start a conversation. Friends who tried to help him wasted their time by offering help he didn't need and advice he didn't want.

Some people who take words out of context just want to gain attention or win an argument. But others are more sinister. They twist truth to gain power over others. They endanger not only lives but also souls.

When people use words to manipulate others to behave in certain ways—or worse, when they quote the Bible out of context to convince others to do wrong—there's only one defense: We need to know what God truly says in His Word. Jesus was able to resist temptation with the truth (LUKE 4). We have the same resource. God has given us His Word and Spirit to guide us and keep us from being deceived or misled.

Julie

June 19

RETIREMENT TIME

MATTHEW 16:24–28

"For whoever wants to save their life will lose it, but whoever loses their life for me will find it."

Matthew 16:25

After working for forty years as a teacher, Jane Hanson retired. She and her husband were looking forward to relaxing, traveling, and enjoying the arrival of their first grandchild.

Then Jane heard about a ministry to at-risk youth, and she knew she had to get involved. "I realized there are kids just waiting, and I could make a difference," she said. She began teaching English to a young Liberian man who had been forced to flee his home country because of civil war. Of this ministry opportunity, Jane said, "I could just go shopping to stay busy, but what fun would that be?"

Jane is making a difference. Perhaps she has learned a little of what Jesus meant when He said, "Whoever wants to save their life will lose it, but whoever loses their life for me will find it" (MATTHEW 16:25). Giving ourselves to the Lord through helping others takes self-denial, yet one day Jesus will reward that effort (V. 27).

Let's follow Jane's example of love for God and others—no matter what our stage of life may be.

Anne

June 20

NO LAZY RIVER

PROVERBS 22:1–21

Start children off on the way they should go, and even when they are old they will not turn from it.

Proverbs 22:6

One of our favorite family vacation sites is a beautiful beach community located in an adjoining state. That location offers an indoor swimming pool with a surrounding lazy river that holds a special appeal for our kids. They enjoy trying to swim against its current, only to be carried in the opposite direction.

My husband and I must frequently swim against the flow of society's values in order to bring our children into a healthy, godly understanding of who they are. Whether we're considering our experience in youth ministry or my work in Christian education, we return to this truth: we're ultimately responsible for the spiritual education of our children.

While the greatest spiritual deposit I can make in my children's lives is to bring God's knowledge and discipline to them (PROVERBS 22:15, 17–19), I must also understand that they'll never learn to persevere in their faith if I remove every obstacle from their paths. The training pool isn't always easy, but as we look to God's Word, we can rest in His promise that "the Lord preserves those with knowledge" (22:12 NLT).

Regina

June 21

LESSONS FOR LITTLE ONES

PROVERBS 22:1-6

> Being found in appearance as a man, he humbled himself by becoming obedient to death—even death on a cross!
>
> *Philippians 2:8*

Tibetan-born Sherpa Nawang Gombu and American Jim Whittaker reached the top of Mount Everest on May 1, 1963. As they approached the peak, each considered the honor of being the first of the two to step to the summit. Whittaker motioned for Gombu to move ahead, but Gombu declined with a smile, saying, "You first, Big Jim!" Finally, they decided to step to the summit at the same time.

Paul encouraged the Philippian believers to demonstrate this kind of humility. He said, "Let each of you look out not only for his own interests, but also for the interests of others" (PHILIPPIANS 2:4 NKJV). Selfishness and superiority can divide people, but humility unites us, since it is the quality of "being one in spirit and of one mind" (V. 2).

Practicing humility helps us to become more like Jesus who, for our sake, "humbled himself by becoming obedient to death" (VV. 7-8). Following in Jesus's footsteps means backing away from what is best for us and doing what is best for others.

Jennifer

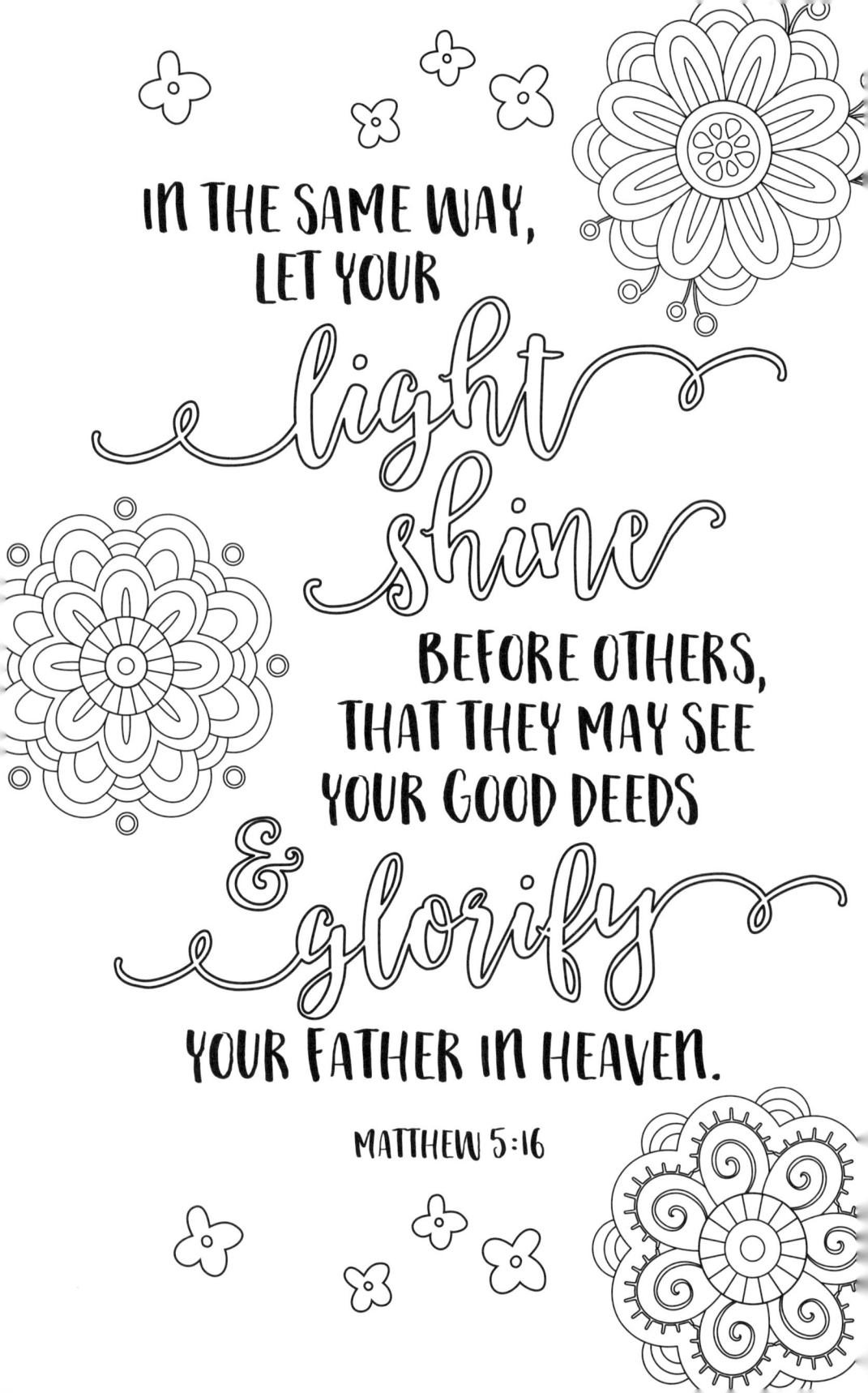

IN THE SAME WAY,
LET YOUR
light
shine
BEFORE OTHERS,
THAT THEY MAY SEE
YOUR GOOD DEEDS
& *glorify*
YOUR FATHER IN HEAVEN.

MATTHEW 5:16

June 22

SHINE THROUGH
MATTHEW 5:13–16

"In the same way, let your light shine before others, that they may see your good deeds and glorify your Father in heaven."

Matthew 5:16

A little girl wondered what a saint might be. One day her mother took her to a great cathedral to see the gorgeous stained-glass windows with scenes from the Bible. When she saw the beauty of it all she cried out loud, "Now I know what saints are. They are people who let the light shine through!"

Some of us might think saints are people of the past who lived perfect lives and did Jesus-like miracles. But when Scripture uses the word *saint*, it is actually referring to anyone who belongs to God through faith in Christ. In other words, saints are people like us who have the high calling of serving God while reflecting our relationship with Him in whatever we do. That is why the apostle Paul prayed that his readers would think of themselves as the treasured inheritance of Christ and saints of God (EPHESIANS 1:18).

If we are fulfilling our calling, we will look like people who, maybe even without realizing it, are letting the rich colors of the love, joy, peace, patience, kindness, gentleness, faithfulness, and self-control of God shine through.

Keila

June 23

TRAIL TREES
ISAIAH 53:4–12

> Dogs surround me, a pack of villains encircles me; they pierce my hands and my feet. All my bones are on display; people stare and gloat over me. They divide my clothes among them and cast lots for my garment.
>
> Psalm 22:16-18

My daughter is fascinated with the history of the indigenous people in northern Michigan where she lives. One afternoon when I was visiting, she showed me a road that had a sign designating "Trail Trees." She explained that long ago Native Americans bent young trees to point the way to specific destinations, and they have continued to grow in unusual shapes.

The Old Testament serves a similar purpose. Its many commands and teachings direct our hearts to the way the Lord wants us to live—the Ten Commandments, for example. In addition, Old Testament prophets pointed the way to a coming Messiah. Thousands of years before Jesus came, they spoke of Bethlehem—Jesus's birthplace (SEE MICAH 5:2 AND MATTHEW 2:1–6). And Isaiah 53:1–12 points to the sacrifice Jesus would make as the Lord "laid on him the iniquity of us all" (V. 6; SEE LUKE 23:33).

God's servants pointed to God's Son—Jesus—the One who "took up our pain and bore our suffering" (ISAIAH 53:4). He is the way to life.

Cindy

June 24

NEW WAY OF SEEING
1 PETER 3:3-6

Rather, [your beauty] should be that of your inner self, the unfading beauty of a gentle and quiet spirit, which is of great worth in God's sight.

1 Peter 3:4

God gave me new things to treasure and value after I left the United States for Uganda a few years ago. Some of the interests and things I enjoyed before moving to my new ministry have, to my surprise, been replaced.

In Africa, I've discovered beauty in watching the face of an impoverished child light up after receiving a gift of clothing, in witnessing a mother as she loves and cares for her sick child, and in seeing a starving child share his meager food portions with a sibling.

Among the poor in Sub-Saharan Africa, I've gained deeper understanding of "the unfading beauty of a gentle and quiet spirit, which is of great worth in God's sight" (1 PETER 3:4). I have better understood how this type of loveliness, observed by pure and reverent living, pleases God more than "the outward beauty of fancy hairstyles, expensive jewelry, or beautiful clothes" (1 PETER 3:3 NLT).

God provides what we need to grow in faith. By His work, we're better primed to see beauty—and all of life—as He does.

Roxanne

June 25

PEOPLE POWER
EPHESIANS 4:7–16

From him the whole body, joined and held together by every supporting ligament, grows and builds itself up in love, as each part does its work.

Ephesians 4:16

A man was boarding a train in Perth, Australia, when he slipped. His leg got caught in the gap between the train carriage and the station platform. Dozens of passengers quickly came to his rescue. They used their sheer might to tilt the train away from the platform, and the trapped man was freed!

In Ephesians 4, we read that people power is God's plan for building up His family. He has given each of us a special gift of His grace (V. 7) for the specific purpose that "the whole body, joined and held together by every supporting ligament, grows and builds itself up in love, as each part does its work" (V. 16).

Every person has a job to do in God's family; there are no spectators. In God's family we weep and laugh together. We bear each other's burdens. We pray for and encourage one another. We challenge and help each other to turn from sin. Show us, Father, our part in helping your family today.

Poh Fang

June 26

THE PRICE OF LOVE

ISAIAH 53:9–12

He poured out his life unto death.

Isaiah 53:12

Our daughter burst into tears as we waved goodbye to my parents. After visiting us in England, they were starting their long journey back to their home in the United States. "I don't want them to go," she said. As I comforted her, my husband remarked, "I'm afraid that's the price of love."

We might feel the pain of being separated from loved ones, but Jesus felt the ultimate separation when He paid the price of love on the cross. He who was both human and God fulfilled Isaiah's prophecy seven hundred years after Isaiah gave it when He "bore the sin of many" (ISAIAH 53:12). In this chapter we see rich pointers to Jesus being the Suffering Servant, such as when He was "pierced for our transgressions" (V. 5).

Because of love, Jesus came to earth and was born a baby. Because of love, He received the abuse of the teachers of the law, the crowds, and the soldiers. Because of love, He suffered and died to be the perfect sacrifice, standing in our place before the Father. We live because Jesus paid the price of love.

Amy

June 27

WHEN YES MEANS NO

ROMANS 8:22–28

I call on the Lord in my distress, and he answers me.
Psalm 120:1

I thanked God for the privilege of serving as my mom's live-in caregiver during her battle against leukemia. When medicines began to hurt more than help, she decided to stop treatment. "I'm ready to go home," she said.

I pleaded with our loving heavenly Father—confident He could work miracles. Finally, I surrendered, praying, "Your will be done, Lord."

Soon after, Jesus welcomed my mama into a pain-free eternity.

In this fallen world, we'll experience suffering until Jesus returns (ROMANS 8:22–25). Thankfully, "the Spirit intercedes for God's people in accordance with the will of God" (V. 27). He reminds us that in all things God works for the good of those who love Him (V. 28), even when His yes to someone else means a heartbreaking no for us.

When we accept our small part in God's greater purpose, we can echo my mom's watchword: "God is good, and that's all there is to it. Whatever He decides, I'm at peace." With confidence in the Lord's goodness, we can trust Him to answer every prayer according to His will and for His glory.

Xochitl

June 28

REFLECTIONS ON WINDOWS

PSALM 34:1–10

Open my eyes that I may see wonderful things in your law.

Psalm 119:18

Much of the scenery I saw during our vacation in Alaska was through the windows of moving vehicles. I was thankful for glass, but it also presented a challenge. Rain and condensation on the windows sometimes obscured the view.

Those challenges help me understand why it's impossible for us to see life the way God intended it. Sin obscures the beauty of life. Sometimes sin is inside—our selfishness creates a fog that makes us see ourselves as more important than we are and causes us to forget about others' interests. Sometimes sin is outside. The injustice of others causes our tears to fall like rain, preventing us from seeing the goodness of God. Sin of any kind keeps us from seeing the wonder and glory of life as God designed it.

For now, even though "we see things imperfectly, like puzzling reflections in a mirror" (1 CORINTHIANS 13:12 NLT), we see enough to know that God is good (PSALM 34:8). The many wonderful things that God has revealed will help us to forsake sin and work to minimize its consequences in the world.

Julie

June 29

PLANTING GOOD SEEDS

HOSEA 10:12–15

> Sow righteousness for yourselves, reap the fruit of unfailing love, and break up your unplowed ground; for it is time to seek the Lord, until he comes and showers his righteousness on you.
>
> Hosea 10:12

As a new gardener, I soon learned that uncultivated soil was resistant to seed planting and growth. But when I planted good seeds in well-prepared soil, heaven's sun and rain did their part until the harvest came. This is true not only in gardening but also in Christian living.

God's prophet Hosea preached this principle to the people of Israel. They had sown seeds of wickedness and trusted in their own way instead of God's. Now they were eating the bitter fruit of lies, especially the lie that their safety and success came from their own military strength (HOSEA 10:13).

Hosea pleaded with Israel to go God's way—to break up the sin-hardened soil of their hearts and to "seek the Lord" (V. 12). If they would sow seeds of righteousness, they would reap the Lord's mercy, and He would rain blessings on them.

When the soil of our heart is receptive to God and His Word, we will trust God's way. We will sow right actions and attitudes in our lives and we will grow His way. And He will make us fruitful.

Joanie

June 30

WATCH AND PRAY

MARK 14:32–42

"Watch and pray so that you will not fall into temptation. The spirit is willing, but the flesh is weak."

Mark 14:38

From my window I can see a 1,700-meter-high hill called the Cerro del Borrego. In 1862 the French army invaded Mexico. While the enemy camped in the central park of Orizaba, the Mexican army established its position at the top of the hill. However, the Mexican general neglected to guard access to the top. While the Mexican troops slept, the French attacked and killed two thousand of them.

This reminds me of another hill, the Mount of Olives, and the garden at its foot where a group of disciples fell asleep. Jesus rebuked them, saying, "Watch and pray so that you will not fall into temptation. The spirit is willing, but the flesh is weak" (MARK 14:38).

Temptation strikes when we are most vulnerable. When we neglect certain areas of our spiritual lives—such as prayer and Bible study—we become drowsy and let our guard down, making us easy targets for our enemy, Satan, to strike (1 PETER 5:8).

If we remain watchful and pray, the Spirit will enable us to resist temptation.

Keila

July 1

SEEING WELL

JOHN 15:12-17

"You are my friends if you do what I command."

John 15:14

Raleigh is a powerful dog—large, muscular, and weighing one hundred pounds! Yet Raleigh connects well with people.

Once, a four-year-old girl spotted Raleigh across a room. At first she was afraid, but then she approached him and spent several minutes talking to him and petting him. She discovered that he's both gentle and powerful.

This combination of qualities reminds me of what we read about Jesus. Jesus was approachable—He welcomed little children (MATTHEW 19:13-15) and was kind to an adulterous woman in a desperate situation (JOHN 8:1-11). At the same time, Jesus's power was astounding. Heads turned and jaws dropped as He subdued demons, calmed violent storms, and resurrected dead people (MARK 1:21-34; 4:35-41; JOHN 11)!

How we see Jesus determines how we relate to Him. If we focus only on His power, we may treat Him with the detached worship of a comic book superhero. Yet, if we overemphasize His kindness, we risk treating Him too casually. The truth is that Jesus is both at once—great enough to deserve our obedience yet humble enough to call us friends.

Jennifer

"Come to me, all you who are weary & burdened, and I will give you rest."

— Matthew 11:28

July 2

ONE MISSION
LUKE 9:46–62

"Do not stop him," Jesus said, "for whoever is not against you is for you."

Luke 9:50

My husband and I often must act as referees while moderating disagreements between our two children. While they focus on their differences, we remind them that they need each other—something that's hard for them to see.

The church of Jesus Christ is sometimes like that: recognized more for its divisions than its unity.

As Luke 9:46–62 illustrates, the struggle isn't a new one. While the disciples may have been trying to protect the integrity of Jesus's ministry, their desire for distinction went beyond a passion for truth. Telling Jesus, "We saw someone driving out demons in your name and we tried to stop him, because he is not one of us," they drew a line of separation Christ had not drawn (V. 49).

The disciples were committed to following Christ (V. 62). But their radical faith didn't guarantee that their perspective always revealed the full picture (1 CORINTHIANS 13:12).

When it comes to the unity of believers, we must remember: His body was broken and His clothes were divided so His church wouldn't have to be (1 CORINTHIANS 13:13; EPHESIANS 2:14; COLOSSIANS 1:16–20).

Regina

July 3

"Come to Me"
MATTHEW 11:25–30

"Come to me, all you who are weary and burdened, and I will give you rest."
Matthew 11:28

I was stressed about mounting medical bills after we had our third daughter. I couldn't sleep as I tried to figure out how we'd pay the bills. My muscles were tense. I was exhausted. So I cried out to God.

Experts tell us to combat stress by getting plenty of rest, eating right, and exercising. But Jesus tells us about something else that provides true peace and rest: prayer.

As I prayed, I was reminded of Matthew 11:28 where Jesus said, "Come to me, all you who are weary and burdened, and I will give you rest." Jesus invited me to come to Him to gain perspective and real rest. In the next verse, He said, "Take my yoke upon you and learn from me . . . and you will find rest for your souls" (v. 29). Our loving Savior doesn't scold us for being unable to handle the pressures of life by ourselves. Instead, He wants us to *give* our burdens to Him (PSALM 55:22).

Go to Him today!

Marlena

July 4

EVERYTHING COMES FROM GOD
1 CHRONICLES 29:14-19

"Lord our God, all this abundance that we have provided for building you a temple for your Holy Name comes from your hand, and all of it belongs to you."

1 Chronicles 29:16

By the time I was eighteen, I had worked and saved until I had enough money for a year of school. Then my mom had emergency surgery, and I realized I had the money in the bank to pay for her operation.

My love for my mother suddenly took precedence over my plans. These words from *Passion and Purity* by Elisabeth Elliot took on new meaning: "If we hold tightly to anything given to us, unwilling to let it go when the time comes to let it go . . . we stunt the growth of the soul." She was saying that what we have "is ours to thank Him for and ours to offer back to Him."

I saw my savings as a gift from God! I could give to my family because I was sure God could get me through school another way, and He did.

Today, think about David's prayer from 1 Chronicles 29:14, "Everything we have has come from you, and we give you only what you first gave us" (NLT).

Keila

July 5

WALKING IN HIS DUST
MARK 1:16–20

Without delay he called them, and they left their father Zebedee in the boat with the hired men and followed him.

Mark 1:20

In the first century, if a Jewish man wanted to become a disciple of a rabbi (teacher), he was expected to leave his family and job to join his rabbi. They would live together twenty-four hours a day—discussing and memorizing the Scriptures and applying them to life.

The disciple's calling was to "cover himself in the dust of [the rabbi's] feet," as the common saying goes, drinking in his every word. He followed his rabbi so closely that he would "walk in his dust." In doing so, he became like the rabbi, his master.

Simon, Andrew, James, and John knew that this was the type of relationship to which Jesus was calling them (MARK 1:16–20). So immediately they walked away from their work and "followed him" (V. 20). For three years they stayed close to Him—listening to His teaching, watching His miracles, learning His principles, and walking in His dust.

As Jesus's followers today, we too can "walk in His dust." By spending time studying and meditating on His Word and applying its principles to life, we'll become like our rabbi—Jesus.

Anne

July 6

A PERFECT FATHER
PROVERBS 20:3-7

The righteous lead blameless lives; blessed are their children after them.
Proverbs 20:7

My father once admitted to me, "When you were growing up, I was gone a lot."

I don't remember that. Besides working full time, he was occasionally gone to direct choir practice at church or to travel briefly with a men's quartet. But for all the significant moments of my life—he was there.

For instance, when I was eight, I had a tiny part in an afternoon school play. All the mothers came, but only one dad—mine. He has always let my sisters and me know that we are important to him and that he loves us. And seeing him tenderly caring for my mom in the last few years of her life taught me what unselfish love looks like. Dad isn't perfect, but he gives me a good glimpse of my heavenly Father. That's what a Christian dad should do.

At times earthly fathers disappoint or hurt their children. But our Father in heaven is "compassionate and gracious, slow to anger, abounding in love" (PSALM 103:8). A godly dad models for his children our perfect Father in heaven.

Cindy

July 7

GENTLE LIGHTS
1 PETER 3:13–17

"In the same way, let your light shine before others, that they may see your good deeds and glorify your Father in heaven."

Matthew 5:16

Wang Xiaoying (pronounced Shao-ying) lives in a rural area of China's Yunnan Province. Due to health problems, her husband couldn't find work, causing hardship for the family. Her mother-in-law blamed the trouble on Xiaoying's faith in God. So she mistreated Xiaoying and urged her to go back to the traditional religion of her ancestors.

But because Xiaoying's husband had observed her transformed life, he said, "Mother, it isn't enough for Xiaoying alone to believe in God; we too should put our faith in God!" He is now considering the good news of Jesus.

People are watching. The best witness combines good behavior with appropriate words, reflecting the difference Christ makes in our lives.

This was the apostle Peter's instruction to the first-century believers, and to us: Be "eager to do good" (1 PETER 3:13), live obediently in Christ, have a good conscience, and be prepared to explain to others why we have such hope (V. 15).

Let's shine for Jesus where we are. He can help us reach even those who don't agree with us.

Poh Fang

July 8

FAITH IN ACTION

JAMES 2:14–26

Show me your faith without deeds, and I will show you my faith by my deeds.

James 2:18

As a friend drove to the store, she noticed a woman walking alongside the road and felt she should offer her a ride. When she did, she learned that the woman didn't have money for the bus. She was walking many miles home from work in the hot and humid weather. And she had walked that same road that morning to get to work by 4 a.m.

By offering a ride, my friend acted on James's instruction for Christians to live out their faith with their deeds: "Faith by itself, if it is not accompanied by action, is dead" (V. 17). He was concerned that the church take care of the widows and the orphans (JAMES 1:27), and he also wanted them to rely not on empty words but to act on their faith with deeds of love.

We are saved by faith, not works, but we live out our faith by loving others and caring for their needs. May we, like my friend who offered the ride, keep our eyes open for those who might need our help as we walk together in this journey of life.

Amy

July 9

FACING MY FEARS
PSALM 138

*When I called, you answered me;
you greatly emboldened me.*

Psalm 138:3

After Bill and I married, I became overly dependent on him, rather than depending on God for my security and strength. Secretly I worried, "What if one day I don't have Bill anymore?"

When our missionary work took Bill from home for weeks at a time, I began to depend on myself instead of Bill. Feeling even more inadequate, I reduced the risks of life whenever possible and lived within a cocoon of anxiety, even being afraid to go out in public.

Finally, at rock bottom, I followed David's example in Psalm 138:3. I too cried out, and God answered me. His answer gave me the understanding and strength to crack open the cocoon of fear and begin spreading my wings in dependence on God. Slowly but surely He made me a bold servant at Bill's side.

Years later, when Bill died, I recognized how compassionately God had dealt with my earlier fear: "What if one day I don't have Bill anymore?" Instead of removing my fear, God gave me the strength and ability to face it. And He will enable you too as you depend on Him.

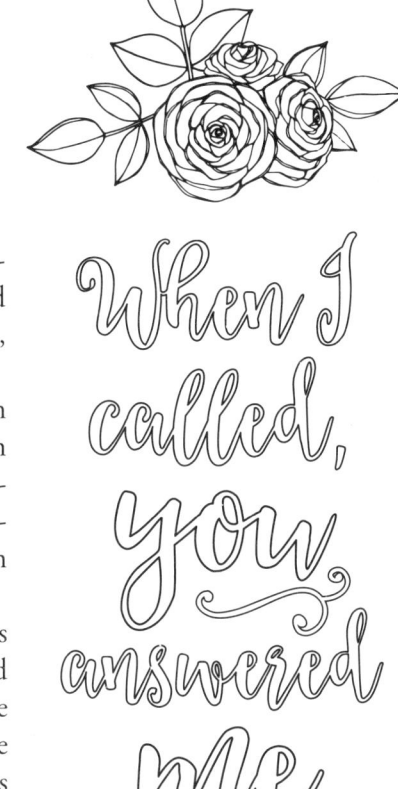

Joanie

When I called, you answered me.

PSALM 138:3

July 10

NOWHERE TO HIDE

AMOS 5:14-24

Jesus Christ, who is the faithful witness, the firstborn from the dead, and the ruler of the kings of the earth.
Revelation 1:5

I smelled something burning, so I hurried to the kitchen. Nothing was on the stove or in the oven. I followed my nose through the house. My nose led me to my office and then to my desk. I peeked beneath it, and there, peering back at me with big eyes pleading for help, was Maggie, our dog—our very "fragrant" dog. That "burning" smell now had the distinct odor of skunk. Maggie had gone to the farthest corner of our house to escape the foul smell, but she couldn't get away from herself.

Maggie's dilemma brought to mind the many times I have tried to run away from unpleasant circumstances only to discover that the problem was not the situation I was in but me. We run away from situations thinking we can escape the unpleasantness—only to discover that the unpleasantness is us.

The only way to escape ourselves is to stop hiding, acknowledge our waywardness, and let Jesus wash us clean (REVELATION 1:5). I am grateful that when we do sin, Jesus is willing to give us a brand-new start.

Julie

July 11

A BUBBLE BREAK
2 CORINTHIANS 4:7–18

> So we fix our eyes not on what is seen, but on what is unseen, since what is seen is temporary, but what is unseen is eternal.
>
> *Corinthians 4:18*

A young boy showered my husband, Carl, and me with bubbles as he came running by us on the Atlantic City boardwalk. It was a light and fun moment on a difficult day. We had come to the city to visit our brother-in-law in the hospital and to help Carl's sister who was struggling and having trouble getting to her doctors' appointments. So as we took a break and walked along the seaside boardwalk, we were feeling a bit overwhelmed by the needs of our family.

Then came the bubbles. They had a special significance to me. I love bubbles and keep a bottle in my office to use whenever I need the smile of a bubble break. Those bubbles and the vast Atlantic Ocean reminded me of what I can count on: God is always close. He is powerful. He always cares. And He can use even the smallest experiences and briefest moments to help us remember that His presence is like an ocean of grace in the middle of our heavy moments.

Maybe one day our troubles will seem like bubbles—momentary in light of eternity for "what is seen is temporary, but what is unseen is eternal" (2 CORINTHIANS 4:18).

Anne

July 12

BECAUSE

JOB 2

He replied, "You are talking like a foolish woman. Shall we accept good from God, and not trouble?" In all this, Job did not sin in what he said.

Job 2:10

One day my toddler exclaimed, "I love you, Mom!" When I asked him why he loved me, he answered, "Because you play cars with me." "Any other reason?" "Nope. That's it." My toddler's response made me smile—and think about the way I relate to God. Do I love and trust Him just because of what He does for me? What about when the blessings disappear?

Job had to answer these questions when catastrophe hit. His wife advised him, "Curse God and die!" (2:9). Instead, Job asked, "Shall we accept good from God, and not trouble?" (v. 10). Yes, Job struggled after his tragedy—he became angry with his friends and questioned the Almighty. Still, he vowed, "Though he slay me, yet will I hope in him" (13:15).

Job's affection for his heavenly Father didn't depend on a tidy solution to his problems. Rather, he loved and trusted God because of all that He is. Job said, "God is wise in heart and mighty in strength" (9:4 NKJV).

Our love for God must not be based solely on His blessings but on who He is.

Jennifer

July 13

PROTECTING A PROMISE
MATTHEW 2:13-23

> When they had gone, an angel of the Lord appeared to Joseph in a dream. "Get up," he said, "take the child and his mother and escape to Egypt. Stay there until I tell you, for Herod is going to search for the child to kill him."
>
> *Matthew 2:13*

What a series of events it had been for Joseph! He had seen angelic visitations, heard the voice of God, and witnessed the miracle of a virgin birth. Then came another dream. The message was clear: "Flee, for danger is near" (MATTHEW 2:13).

Screaming and wailing rang out in Bethlehem (V. 16), but Joseph's son—God's Son—would not be numbered among the dead. Scripture had foretold that the Messiah would prevail: "Of . . . his government and peace there will be no end" (ISAIAH 9:7). But Joseph realized he had been entrusted with a promise from God (1:20–23). His responsibility to protect the Messiah was fraught with danger, questions, and uncertainties.

Why then, do we think our path should be without struggle? Ultimately, the fulfillment of God's covenant to His people would come through His hand. But we also have a part to play—just as Joseph did.

As we persevere by God's power and provision, may we guard His truth (2 TIMOTHY 1:14) and remain steadfast. God will fulfill His promises (ISAIAH 46:11)!

Regina

July 14

THE SONGS OF OUR LIVES

JOB 29:1-6; 30:1-9

"Surely God is my salvation; I will trust and not be afraid. The Lord, the Lord himself, is my strength and my defense; he has become my salvation."

Isaiah 12:2

The members of an orchestra hear most clearly the sound of the instruments closest to them.

In a sense, we are the members of God's orchestra. We hear only the music closest to us. Because we don't hear a balanced work, we are like Job, who cried as he suffered: "Now those young men mock me in song; I have become a byword among them" (JOB 30:9).

Job recalled how princes and officials had respected him. But now, after his troubles, he had become the target of mockers. "My harp plays sad music," he lamented (30:31 NLT). Yet there was much, much more to the symphony. Job simply couldn't hear the whole song.

Maybe today you hear only the sad notes of your own violin. Don't lose heart. Every detail in your life is part of God's composition.

God's masterpiece of redemption is the symphony we are playing, and ultimately everything will work together for His good purposes. God is the composer of our lives. His song is perfect, and we can trust Him.

Keila

July 15

JESUS'S COMPASSION
LUKE 7:11-17

> When the Lord saw her, his heart went out to her and he said, "Don't cry."
>
> Luke 7:13

Greg Boyle, who helped launch a ministry to former gang members, knows about loving and caring for others. In his book *Tattoos on the Heart*, he writes, "Compassion isn't just about feeling the pain of others; it's about bringing them in toward yourself."

Compassion bridges the distance between us and another person. It enables us to lovingly move toward another instead of bolting in the opposite direction. In imitating Jesus's compassion, we would never act like the priest or Levite who moved away from the wounded man described in the parable of the good Samaritan (LUKE 10:30-37). It was the least expected person, a Samaritan, who acted the most like Christ. The parable reminds us that we are capable of acting without love toward our neighbor.

Instead, may we live out Jesus's compassion as revealed in His encounter with the widow of Nain. When Jesus learned her only son had died, "his heart went out to her," and He raised her son (7:11-15). Jesus moved *toward* her and lovingly addressed her need. May we, like Christ, move toward others with a heart of compassion.

Marlena

July 16

LESSON OF THE HORSE MASK

PSALM 119:33–40

Turn my eyes away from worthless things; preserve my life according to your word.

Psalm 119:37

At a horse farm near our house, some of the horses often have masks over their eyes. At first I felt sorry for the horses that weren't allowed to see. But then I learned that my assumption was wrong. The masks are made of mesh, so horses can see through them. But flies, which cause eye disease, are kept out. The masks don't keep the horses from seeing; they keep them from going blind!

Non-Christians often make conclusions about the Bible similar to the one I made about the mask. They think of it as something God "puts over our eyes" to keep us from seeing all the fun we could be having. They feel sorry for Christians because they think the Lord keeps us from enjoying life. What I didn't know about the horse mask, they do not know about the Bible. It keeps us from being infected by lies that cause spiritual blindness. The Bible doesn't keep us from enjoying life; it makes true enjoyment possible.

As we learn the lesson of the horse mask, we can rejoice that through God's Word we can really see!

Julie

July 17

HOW TO HAVE PEACE

COLOSSIANS 1:15–23

> Therefore, since we have been justified through faith, we have peace with God through our Lord Jesus Christ.
>
> *Romans 5:1*

The Kamppi Chapel of Silence in Helsinki, Finland, stands out in its urban setting. The curved structure, covered with wood, buffers the noise from the busy city outside. Designers created the chapel as a quiet space and a "calm environment for visitors to compose themselves." It's a welcome escape from the hustle and bustle of the city.

Many people long for peace, and a few minutes of silence may soothe our minds. But the Bible teaches that real peace—peace with God—comes from His Son. The apostle Paul said, "Therefore, since we have been justified through faith, we have peace with God through our Lord Jesus Christ" (ROMANS 5:1). Without Christ, we are enemies of God because of our sin. Thankfully, accepting Jesus's sacrifice reconciles us to God and ends the hostility that existed between us (COLOSSIANS 1:19–21).

Having peace with God does not ensure problem-free living. Jesus told His followers, "In this world you will have trouble," but He also said, "In me you may have peace" (JOHN 16:33). Because of Christ, the true peace of God can fill our hearts (COLOSSIANS 3:15).

Jennifer

July 18

Common Sense
PROVERBS 1:20-23

For the Lord gives wisdom; from his mouth come knowledge and understanding.

Proverbs 2:6

Eighteenth-century French philosopher Voltaire said, "Common sense is not so common." He was right! In a society that has grown increasingly litigious, we are inundated with warnings on products, mostly because some people lack common sense. Just read the following instructions.

On a hair dryer: Do not use while sleeping.

On a chain saw: Do not stop chain with hand.

Common sense can be learned from experience or the teaching we receive from those we trust. But God's Word is the best source of all to develop discernment and good judgment.

Three words echo throughout the book of Proverbs: wisdom, knowledge, and understanding. God has packed this book with common sense.

Proverbs 11:12 advises restraint: "A man of understanding holds his peace" (NKJV).

Proverbs 20:13 is practical: "Do not love sleep, lest you come to poverty" (NKJV).

To get more common sense, consult God's Word—the source of wisdom—daily.

Cindy

July 19

MISTAKEN IDENTITY

PSALM 115:1–18

Not to us, Lord, not to us but to your name be the glory, because of your love and faithfulness.

Psalm 115:1

People often confuse me with my older sister. From the staff at my favorite coffee shop to my sister's nursing students, we have many stories of people who try to ask me a medical question or who talk to her about writing. The mix-up seems humorous to us because we don't see the similarities others view so clearly.

With God, there is no mistaken identity regarding any of us. "Yet to all who did receive him, to those who believed in his name, he gave the right to become children of God—children born not of natural descent, nor of human decision or a husband's will, but born of God" (JOHN 1:12–13). Sometimes, though, experiences, people, and powers of darkness try to destroy our understanding of who we *truly* are.

In places of uncertainty, we at times construct a sense of self based in the temporary. True security, though, comes when we tear down the idols of self and choose Jesus (vv. 9–11). The cross brings us into fellowship with Him. In Him, our identity is restored to its God-given potential and meaning (139:13–16).

Regina

July 20

RED FLAGS

PROVERBS 13:1-14

The teaching of the wise is a fountain of life, turning a person from the snares of death.
Proverbs 13:14

Swans frequently visit Mill Pond, England, where a friend of mine lived. He calls it "a beautiful place where ducks, geese, and other waterfowl frolic playfully." Yet even in this idyllic setting there's danger. Near the pond are some power lines. A number of swans have been killed because they didn't see them as they approached the pond.

He talked with some officials about this problem, and eventually the power company installed red flags on the lines. Now the swans can see the danger and avoid it. Since the red flags were installed, not a single swan has died.

God has provided some "red flags" for our protection. The book of Proverbs contains many warnings about evil, and it encourages us to seek wisdom. In Proverbs 13:1–14, we find several red flags, including:

- Don't ignore instruction and rebuke (V. 1).
- Guard what you say (V. 3).
- Beware of the pursuit of riches (V. 7).

We can be thankful that the Bible gives us warnings that can keep us out of danger.

Anne

July 21

DESIRING GROWTH
HEBREWS 5:11-14

> Anyone who lives on milk, being still an infant, is not acquainted with the teaching about righteousness.
>
> *Hebrews 5:13*

The axolotl (pronounced ACK-suh-LAH-tuhl) is a biological enigma. Instead of maturing into adult form, this endangered Mexican salamander retains tadpole-like characteristics throughout its life. Writers and philosophers have used the axolotl as a symbol of someone who fears growth.

In Hebrews 5 we learn about Christians who were avoiding healthy growth—remaining content with spiritual "milk" intended for new believers. They were in danger of sliding backward spiritually from the Christlike attitudes they had already shown (6:9-11). They weren't ready for a solid diet of self-sacrifice (5:14). So the author wrote, "We have much to say about this, but it is hard to make it clear to you because you no longer try to understand" (v. 11).

Axolotls follow the natural pattern set for them by their Creator. But followers of Christ are designed to grow into spiritual maturity. As we do, we discover that growing up in Him involves more than our own peace and joy. Growth in His likeness honors God as we unselfishly encourage others.

Keila

July 22

NOT MY WORRY
ISAIAH 40:25–31

> Cast your cares on the Lord and he will sustain you; he will never let the righteous be shaken.
>
> *Psalm 55:22*

A man worried constantly about everything. Then one day his friends heard him whistling happily and looking noticeably relaxed. "What happened?" they asked him in astonishment.

He said, "I'm paying a man to do my worrying for me."

"How much do you pay him?" they asked.

"Two thousand dollars a week," he replied.

"Wow! How can you afford that?"

"I can't," he said, "but that's his worry."

Need someone to give your worries to?

The prophet Isaiah reminds us that God brings out the stars and calls them all by name (40:25–26). Because of "his great power and mighty strength", not one of them is missing (v. 26). And just as God knows the stars by name, He knows you and me individually and personally. You are each under His watchful care (v. 27).

You can turn your worries over to the Lord. He is never too weary or too tired to pay attention. He has all wisdom and all power, and He loves to use it on your behalf. The Holy One who directs the stars has His loving arms around each of us.

Poh Fang

July 23

From Mourning to Dancing
ISAIAH 61:1-4

> The Spirit of the Sovereign Lord is on me, because the Lord has anointed me to proclaim good news to the poor. He has sent me to bind up the brokenhearted, to proclaim freedom for the captives and release from darkness for the prisoners.
>
> *Isaiah 61:1, 3*

"We're cutting your job." A decade ago those words sent me reeling. At the time, I felt shattered, partly because my identity was so intertwined with my role as editor. Recently, I felt a similar sadness when I heard that my freelance job was ending. But this time was not as traumatic because I have seen God's faithfulness and how He can turn my mourning to joy.

The Lord can move us from despair to rejoicing, as we see in Isaiah's prophecy about the coming of Jesus (ISAIAH 61:1-3). The Lord gives us hope when we feel hopeless; He helps us to forgive when we think we can't; He teaches us that our identity is in Him and not in what we do. He gives us courage to face an unknown future. When we wear the rags of "ashes," He gently gives us a coat of praise.

When we think about God's faithfulness over the years, we know that He's willing and able to turn our grief to dancing once again—to give us sufficient grace in this life and full joy in heaven.

Amy

July 24

LIFE BEYOND THE GRAVE

JOHN 11:1-44

"And whoever lives by believing in me will never die. Do you believe this?"

John 11:26

My beloved husband, Bill, died of cancer at the age of forty-eight. One tearful morning I read John 11—the story about Jesus raising Lazarus from the dead. I was reassured by two truths from that passage.

The first truth was revealed when Jesus said Lazarus was asleep and He would wake him (vv. 11-14). His disciples responded, "Lord, if he sleeps, he will get better." Jesus replied, "Lazarus is dead." This was Jesus's gentle way of teaching them not to dread death any more than sleep. Because of His power, resurrecting someone from the grave was like waking someone from sleep.

I saw a second truth in Jesus's statement to Martha: "The one who believes in me will live, even though they die; and whoever lives by believing in me will never die" (vv. 25-26). As the resurrection and the life, Jesus will "waken" the bodies of believers someday. His power to do this was demonstrated when He raised Lazarus (vv. 43-44).

Have you lost someone close? Perhaps these promises can give you comfort and assurance.

Joanie

July 25

IMAGE CONSCIOUS
2 CORINTHIANS 3:1-3, 17-18

> And we all, who with unveiled faces contemplate the Lord's glory, are being transformed into his image with ever-increasing glory, which comes from the Lord, who is the Spirit.
>
> *2 Corinthians 3:18*

When going through old family photos, my cousins and I joke about which physical characteristics we've inherited. We notice primarily the negative ones: short legs, crooked teeth, unruly cowlicks. In addition to physical attributes, we also inherited character traits—some good, some not so good. We don't always pay as much attention to those.

According to my unscientific observations, people try all kinds of things to overcome physical imperfections—exercise routines, weight-loss programs, makeup, hair coloring, cosmetic surgery. But with our character flaws, we do something different. We tend to use them as an excuse for behaving badly. Changing our looks, I suppose, is easier than changing our character. Imagine how much better off we'd be if we put our energy into character development.

As believers, we're not limited by our genetic makeup. We can surrender our flaws to Him and allow Him to fulfill the potential He has in mind for us. The power of God's Spirit and the life of God's Son are at work in us, conforming us to His image (2 CORINTHIANS 3:18).

Julie

July 26

LOVE REVEALED
1 JOHN 4:9-16

This is how God showed his love among us: He sent his one and only Son into the world that we might live through him.
1 John 4:9

When a series of pink "I love you" signs mysteriously appeared in Welland, Ontario, local reporter Maryanne Firth decided to investigate. Her sleuthing turned up nothing. Weeks later, new signs appeared featuring the name of a local park along with a date and time.

Accompanied by a crowd of curious townspeople, Firth went to the park at the appointed time. There she saw a man wearing a suit, but he had cleverly concealed his face. Imagine her surprise when he handed her a bouquet and proposed marriage! The mystery man was Ryan St. Denis—her boyfriend. She happily accepted.

If you think Ryan's expression of love for Maryanne is neat, think of God's expression of love for us! "This is how God showed his love among us: He sent his one and only Son into the world that we might live through him" (1 JOHN 4:9). Jesus willingly gave up His life so anyone who believes in Him can have an everlasting relationship with God.

Nothing can separate a Christian "from the love of God that is in Christ" (ROMANS 8:39). Now, that's true love!

Jennifer

July 27

MY PEOPLE
1 PETER 2:1–10

> Once you were not a people, but now you are the people of God; once you had not received mercy, but now you have received mercy.
>
> 1 Peter 2:10

A little girl was being punished for bad behavior, and her parents were making her eat dinner by herself in the corner of the room. They paid no attention to her until they heard her pray part of Psalm 23: "I thank you, Lord, for preparing a table before me in the presence of my enemies."

Cute story. But in reality, our families can at times feel like the enemy. Even our spiritual family at church lets us down occasionally. But if we learn to give up the naive idea that others will always meet our lofty expectations, we might also change our focus.

Instead of focusing on others, we can find hope in the truth that we are God's very own children through faith in Jesus (1 PETER 2:10). He has chosen us as His own "special possession" (V. 9). The Lord has brought us into His family, and He'll never treat us as an enemy.

When others let us down, let's change our focus and remind ourselves that we who have put our faith in Jesus are God's children—cherished and cared for by Him.

Anne

July 28

SAFE

PSALM 33:1–22

We wait in hope for the Lord; he is our help and our shield.

Psalm 33:20

Overwhelmed with work and tired from a busy weekend of ministry, I couldn't stop the tears when I came home to a leak in the kitchen ceiling of our new house. Compounding the situation were the challenges of moving to a new town and opposition from our neighbors for having a home Bible study. As I watched each drip fall from the bulging drywall, I longed for something to be easy.

Sometimes we simply need to be reminded: God has us covered. Psalm 33:20 says, "We wait in hope for the Lord; he is our help and our shield." And Psalm 33:18 declares that "the eyes of the Lord are on those who fear him, on those whose hope is in his unfailing love."

Moved by love, God faithfully watches over us (PSALM 33:18). To make our victory dependent on circumstances and others' choices is to place our hope in the warhorse and the armor (PSALM 33:16–17). Instead, we trust in Him: "In him our hearts rejoice, for we trust in his holy name" (PSALM 33:21–22). He alone keeps us safe.

Regina

July 29

ROYAL WEDDING
REVELATION 19:1–10

Let us rejoice and be glad and give him glory! For the wedding of the Lamb has come, and his bride has made herself ready.

Revelation 19:7

Weddings and extravagance sometimes go together. Modern weddings have become a chance for young women to live out the fantasy of being "a princess for a day." An elegant gown, an elaborate hairstyle, attendants in color-coordinated dresses, bouquets of flowers, an abundance of food, and lots of celebrating with friends and family contribute to the fairy tale atmosphere. Royal weddings take extravagance to a level we "commoners" seldom see. In 2011 we got a peek at that when the wedding of Prince William and Kate Middleton was broadcast worldwide.

Another royal wedding is in the planning stages—the most extravagant ever. In this wedding, the most important person will be the groom, Christ himself; and we, the church, will be His bride. John's revelation says that the bride will make herself ready (19:7) and that our wedding gown will be our righteous acts (v. 8).

Though earthly marriages last only a lifetime, every bride works hard to make her wedding perfect. How much more, as the bride of Christ, should we be doing to prepare ourselves for a marriage that will last for eternity.

Julie

July 30

COME TO ME

JOHN 6:30-40

> Then Jesus declared, "I am the bread of life. Whoever comes to me will never go hungry, and whoever believes in me will never be thirsty."
>
> *John 6:35*

When Jesus lived on earth, He invited people to come to Him, and He still does (JOHN 6:35). But what do He and the heavenly Father have that we need?

Salvation. Jesus is the only way to have forgiveness of sin and the promise of heaven. "Everyone who believes may have eternal life in him" (JOHN 3:15).

Purpose. We are to give all of our heart, soul, mind, and strength to following Jesus. "Whoever wants to be my disciple must deny themselves and take up their cross and follow me" (MARK 8:34).

Comfort. In trial or sorrow, the "God of all comfort . . . comforts us in all our troubles" (2 CORINTHIANS 1:3–4).

Wisdom. We need wisdom beyond our own. "If any of you lacks wisdom, you should ask God . . . and it will be given to you" (JAMES 1:5).

Abundant Life. The fullest life is found in Jesus. "I have come that they may have life, and have it to the full" (JOHN 10:10).

Jesus said, "Whoever comes to me I will never drive away" (JOHN 6:37). Come!

Anne

July 31

DRINK UP!

JOHN 4:7–14

"Whoever drinks the water I give them will never thirst. Indeed, the water I give them will become in them a spring of water welling up to eternal life."

John 4:14

Before the turn of the century, Ida's Pastry Shoppe in Jenison, Michigan, advertised this offer: "Buy one of our coffee mugs for $4.79 and fill up your cup for a dime each time you visit."

The owners never expected that more than thirty-five years later, four longtime customers would still be getting their coffee every day—for ten cents.

You won't find many deals like that anymore. But Jesus offered something far greater to the woman at the well (JOHN 4:10). He said, "Everyone who drinks this water will be thirsty again, but . . . the water that I shall give them will become in them a spring of water welling up to eternal life" (VV. 13–14).

The woman was ready to listen. Each of her many personal relationships had left her empty. Then Jesus offered her "water" that would give her something more—eternal life.

Jesus has made you the same offer, "I have come that they may have life, and have it to the full" (JOHN 10:10).

God's grace and love come from a bottomless reservoir. Drink from the water He offers. You'll never thirst again.

Cindy

August 1

CONTENT WHERE WE ARE

PHILIPPIANS 4:11-13

I am not saying this because I am in need, for I have learned to be content whatever the circumstances.

Philippians 4:11

We've heard the stories: A couple, longtime pillars of their local church, suddenly bolt to join a new church—prompting their home church to wonder what went wrong. A family is ripped from its community when an unexpected job change demands relocation.

Stories of displacement and disruption—circumstances that can easily and understandably lead to discontentment. We're troubled with the way our stories have unfolded, unhappy with life.

The apostle Paul had every reason to be discontent. He endured shipwrecks, beatings, whippings, and more (2 CORINTHIANS 11:22–27). Undoubtedly he struggled with discontentment. But he wrote, "I have learned to be content whatever the circumstances" (PHILIPPIANS 4:11). With God's help, this is something we can develop by treasuring our good gifts no matter the circumstances.

Even in our most difficult times, we can find things to be thankful for—God's comfort, for instance. Because of what God has provided, we can be content with the good in our hard situations. May we rest in Him as we pray for His kingdom to come (MATTHEW 6:10).

Marlena

I have learned to be content whatever the circumstances.

PHILIPPIANS 4:11

August 2

LITTLE BY LITTLE
EXODUS 23:20-33

"Little by little I will drive them out before you, until you have increased enough to take possession of the land."

Exodus 23:30

When I was a little girl, I cherished one particular story I read—never dreaming how much it would affect me years later.

It was about a little boy with a small shovel. He was trying to clear a pathway through deep snow in front of his house. A man saw the child's enormous task and said, "Little boy, how can someone as small as you expect to finish a task as big as this?" The boy looked up and replied, "Little by little, that's how!" And he continued shoveling.

God reminded me of that story when I was recovering from a breakdown. I remember how my "adult" self taunted the weak "child" within me: "How can someone as inadequate as you climb so great a mountain as this?" That little boy's reply became my reply: "Little by little, that's how!" And I did overcome—by depending on God. Together we claimed one small victory after another.

The obstacles facing Israel as they prepared to enter the Promised Land must have seemed insurmountable. But He didn't ask them to do it all at once. "Little by little" is the strategy for victory.

Joanie

August 3

RESTING IN GOD
ROMANS 4:16–22

Yet he did not waver through unbelief regarding the promise of God, but was strengthened in his faith and gave glory to God, being fully persuaded that God had power to do what he had promised.

Romans 4:20-21

It was our last family holiday before our eldest son went off to college. As we filled the back pew in the little seaside church, my heart filled with love as I glanced at my five reasonably tidy children. "Please protect them spiritually and keep them close to you, Lord," I prayed silently.

The final hymn had a rousing chorus based on 2 Timothy 1:12. "I know whom I have believed, and am persuaded that he is able to keep that which I have committed unto him." I was assured that God would keep their souls.

In the years since, there have been times of wandering for some of my children and outright rebellion for others. Sometimes I wondered about God's faithfulness. Then I remembered Abraham. He never failed to trust the promise he had received (GENESIS 15:5–6). Through years of waiting and mistaken attempts to help things along, Abraham hung on to God's promise until Isaac was born.

What an encouraging reminder! We tell God our request. We know He is powerful. We thank Him for His faithfulness.

Marion

August 4

MAKE MY BROWN EYES BLUE

MATTHEW 16:24-28

"For whoever wants to save their life will lose it, but whoever loses their life for me will find it."

Matthew 16:25

As a young girl, Amy Carmichael (1867–1951) wished she had blue eyes instead of brown. She even prayed that God would change her eye color (which never happened). At age twenty, Amy sensed God's call to serve Him as a missionary. She ended up in India, where she recognized God's wisdom in the way He made her. She knew she might have had a more difficult time gaining acceptance from the predominately brown-eyed people if her eyes had been blue. She served God in India for fifty-five years.

We can't know for sure that Amy was more readily accepted because of her eye color, but we do know that it is the Lord "who has made us, and we are his" (PSALM 100:3). As we submit to His wisdom in everything, we can serve Him effectively.

Amy knew what submission was. When asked about missionary life, she replied, "Missionary life is simply a chance to die." Then she quoted Matthew 16:25.

That describes the devoted Christian's life as well—surrender to God's plans and will for us. May we submit to Him today.

Anne

August 5

A MODEST PROPOSAL
PHILIPPIANS 2:1-11

> And being found in appearance as a man, he humbled himself by becoming obedient to death—even death on a cross!
>
> *Philippians 2:8*

As a college student, I heard countless engagement stories. My starry-eyed friends told about glitzy restaurants, mountaintop sunsets, and rides in horse-drawn carriages. Then there was the guy who simply washed his girlfriend's feet. His "modest proposal" proved he understood that humility is vital for a lifelong commitment.

The apostle Paul taught about humility and how it holds us together—especially in marriage. Paul said to reject "me-first" urges: "Do nothing out of selfish ambition" (PHILIPPIANS 2:3). Instead, we should value our spouses more than ourselves and look out for their interests.

Humility in action means serving our spouse, and no act of service is too small or too great. After all, Jesus "humbled himself by becoming obedient to death." His selflessness showed His love for us.

What can you do today to humbly serve the one you love? Whatever it is, placing your spouse's needs before your own confirms your commitment to each other through Christlike humility.

Jennifer

August 6

A PLEASING AROMA
2 CORINTHIANS 2:12-17

> For we are to God the pleasing aroma of Christ among those who are being saved and those who are perishing.
>
> *2 Corinthians 2:15*

A perfumer who works in New York declares that she can recognize certain combinations of scents and guess the perfumer behind a fragrance. With just a sniff, she can say, "This is Jenny's work."

When writing to Christians in Corinth, Paul used an example that would have reminded them of a victorious Roman army in a conquered city burning incense (2 CORINTHIANS 2:14). For the Romans, the aroma of the incense meant victory; for the prisoners, it meant death.

Paul said we are to God the pleasing aroma of Christ's victory over sin. God has given us the fragrance of Christ himself so we can become a sweet-smelling sacrifice of praise. But how can we live so we spread this pleasing fragrance to others? We can show generosity and love, and we can share the gospel so others can find the way to salvation. We can allow the Spirit to display through us His gifts of love, joy, and kindness (GALATIANS 5:22–23).

Do others observe us and say, "This is Jesus's work"? Are we allowing Him to spread His fragrance through us?

Keila

August 7

IF OUR HEARTS . . .
LUKE 6:43-45

Bring to an end the violence of the wicked and make the righteous secure—you, the righteous God who probes minds and hearts.

Psalm 7:9

As I stood in rural Uganda watching a rig I had contracted to drill a well for seven hundred impoverished villagers, an elderly man approached me. He grasped my hands and in broken English said, "If you could open my heart and view inside, you would see happiness on top of happiness on top of happiness for this water God has provided."

Those words gave me insight into the overflow of this dear man's heart: gratitude, humility, meekness, and reverence for the Lord were evident. "The mouth speaks what the heart is full of," Jesus said. "A good man brings good things out of the good stored up in his heart, and an evil man brings evil things out of the evil stored up in his heart" (LUKE 6:45).

If our hearts are full of bitterness or hatred, broken relationships and isolation will follow. If our hearts are full of love, compassion, and gratitude, we'll tend to have healthy, edifying relationships.

What's in your heart?

Roxanne

August 8

THE BOND OF PEACE
EPHESIANS 4:1-6

Make every effort to keep the unity of the Spirit through the bond of peace.
Ephesians 4:3

After I confronted my friend by email over a matter on which we had differed, she didn't respond. Had I overstepped?

As she popped into my mind throughout the following days, I prayed for her, unsure of the way forward. Then one morning I went for a walk in our local park and saw her—pain etched on her face as she glimpsed me. "Thank you, Lord, that I can talk to her," I whispered as I approached her with a welcoming smile. We talked openly and were able to resolve matters.

Sometimes when hurt or silence intrudes on our relationships, mending them seems out of our control. But as the apostle Paul says in his letter to the church at Ephesus, we are called to work for peace and unity through God's Spirit—donning the garments of gentleness, humility, and patience as we seek God's healing in our relationships. The Lord yearns for us to be united, and through His Spirit He can bring His people together—even unexpectedly during a walk in the park.

Amy

August 9

IT'S WORTH IT
2 CORINTHIANS 11:24-33

If I must boast, I will boast of the things that show my weakness.
2 Corinthians 11:30

"I can't do it," Robert said, throwing his pencil down in despair. "It's just too hard!" Reading, writing, and spelling seemed impossible to our dyslexic nine-year-old. At last, someone offered a solution—but it would be tough: Reading and spelling practice for twenty minutes every evening. Sometimes we just didn't feel like doing it, and at times we despaired of seeing progress. But we were committed to helping Robert, so we battled on.

After a couple of years, all the tears and struggles seemed worthwhile. Robert learned to read and spell. And we all learned patient endurance.

The apostle Paul suffered all sorts of hardships as he pursued his goal of sharing the good news of Jesus with those who had never heard. Persecuted, beaten, imprisoned, and misunderstood, sometimes he faced death itself (2 CORINTHIANS 11:25). But the joy of seeing people respond to his message made it all worthwhile.

If you feel that the task God has called you to is too hard, remember this: The spiritual lessons and joy may seem hidden at first, but they are certainly there! God will help you find them.

Marion

August 10

LIGHT UP THE NIGHT
DANIEL 12:1–3

"Those who are wise will shine like the brightness of the heavens, and those who lead many to righteousness, like the stars for ever and ever."

Daniel 12:3

One mild fall evening, thousands of people in my hometown gathered along the banks of the Grand River to light sky lanterns. They released them into the darkness and watched as they rose to join the moon in a dazzling display that turned the night sky into a sparkling work of art.

When I saw pictures of the event, I was disappointed that I was out of town and had missed it. But I realized that what had happened in Grand Rapids could be seen as a symbol of the conference I was attending in New York City. More than a thousand people from a hundred cities around the world had gathered to plan a "work of art"—lighting up the darkness of their own cities by planting churches and spreading the gospel of Christ, the Light of the World.

The prophet Daniel wrote about a time when those who turn others to the Lord will shine like stars forever (DANIEL 12:3). We can all join in that great event. Let's shine the light of Christ in dark places where we live and work.

Julie

August 11

WORTH THE CALORIES?

PHILIPPIANS 4:4–9

> Finally, brothers and sisters, whatever is true, whatever is noble, whatever is right, whatever is pure, whatever is lovely, whatever is admirable—if anything is excellent or praiseworthy—think about such things.
>
> *Philippians 4:8*

I love egg *roti prata*, a popular pancake here in Singapore. But I discovered that it would take me thirty minutes of running to burn away the 240 calories in one of those pancakes.

When I started working out in the gym, I began asking myself, *Is that food worth the calories?*

While it is wise to watch our food consumption, there's a more important area of life that needs to be monitored: our media consumption. Research shows that what we see stays in our minds a long time. It has a "clingy effect," sticking to us like that stubborn fat we find so hard to lose. And it can influence us for good or for bad.

We need to be discerning media consumers. We need to ask ourselves: Are we careful about what we allow our eyes to see?

In Philippians 4:8, Paul tells us in essence, "Feed on things that are true, noble, just, pure, lovely, of good report, virtuous, and praiseworthy." This is a "diet" worthy of what Christ has done for us.

Poh Fang

August 12

NOT WHAT WE PLANNED

ISAIAH 55:6–9

"For my thoughts are not your thoughts, neither are your ways my ways," declares the Lord.

Isaiah 55:8

In 1915 Dr. Frank Laubach's church commissioned him to serve as a professor at Union Theological Seminary in Manila. When he and another man were being considered for the office of seminary president, a vote was held to determine which candidate would win. Dr. Laubach did what he thought honorable; he voted for his opponent. Consequently, he lost the election by one vote—his own. He was disappointed and depressed, and he even questioned God. Yet God used that incident to redirect his life. He eventually developed a literacy program that taught an estimated sixty million people to read.

Sometimes our desired plans for our lives and God's kingdom don't come to pass. They don't turn out to be His perfect plans (ISAIAH 55:8). It's easy to lose heart.

Still, God reveals that He is *for* us. He is the God of hope who always seeks our best—providing what it means for us to truly flourish even when we can't see it (V. 9).

Our Father is far more generous than we can ever imagine. As we trust in God, we find that His plans are always best.

Marlena

August 13

TIMING IS EVERYTHING
PSALM 37:3-11

We know that in all things God works for the good of those who love him, who have been called according to his purpose.
Romans 8:28

What I thought was a coincidental meeting had been good timing on my future husband's part.

From the balcony of the church, he had seen me, deduced which exit I might be using, raced down two flights of stairs, and arrived seconds before I did. As he casually held the door and struck up a conversation, I was oblivious to the fact that his "impromptu" dinner invitation had been premeditated. It was perfect timing.

Perfect timing is rare—at least where humans are concerned. But God has specific purposes and plans for us, and His timing is always perfect.

We see that timing in the life of Bible characters: Abraham's servant prayed for a wife for Isaac. God answered his prayer by bringing the young woman to him (GENESIS 24). And we marvel at Esther's courage as Mordecai reminded her, "Who knows but that you have come to your royal position for such a time as this?" (ESTHER 4:14).

Disappointed in the pace of God's plans? "Trust in the LORD" (PSALM 37:3). God will open doors when the timing is perfect.

Cindy

August 14

God, Answer Me!
PSALM 6

Away from me, all you who do evil, for the Lord has heard my weeping.
Psalm 6:8

Theresa left Sue a message, saying she had great news. Sue was sure the news was that her friend had received Jesus as Savior. After all, she had been praying for Theresa's salvation for thirty years.

A few days later, Theresa revealed very different "great news": She had a new boyfriend and was moving in with him. Sue cried out in desperation, "Lord, what makes me think you would answer me after thirty years of praying?"

Some of our hardest struggles are those deep desires that go unmet. The psalmist David could relate. He cried, "Have mercy on me, Lord. . . . My soul is in deep anguish. How long, Lord, how long?" (PSALM 6:2–3). Later in the psalm, we read that David knew the Lord had heard him (V. 9).

A month after Theresa's "great news," she called and left another message: "I have wonderful news! I trusted Jesus as my Savior! I don't know why I didn't do it long ago." Thirty years of prayer paid off.

Keep praying. In His time, God will answer.

Anne

August 15

ENOUGH TO SHARE
DEUTERONOMY 15:4–11

Give generously to them and do so without a grudging heart; then because of this the Lord your God will bless you in all your work and in everything you put your hand to.

Deuteronomy 15:10

I recall when my son and I had twelve little guests at our dinner table in Uganda every night for three years. Before that, the children had gone entire days without food.

Our meals were filled with laughter as the boys and girls tried spaghetti and other foods for the first time. I watched with joy as children who had been hungry and weak gained the energy to run and play. Wasswa and I discovered that the more we shared, the more God provided for us to give away (DEUTERONOMY 15:8, 10).

Perhaps we hesitate to help others because we don't think we have enough to give. Consider what happened when the disciples faced the prospect of feeding a huge crowd and told Jesus to send them away. He said, "That isn't necessary—you feed them." "But we have only five loaves of bread and two fish!" they answered (MATTHEW 14:15–17 NLT). They forgot who Jesus was—the One who could feed them all.

Today, ask Him to open your eyes to the need of those around you—and let Him provide.

Roxanne

August 16

GOD IS ALIVE!
PSALM 30

That my heart may sing your praises and not be silent. Lord my God, I will praise you forever.

Psalm 30:12

Sixteenth-century theologian Martin Luther once experienced a period of worry and despondency. One day his wife dressed in black mourning clothes.

"Who has died?" asked Luther.

"God," said his wife.

"God!" said Luther, horrified. "How can you say such a thing?"

She replied, "I'm only saying what you are living."

Luther realized that he indeed was living as if God were no longer alive and watching over them in love. He changed his outlook from gloom to gratitude.

Occasionally we too live as if God were dead. For encouragement, we can turn to the Psalms. The writers may have faced bleak times, but they had one habit that kept them from going sour: giving thanks to God. For example, David wrote, "You have turned for me my wailing into dancing. . . . Lord my God, I will give praise to you forever" (PSALM 30:11–12).

Meeting every situation with thanksgiving helps us see those situations from God's perspective—opportunities to discover His power and love.

Each time you express gratitude to God in a difficult situation, you're declaring, "God is alive!"

Joanie

August 17

LANGUAGE OF LOVE
JAMES 3:1-12

With the tongue we praise our Lord and Father, and with it we curse human beings, who have been made in God's likeness.

James 3:9

When my grandmother came to Mexico as a missionary, she had a hard time learning Spanish. One day she went to the market. She showed her shopping list to the girl helping her and said, "It's in two tongues (*lenguas*)." But she should have said it was written in two languages (*idiomas*). The butcher overheard them and assumed she wanted to purchase two cow tongues. My grandmother didn't realize what she had till she got home!

Mistakes are inevitable when we are learning a second language, including learning the new language of God's love. For example, we might praise the Lord but then speak badly of others. Our old sinful nature opposes our new life in Christ. What comes out of our mouths shows us how much we need God's help.

Our old "tongue" must go away. And we learn the new language of love by making Jesus the Lord of our speech. When the Holy Spirit works in us, He gives us self-control to speak words that please the Father. Lord, "keep watch over the door of my lips" (PSALM 141:3).

Keila

August 18

FULL SUN

EPHESIANS 5:1–16

For you were once darkness, but now you are light in the Lord. Live as children of light.

Ephesians 5:8

I know better, but I still keep trying. The instructions on the label are clear: "Needs full sun." Our yard has mostly shade. It is not suitable for plants that need full sun. But I like the plant. So I buy it, bring it home, plant it, and take really good care of it. But the plant is not happy! My care and attention are not enough. It needs sunlight, which I cannot provide. Plants need what they need.

And so do people. Although we can survive for a while in less-than-ideal conditions, we can't thrive. In addition to our basic physical needs, we also have spiritual needs that can't be met by any substitute.

Scripture says that believers are children of light. This means that we need to live in the full light of God's presence to thrive (PSALM 89:15). If we try to live in darkness, we will produce nothing but "fruitless deeds" (SEE EPHESIANS 5:3–4, 11). But if we are living in the light of Jesus, the Light of the World, we will produce the fruit of His light, which is good, faithful, and true.

Julie

August 19

MIRACLE RAIN

1 KINGS 18:1, 41–45

"Remember the former things, those of long ago; I am God, and there is no other; I am God, and there is none like me."

Isaiah 46:9

Life is hard for the villagers in China's Yunnan Province. Their main food source is corn and rice. One year a severe drought hit, and the crops withered. Many superstitious practices were carried out as the people attempted to end the drought. When nothing worked, people blamed the five Christians in the village for offending their ancestors' spirits.

Those five believers gathered to pray. Before long, the sky darkened and long, drenching rains came. The crops were saved! Most of the villagers did not believe God sent the rain, but some did and sought to find out more about Him.

In 1 Kings we read of a severe drought in Israel. It was a result of God's judgment on His people (17:1), who worshiped the false god Baal, whom they thought could send rain for their crops. Then God, through His prophet Elijah, showed that He is the one true God who determines when rain falls.

Our all-powerful God desires to hear our prayers and answer our pleas. Although we don't always understand His timing or His purposes, God always responds with His best for our lives.

Poh Fang

August 20

HARD CONVERSATIONS
GALATIANS 2:1-21

For through the law I died to the law so that I might live for God.
Galatians 2:19

I remember when someone on our church ministry team responded with disbelief upon discovering that my husband and I have disagreements. It's true. We—like any family—have to work through conflict. Spiritual maturity doesn't mean we're exempt from challenges, or that we try to hide behind a squeaky-clean façade.

Guarding our image is a temptation we all face. The opinions of others can make us lose sight of the real call to discipleship (LUKE 9:23–24) and choose to focus on how others see us. But this truth remains: *A desire to protect our reputation is nothing more than a fear of other people* (JOHN 12:42–43).

Disappointed with Peter's response to the Gentile believers (GALATIANS 2:11-16), Paul was unafraid to engage him in a hard conversation. He reminded Peter that caving in to people's desires was not the answer (GALATIANS 2:20–21).

Being authentic in the church means holding Christ's reputation above our own. Only then will we be the city set on a hill—the hope of Jesus shining in a world shrouded in the deception of appearances (MATTHEW 5:14-16).

Regina

August 21

ROCK-SOLID
PSALM 34:15–22

The eyes of the Lord are on the righteous, and his ears are attentive to their cry.

Psalm 34:15

It was a sad day in May 2003 when the Old Man of the Mountain broke apart and slid down the mountainside. This forty-foot profile of an old man's face, carved by nature in the White Mountains of New Hampshire, had long been an attraction to tourists, a solid presence for residents, and the official state emblem. It was written about by Nathaniel Hawthorne in his short story "The Great Stone Face."

Nearby residents were devastated when the Old Man fell. One woman said, "I grew up thinking that someone was watching over me. I feel a little less watched-over now."

In life a dependable presence sometimes disappears. Something or someone we've relied on is gone, and our life is shaken. The loss makes us feel off-balance, unstable. We might even conclude that God is no longer watching over us.

But "the eyes of the Lord are on the righteous" (PSALM 34:15). He "is near to those who have a broken heart" (V. 18 NKJV). He is the Rock whose presence we can always depend on (DEUTERONOMY 32:4).

God's presence is real. He continually watches over us. He is rock-solid.

Anne

August 22

FOR OUR HEALTH
1 CHRONICLES 16:7–14

> Give praise to the Lord, proclaim his name; make known among the nations what he has done.
>
> *1 Chronicles 16:8*

According to a prominent Duke University Medical Center researcher, "If thankfulness were a drug, it would be the world's best-selling product with [health benefits] for every major organ system."

The Bible takes the idea of thankfulness to a deeper level. The act of giving thanks causes us to recognize the One who provides our blessings (JAMES 1:17).

David knew that God was responsible for the safe delivery of the ark of the covenant in Jerusalem (1 CHRONICLE 15:26). As a result, he penned a song of gratitude that centered on God instead of the event. The ballad began: "Give praise to the Lord, proclaim his name; make known among the nations what he has done" (16:8). David's song went on to rejoice in God's greatness, highlighting God's salvation, creative power, and mercy (VV. 25–36).

True thankfulness is worshiping the Giver and not the gifts we enjoy. Focusing on the good things in our lives may benefit our bodies, but directing our thanks to God benefits our souls.

Jennifer

August 23

TRUE COMMUNICATION
ACTS 2:1-12

When they heard this sound, a crowd came together in bewilderment, because each one heard their own language being spoken.

Acts 2:6

Walking in my North London neighborhood, I hear snatches of conversation in many languages—Polish, Japanese, Hindi, and Italian, to name a few. This diversity feels like a taste of heaven, yet I can't understand what they're saying. As I step into the Russian café or the Polish market and hear the different accents and sounds, I reflect on how wonderful it must have been on the day of Pentecost when people of many nations could understand what the disciples were saying.

On that day, pilgrims gathered together in Jerusalem to celebrate the festival of the harvest. The Holy Spirit rested on the believers so that when they spoke, the hearers (who had come from all over the world) could understand them in their own languages (ACTS 2:5-6). What a miracle! Many were spurred on to find out more about Jesus.

We may not speak many languages, but the Holy Spirit equips us to connect with people in other ways. Amazingly, we are God's hands and feet—and mouth—to further His mission. Today, how might we—with the Spirit's help—reach out to someone unlike us?

Amy

August 24

THE GIFT OF TEARS

JOHN 11:32-44

Jesus wept.
John 11:35

I called a longtime friend when his mother died. She had been a close friend of my mother, and now both had passed on. As we spoke, our conversation slipped easily into a cycle of emotion—tears of sorrow that Beth was gone and tears of laughter as we recalled the caring and fun person she had been.

Have you experienced that strange crossover from crying one moment to laughing the next? It's amazing that sorrow and joy can both provide a physical release.

Since we are made in God's image (GENESIS 1:26), and humor is such an integral part of almost every culture, I imagine that Jesus must have had a wonderful sense of humor. We know that He also knew the pain of grief. When his friend Lazarus died, Jesus saw Mary weeping, and "He was deeply moved in spirit." A short time later, He too began to weep (JOHN 11:33–35).

Our ability to express our emotions with tears is a gift, and God keeps track of each tear we cry (SEE PSALM 56:8).

Cindy

August 25

ON THE FRINGE
PHILIPPIANS 4:10–20

And my God will meet all your needs according to the riches of his glory in Christ Jesus.
Philippians 4:19

When butterflies hatch at Frederik Meijer Gardens in Grand Rapids, Michigan, they do so in an indoor tropical paradise perfectly suited to meet their every need. The temperature is perfect. The humidity is perfect. The food is a perfect balance of calories and nutrition to keep them healthy. No need to go elsewhere. Yet some butterflies see the bright blue sky outside the conservatory and spend their days fluttering near the glass ceiling far away from the plentiful food supply.

I want to say to those butterflies, "Don't you know everything you need is inside? The outside is cold and harsh, and you will die within minutes if you get what want."

I wonder if that's God's message to us. So I ask myself, *Do I look longingly at things that would harm me? Do I ignore God's plentiful provision because I imagine that something just beyond my reach is better? Do I spend my time on the fringes of faith?*

God supplies all our needs from His riches (PHILIPPIANS 4:19). May we be grateful and content with what He has provided.

Julie

August 26

TASTE AND SAY!
PSALM 34

*Taste and see that the L*ORD *is good; blessed is the one who takes refuge in him.*
Psalm 34:8

Do you believe God is good, even when life isn't? Mary did, and I gasped in amazement the day I heard her pastor share her story at her funeral.

Mary had been a widow—very poor, and housebound because of her ailments in old age. But like the psalmist, she had learned to praise God amid her hardships. Over the years, she had come to savor with deep gratitude every good thing He sent her way.

Her pastor had occasionally visited her at home. Because of her crippling pain, it took her a long time to inch her way to the door to let him in. So he would call on the telephone and tell her that he was on his way and what time he would get there. Mary would then begin the slow, arduous journey to the door, reaching it about the time he arrived. Without fail, she would greet him with these triumphant words: "God is good!"

Mary's example challenges us not only to "taste and see" but also to taste and *say* that the Lord is good—even when life isn't.

Joanie

August 27

A FAITHFUL SERVANT

JOSHUA 14:6–15

If anyone speaks, they should do so as one who speaks the very words of God. If anyone serves, they should do so with the strength God provides, so that in all things God may be praised through Jesus Christ. To him be the glory and the power for ever and ever. Amen.

1 Peter 4:11

Madaleno is a bricklayer. From Monday to Thursday he builds walls and repairs roofs. He is quiet, reliable, and hardworking. Then from Friday to Sunday he goes up to the mountains to teach the Word of God. At age seventy, he still works with his hands building houses, but he also works to build the family of God.

His life has been threatened several times. He has slept under the stars. He has been kicked out of towns. But he thinks God has called him to do what he does, and he serves happily.

Madaleno's faithfulness reminds me of Caleb and Joshua, two of the men Moses sent to explore the Promised Land (NUMBERS 13; JOSHUA 14:6–13). Their companions were afraid of the people who lived there, but Caleb and Joshua trusted God and believed He would help them conquer the land.

The work entrusted to us may be different from Madaleno's. But our confidence can be the same. In reaching out to others, we rely not on ourselves but on the strength of our God.

Keila

August 28

REFLECTING GOD'S LOVE

EXODUS 34:29-35

> When Moses came down from Mount Sinai ... he was not aware that his face was radiant because he had spoken with the Lord.
>
> Exodus 34:29

When I served as my mom's caregiver during her treatment at a live-in cancer care center, even on her hardest days, she read Scripture and prayed for others before getting out of bed.

She spent time with Jesus daily, expressing her faith through her dependence on God, her kind deeds, and her desire to encourage and pray for others. Although she didn't realize it, her smiling face glowed with the Lord's loving grace as she shared His love with everyone around.

After Moses spent forty days and nights communing with God (EXODUS 34:28), he descended Mount Sinai. He had no idea his intimate connection with the Lord actually changed his appearance (V. 29). But the Israelites could tell by the glow on his face that Moses had spoken with the Lord (VV. 30–32).

While our transformation will definitely not be as apparent as Moses's beaming face, as we spend time with the God who hears us and as we surrender to Him each day, we reflect His love. God can draw others closer to Him as the evidence of His presence shows through us.

Xochitl

August 29

CLEANING HOUSE
1 PETER 1:22–25

Rid yourselves of all malice and all deceit, hypocrisy, envy, and slander of every kind.

1 Peter 2:1

Recently, I switched rooms in the home I rent. This took longer than expected because I wanted a completely fresh and uncluttered start. After I spent hours and hours cleaning and sorting, bags of stuff sat by the front door to be thrown away, donated, or recycled. But at the end of this exhausting process was a fresh, beautiful room.

My housecleaning project gave me a fresh perspective on 1 Peter 2:1, as paraphrased in *The Message*: "So clean house! Make a clean sweep of malice and pretense, envy, and hurtful talk." Interestingly, it's after a joyful confession of believers' new life in Christ (1:1–12) that Peter urges them to throw away destructive habits (1:13–2:3). We don't change our lives to be saved, but because we are saved (1:23).

As real as our new life in Christ is, bad habits do not disappear overnight. So we need to "clean house," throwing away all that prevents us from fully loving others (1:22) and growing (2:2). Then, in that new, clean space, we can experience the wonder of being freshly built by Christ's power and life (v. 5).

Monica

August 30

PAINFUL WORDS
MATTHEW 5:1-16

"God blesses those who are humble, for they will inherit the whole earth."

Matthew 5:5 (NLT)

While walking to our car, my daughter and I were savoring a school musical performance we had just witnessed. Our happiness came to a screeching halt, however, as we watched a man approach a car and denigrate the driver for failing to pull forward far enough into the student loading zone. The diatribe was particularly painful because it took place in the context of Christian community.

Individual rights and freedoms can be a blessing, but living in surrender to Jesus means we humbly serve and love others as He did. Reminding us that the humble will "inherit the whole earth" (MATTHEW 5:5 NLT), Jesus challenges us about the importance of the death of self.

Our greatest evidence of strength isn't in demanding our rights but in demonstrating mercy (MATTHEW 5:7). Anger and frustration can be legitimate responses in certain situations, but they're a problem when we use them as an excuse to behave poorly toward others.

Serving a Savior who "took the humble position of a slave" (PHILIPPIANS 2:7 NLT), let's remember that power doesn't come in what we demand of others, but in what we offer because of Him.

Regina

August 31

HEAVY LIFTING
MATTHEW 11:25–30

"Come to me, all you who are weary and burdened, and I will give you rest."

Matthew 11:28

One day I found my son straining to lift a pair of four-pound barbells over his head—an ambitious feat for a toddler. I offered to help, and together we heaved the weight toward the ceiling. The heavy lifting that was so hard for him was easy for me.

Jesus has this perspective on the stuff that's hard for us to manage. When life seems like a carousel of catastrophes, Jesus isn't fazed by a fender-bender, troubled by a toothache, or harassed by a heated argument—even if it all happens in one day! He can handle anything, and that is why He said, "Come to me, all you who are weary and burdened" (MATTHEW 11:28).

Are you worn out from ongoing problems? Jesus is the only real solution. Approaching the Lord in prayer allows us to cast our burdens on Him so He can sustain us (PSALM 55:22). Today, ask Him to assist you with everything. He can supply rest for your soul, for His yoke is easy and His burden is light (MATTHEW 11:29–30).

Jennifer

September 1

A JOYFUL HEART
2 CHRONICLES 7:1–10

Shout for joy to the Lord, all the earth.
Psalm 100:1

My granddaughter's favorite tune is a John Philip Sousa march. Sousa was a US composer in the late nineteenth century. Moriah is just a toddler, but she loves the Sousa tune and can even hum a few notes. She associates it with joyful times. When our family gets together, we often hum this song, and the grandchildren dance or parade in circles to the beat.

Our joyful noise reminds me of the psalm that implores us to "worship the Lord with gladness" (PSALM 100:2). When King Solomon dedicated the temple, the Israelites celebrated with praises (2 CHRONICLES 7:5–6). Psalm 100 may have been one of the songs they sang: "Shout for joy to the Lord, all the earth. Worship the Lord with gladness; come before him with joyful songs. . . . Enter his gates with thanksgiving and his courts with praise; give thanks to him and praise his name" (VV. 1–2, 4). Why? "For the Lord is good and his love endures forever" (V. 5)!

God loves us! In grateful response, let's "shout for joy to the Lord" (PSALM 100:1)!

Alyson

SHOUT FOR JOY

TO THE *Lord*, ALL THE EARTH. *Worship the Lord with gladness;* COME BEFORE HIM WITH *joyful songs.*

PSALM 100:1-2

September 2

REMOVING THE BARRIERS
PHILEMON 1:8–16

> He is very dear to me but even dearer to you, both as a fellow man and as a brother in the Lord.
> Philemon 1:16

I saw Mary every Tuesday when I visited "the House"—a home that helps former prisoners reintegrate into society. Fresh out of jail, fighting addictions, separated from her son, she lived on the edge of society.

Like Mary, Onesimus knew what it meant to live on society's edge. As a slave, Onesimus had apparently wronged his Christian master, Philemon, and was in prison. While there, he met Paul and came to faith in Christ (v. 10). Paul sent him back to Philemon with a letter urging him to receive Onesimus "no longer as a slave, but better than a slave, as a dear brother" (PHILEMON 1:16).

Like Philemon I had a choice to make: Would I see Mary as an ex-convict and a recovering addict—or as a sister in the Lord? We were privileged to walk together in our journey of faith, and I'm glad I chose to see her as my spiritual sister.

It's easy to allow society's walls to separate believers. But the gospel of Christ removes those barriers, changing our lives and our relationships forever.

Karen

September 3

INTENTIONAL DEFIANCE

JONAH 1:1–2:2

> I cried out to the Lord in my great trouble, and he answered me. I called to you from the land of the dead, and Lord, you heard me!
>
> *Jonah 2:2* (NLT)

A woman was running a half marathon in Ontario, Canada. Somehow she missed the turn for the half marathon and instead ran twenty-six miles—nearly a complete marathon! Not only did she complete it but she also posted a fast enough time to qualify for the famous Boston Marathon.

While her turn was unintentional, let me tell you about Jonah, who *intentionally* made a wrong turn. After God told Jonah to go to Nineveh and preach, "Jonah . . . went in the opposite direction" (JONAH 1:1–3 NLT).

Jonah hoped he could "escape from the Lord" (JONAH 1:3 NLT). He was so calm about his disobedience that he slept peacefully below deck on his escaping ship—until some frightened sailors woke him because of a violent storm. The sailors threw Jonah overboard when they realized it was his fault, and he ended up spending three days and nights inside a huge fish. Jonah finally "cried out to the Lord" (2:2 NLT), and God rescued him.

God hears us when we turn to Him from our wanderings. If we've chosen a wrong turn, let's confess it and find forgiveness in Him today (1 JOHN 1:9)!

Ruth

September 4

A PERFECT SENTENCE

EXODUS 3:13–18

> Who among the gods is like you, Lord?
> Who is like you—majestic in holiness,
> awesome in glory, working wonders?
>
> *Exodus 15:11*

Since I was a young girl, I have sought to compose the perfect sentence.

I realize now that my pursuit of the perfect sentence will never be satisfied, but I have found a statement of perfection. When God called Moses, he told the Lord he was anxious about this responsibility, so he asked what to say if the Israelites doubted him.

The Lord replied, "I am who I am" (EXODUS 3:14). By using His unique name, He offered Moses a glimpse of the nature of His eternal existence in one sentence. You might say it's a statement of perfection!

Biblical scholar George Bush (1796–1859) wrote the following about God's description of himself: "He, in distinction from all others, is the one only true God, the God who really is. . . . The eternal, self-existent, and immutable Being; the only being who can say that He always will be what He always has been."

God says, "I am who I am." He and His name are perfect. In reverence we bow before Him.

Anne

September 5

MY FATHER IS WITH ME

MARK 14:32–50

"A time is coming and in fact has come when you will be scattered, each to your own home. You will leave me all alone. Yet I am not alone, for my Father is with me."

John 16:32

A friend struggling with loneliness posted these words on her Facebook page: "It's not that I feel alone because I have no friends. I have lots of friends. But they can't be with me all the time—for all time."

Jesus understands that kind of loneliness. I imagine that during His earthly ministry He saw loneliness in the eyes of lepers and heard it in the voices of the blind. But above all, He must have experienced it when His close friends deserted Him (MARK 14:50).

He knew they would do that, but He had a better back-up plan. He said to His disciples: "You will leave me all alone. Yet I am not alone, for the Father is with me" (JOHN 16:32). Shortly after Jesus said these words, He took up the cross for us. He made it possible for us to have an intimate relationship with God.

We will all experience loneliness. But Jesus helps us understand that we always have the presence of the Father with us. God is omnipresent and eternal. Only He can be with us all the time—for all time.

Poh Fang

September 6

FIRST RESPONSE
JAMES 5:13–16

Do not be anxious about anything, but in every situation, by prayer and petition, with thanksgiving, present your requests to God. And the peace of God, which transcends all understanding, will guard your hearts and your minds in Christ Jesus.

Philippians 4:6-7

When my husband, Tom, was rushed to the hospital for emergency surgery, I began to call family members. My sister and her husband came right away to be with me, and we prayed as we waited. Tom's sister listened to my anxious voice on the phone and immediately said, "Cindy, can I pray with you?" When my pastor and his wife arrived, he too prayed for us (JAMES 5:13–16).

Prayer should be our first response to life's situations. At its root, prayer is simply a conversation with God, spoken in the expectation that God hears and answers. In His Word, God encourages us to engage Him in prayer (PHILIPPIANS 4:6). We also have His promise that when "two or three gather" in His name, He will be "with them" (MATTHEW 18:20).

For those who have experienced the power of the Almighty, our first inclination often will be to cry out to Him. Nineteenth-century pastor Andrew Murray said, "Prayer opens the way for God himself to do His work in us and through us."

Cindy

September 7

GOD'S WORLD
PSALM 24

The earth is the Lord's, and everything in it, the world, and all who live in it.

Psalm 24:1

I knew my son would enjoy receiving a map of the world for his birthday. After some shopping, I found a colorful chart of the continents, which included illustrations in every region. I loved the map, but I wondered about the label at the bottom of the map: "Our World."

In one sense, the earth is our world because we live in it. We're allowed to drink its water, mine its gold, and fish its seas—but only because God has given us the go-ahead (GENESIS 1:28–30). Really, it's God's world. "The earth is the Lord's, and everything in it" (PSALM 24:1). It amazes me that God has entrusted His incredible creation to mere humans. He knew some of us would mistreat it, deny He made it, and claim it as ours. Still, He allows us to call it home and sustains it through His Son (COLOSSIANS 1:16–17).

Today, take a moment to enjoy life in God's world. Let the world you inhabit inspire you to worship the One who owns it.

Jennifer

September 8

FAMOUS IN GOD'S EYES

MARK 10:42–45

"Whoever wants to be a leader among you must be your servant."

Mark 10:43 (NLT)

In C. S. Lewis's book *The Great Divorce*, he tells of an imagined scene in heaven when a parade is being held in a person's honor. As everyone waits to find out who it is, a guide declares, "It's someone [you] never have heard of. Her name on earth was Sarah Smith. . . . She is one of the great ones. [You] have heard that fame in this country and fame on Earth are two quite different things." She was, it turns out, just an ordinary woman on earth who served others.

Jesus said that the greatest in the kingdom of heaven are the servants of all (MARK 10:43-44). Jesus calls us to love and to serve all people.

Serving others doesn't make for fame in this world. Yet our obedience to God revealed through our faithful service to Him and to others—even in the little things—is what God notices and celebrates (LUKE 16:10).

We might not be famous in the world's eyes, but a posture of love and service makes us "famous" in God's eyes and reflects Jesus's example (MARK 10:45).

Marlena

September 9

BROKEN BUT BEAUTIFUL

JEREMIAH 18:1–6

The pot he was shaping from the clay was marred in his hands; so the potter formed it into another pot, shaping it as seemed best to him.

Jeremiah 18:4

Recently, my daughter showed me her collection of sea glass. Also known as beach glass, the varied bits of colored glass are often remnants of shattered and discarded glass bottles.

If the discarded glass ends up in an ocean, it is relentlessly tossed about by currents and tides. Its jagged edges are ground down by the sand and waves and eventually are smoothed away and rounded off. The result is something beautiful. The jewel-like sea glass has found new life and is treasured by collectors and artists.

In a similar way, a broken life can be renewed when it is touched by God's love and grace. In the Old Testament, we read that when the prophet Jeremiah watched a potter working, he noticed that if an object was marred, the potter simply reshaped it (JEREMIAH 18:1–6). God explained that in His hands the people of ancient Israel were like clay, which He would shape as He saw best.

We are never too badly broken for God to reshape. He loves us in spite of our imperfections and past mistakes, and He desires to make us beautiful.

Cindy

September 10

FEARLESS

JOSHUA 2:1–24

> "I know the Lord has given you this land," she told them. "We are all afraid of you. Everyone in the land is living in terror."
>
> *Joshua 2:9* (NLT)

On the night Rahab encountered the two Israelite spies in Jericho, forty years had passed since God's miraculous deliverance of His people from Egypt. Israel's enemies in Jericho already knew of God's deliverance (JOSHUA 2:9-10). Although the unbelief of God's own children had required His patience as He awaited the readiness of the next generation (PSALM 78:11-12), the people of Jericho didn't have to be convinced of God's greatness (JOSHUA 2:10-11).

Just as God's people in Joshua's day were intended to be conquerers through God's power, we were made to be victorious through the salvation Jesus provided. Through Him, we are sons and daughters of almighty God (ROMANS 8:14-16, 33-39). We are called to declare this truth from God: "My Spirit remains among you, just as I promised when [my children] came out of Egypt. So do not be afraid" (HAGGAI 2:5 NLT). Because of Jesus, we don't have to live in fear. Fear melts before God's love and power!

Regina

September 11

WHAT IS THAT TO YOU?

JOHN 21:15–22

Jesus answered, "If I want him to remain alive until I return, what is that to you? You must follow me."

John 21:22

When you attend a children's choir concert, you're not surprised when the children performers look everywhere but at the director. They wiggle, squirm, and poke each other. Oh, yes, and they occasionally sing. That behavior is cute in children. It's not so cute, though, when adult choir members don't watch the conductor. Good music depends on singers who pay attention to the director so they can stay together as they sing.

Christians sometimes are like singers in a children's choir. Instead of looking at Jesus, the great Conductor, we squirm or look at each other or watch the audience.

Jesus admonished Peter for such behavior. After the Savior told Peter what would be required of him, Peter pointed to John and asked, "What about him?" Jesus answered with a question: "What is that to you? You must follow me" (JOHN 21:22).

God's plan for each of us is the same: Follow Jesus. When we watch Him intently, we'll not be distracted by God's plan for anyone else.

Julie

September 12

RELIEF FROM THE SCORCHING SUN

PSALM 121

The Lord watches over you—the Lord is your shade at your right hand.

Psalm 121:5

Living in Britain, I don't usually worry about sunburn. After all, the sun is often blocked by a thick cover of clouds. But recently I spent some time in Spain, and I quickly realized that with my pale skin, I could be out in the sunshine for only ten minutes before I needed to scurry back under the umbrella.

As I considered the scorching nature of the Mediterranean sun, I began to understand more deeply the meaning of the image of the Lord God as His people's shade at their right hand (PSALM 121:5). Residents of the Middle East knew unrelenting heat, and they needed to find shelter from the sun's burning rays.

When we use Psalm 121 in prayer, we reassure ourselves that the Lord forms a protective covering over us. We find a safe place in the Lord.

We lift our eyes to the "Maker of heaven and earth" (VV. 1–2), because whether we are in times of sunshine or times of rain, we receive His gifts of protection, relief, and refreshment.

Amy

September 13

A WIN EITHER WAY

PHILIPPIANS 1:15–26

For to me, to live is Christ and to die is gain.

Philippians 1:21

Lois had just undergone cancer surgery and was alone with her thoughts. She remembered that she had asked herself before her operation, "Am I ready to die?" Her immediate answer had been, and still was, "Yes, I am. Christ is my Lord and Savior."

With her readiness for death assured, she now needed to concentrate on living. Would it be in fear or in faith? Then God seemed to say, "I have saved you from eternal death. I want to save you from living in fear." Isaiah 43:1 came to mind: "Do not fear, for I have redeemed you; I have summoned you by name; you are mine."

Now Lois testifies, "Yes, I am His! That reality is more important than doctors telling me I have cancer." And then she adds, "I win either way!"

Lois's insight is a convinced echo of Paul's words in today's text, "For to me, to live is Christ and to die is gain" (PHILIPPIANS 1:21). Let's pray that those words will resonate in our heart. That confidence makes us a winner either way.

Joanie

September 14

LIFEBLOOD
HEBREWS 9:19-28

> In fact, the law requires that nearly everything be cleansed with blood, and without the shedding of blood there is no forgiveness.
>
> *Hebrews 9:22*

Mary Ann believed in God and His Son Jesus, but she struggled with why Jesus had to shed His blood to bring salvation. Who would think of cleansing something with blood? Yet the Bible says, "The law requires that nearly everything be cleansed with blood" (HEBREWS 9:22). That, in Mary Ann's opinion, was disgusting!

Then one day she had to go to a hospital. A genetic condition had altered her immune system, and doctors became alarmed when the illness started attacking her blood. As she was in the emergency room she thought, *If I lose my blood, I will die. But Jesus shed His blood so I can live!*

Suddenly everything made sense. In the midst of her pain, Mary Ann felt joy and peace. She understood that blood is life, and a holy life was needed to make peace with God for us. Today she is alive and well, thanking God for her health and for Jesus's sacrifice on her behalf.

How could we ever thank Jesus enough for making His sacrifice our sacrifice, His life our life, and His Father our Father?

Keila

September 15

A FAIR TRADE
PSALM 119:161–168

I rejoice in your promise like one who finds great spoil.
Psalm 119:162

Scott and Mary Crickmore poured fifteen years of their lives into helping translate the New Testament in the Maasina dialect. It was for the Fulani tribe in the West African nation of Mali.

Some people would think that the Crickmores' sacrifice was too great—giving up their comfortable lifestyle, changing their diet to mush and rice, and living in less-than-ideal circumstances for those fifteen years. But the Crickmores say it was "a fair trade," because now the Fulani people have the Word of God in a language they can read.

The psalmist delighted in God's Word. He stood in awe of it, rejoiced over it, loved it, and obeyed it (PSALM 119:161–168). He found great peace and hope in the Word.

The Fulani people are now able to discover the "great treasure" (V. 162 NLT) of God's Word. Would you agree with the Crickmores that any effort and sacrifice to get the Bible to others is "a fair trade"?

Anne

September 16

THE ULTIMATE RESET
ISAIAH 43:14–28

> "I am about to do something new.
> . . . I will make a pathway through
> the wilderness. I will create rivers
> in the dry wasteland."
>
> Isaiah 43:19 (NLT)

When God first told Abram that all nations of the world would be blessed through him, it may have seemed impossible (GENESIS 12:1-3). After all, the man didn't even have a child. And neither he nor his wife was getting any younger. Then Isaac was born—and so was the nation of Israel.

Even so, the promise seemed shaky. The Israelites ended up scattered or in captivity (ISAIAH 5:13). When they emerged from Babylonian bondage, the people had a revived zeal for God's Word that quickly evolved into empty faith. The spirit of God's law was set aside for the letter, and appearances carried the day (MARK 7:4-9).

So God sent His Son to dwell among men. Jesus, fully God and fully man, showed what a sinless life looks like. He offered himself in our place—a perfect sacrifice to take away our sins (JOHN 1:29).

And just like that, the course of humanity was changed—from hopeless to hope fulfilled, from death to life. Thanks be to God who did a new thing (ISAIAH 43:19-20) and who gives us victory through our Lord Jesus Christ!

Remi

September 17

CARRIED THROUGH
PSALM 30:1–12

> Weeping may stay for the night,
> but rejoicing comes in the morning.
> *Psalm 30:5*

I recently reread some of my journals from college. When I did, I realized I didn't feel about myself then as I do today. My struggles with loneliness and doubts about my faith felt overwhelming at the time, but now I can see how God has carried me to a better place. This reminded me that what feels overwhelming today will one day be part of a greater story of His healing love.

Psalm 30 is a celebration psalm that similarly looks back with amazement and gratitude on God's powerful restoration: from sickness to healing, from feeling God's judgment to enjoying His favor, from mourning to joy (vv. 2–3, 11).

The psalm is attributed to David, who experienced restoration so incredible he confessed, "Weeping may stay for the night, but rejoicing comes in the morning" (v. 5). Despite the pain he had endured, David discovered something even greater—God's powerful hand of healing.

If you are hurting today and need encouragement, recall those times in your past when God carried you through to a place of healing. Pray for trust that He will do so again.

Monica

September 18

ORDINARY PEOPLE

JUDGES 6:11–16

> But we have this treasure in jars of clay to show that this all-surpassing power is from God and not from us.
>
> 2 Corinthians 4:7

Gideon was an ordinary person. He was a farmer, and a timid one at that. When God called him to deliver Israel from the Midianites, Gideon's initial response was, "How can I save Israel? Indeed my clan is the weakest in Manasseh, and I am the least in my family" (JUDGES 6:15). God promised that He would be with Gideon and that he would be able to accomplish what he had been asked to do (V. 16). Gideon's obedience brought victory to Israel.

Many others contributed in this plan to save the Israelites from a strong enemy force. God provided Gideon with three hundred men, valiant heroes all, to win the battle. We are not told their names, but their bravery and obedience are recorded in the Scriptures (JUDGES 7:5–23).

Today God is still calling ordinary people to do His work and assuring us that He will be with us as we do. Because we are ordinary people being used by God, it's obvious that the power comes from God and not from us.

Poh Fang

September 19

MEASURE ME

EPHESIANS 4:11–16

And Jesus grew in wisdom and stature, and in favor with God and man.

Luke 2:52

"Can you measure me today?" Caleb, our paperboy, asked.

It was not the first time he had made that request. A few years earlier I had mentioned to him how tall he was getting. So we often measured his height and marked it on the siding of our house. He loved having his growth measured.

It's a good idea to measure our spiritual growth as well. For instance: Do I spend time reading God's Word and talking with Him each day? Do I look forward to fellowshipping with the Lord? What "fruit of the Spirit" is apparent in my life? Do I have a generous and giving spirit? How much better do I know God today than I did a year ago? These questions are good indicators of spiritual growth.

A child seems to grow up all of a sudden, but it's actually a continual process. Just as Jesus grew in both wisdom and stature, we as believers are to continue to "grow in the grace and knowledge of our Lord and Savior Jesus Christ" (2 PETER 3:18). Have you measured yourself lately?

Cindy

September 20

BATTER IN THE BOWL
RUTH 2:1–12

"She said, 'Please let me glean and gather among the sheaves behind the harvesters.' She came into the field and has remained here from morning till now, except for a short rest in the shelter."

Ruth 2:7

One day as my daughter and I were mixing the ingredients of our favorite chocolate treat, she asked if I would leave some batter for her. She wanted to enjoy what was left over. I agreed and then told her, "That's called gleaning, you know, and it didn't start with brownies."

As we enjoyed the remnants of our baking project, I explained that Ruth had gathered leftover grain to feed herself and her mother-in-law Naomi (RUTH 2:2–3). Because both of their husbands had died, the women had returned to Naomi's homeland. There Ruth met a wealthy landowner named Boaz. She asked him, "Please let me glean . . . among the sheaves behind the harvesters" (V. 7). He willingly consented and instructed his workers to purposely let grain fall for her (V. 16).

Like Boaz, who provided for Ruth, God provides for us out of His abundance. His resources are infinite, and He lets blessings fall for our benefit. He willingly provides us with physical and spiritual nourishment. Every good gift we receive comes from Him.

Jennifer

September 21

SECURE
EPHESIANS 3:12-21

"I pray that you, being rooted and established in love, may have power, together with all the Lord's holy people, to grasp how wide and long and high and deep is the love of Christ."

Ephesians 3:17-18

His soft hair brushing against my chin, the tiny bundle snuggled on my shoulder. Though I'm well past the baby stage with our own children, I so enjoy these tender times with friends' babies. Even when they're fussy, I enjoy the opportunity to nestle them close.

This picture is a reflection of God's nurturing care for us. Psalm 68:19 says, "Praise the LORD . . . for each day he carries us in his arms" (NLT). A warrior king, David captured this same idea when he compared his submission to the Lord as being like that of a young child leaning against his mother (PSALM 131:2). *Perfect, peaceful surrender.* It's the kind of restful place we all desire, especially when the storms of life seem strong (PSALM 4:8).

The more we know His love, the greater we trust Him (1 JOHN 4:16). When we understand that we're safe, we come "boldly . . . into God's presence" and live expecting God "to accomplish infinitely more than we might ask or think" (EPHESIANS 3:12, 20 NLT).

Regina

September 22

ARE YOU STRUGGLING?

HEBREWS 12:1-7

Consider him who endured such opposition from sinners, so that you will not grow weary and lose heart.

Hebrews 12:3

I was in my second year of widowhood and I was struggling. Morning after morning my prayer life consisted of one daily sigh: "Lord, I shouldn't be struggling like this!" "And why not?" His still, small voice seemed to ask me.

Then the answer came—unrecognized pride! Somehow I had thought that a person of my spiritual maturity should be beyond such struggle. What a ridiculous thought! I had never been a widow before and needed the freedom to be a true learner—a struggling learner.

At the same time, I was reminded of the story of a man who cut a slit in a cocoon to help an emperor moth inside emerge more easily. However, the moth's wings were shriveled. The narrow opening is God's way to force fluid from its body into its wings, so the "merciful" snip was, in reality, cruel.

Hebrews 12 describes the Christian life as a race requiring endurance, discipline, and correction. We never get beyond the need of a holy striving against self and sin. Sometimes the struggle is exactly what we need to become what God intends us to be.

Joanie

September 23

IGNORANCE AND INNOCENCE

ROMANS 5:12–21

> So that, just as sin reigned in death, so also grace might reign through righteousness to bring eternal life through Jesus Christ our Lord.
>
> Romans 5:21

Some people avoid church for the same reason others avoid going to the doctor: they don't want to find out that anything is wrong. Ignorance of our sin, however, doesn't make us innocent.

Roman law is sometimes considered the source of the idea that ignorance of the law excuses no one. But the concept originated much earlier. When God gave the law to Israel, He established that even unintentional sin required a sacrifice for forgiveness (LEVITICUS 4; EZEKIEL 45:18–20).

The apostle Paul addressed the issue of ignorance. When people were ignorant of God's righteousness, they made up their own (ROMANS 10:3). When we live according to our own standards, we might feel good about ourselves, but that doesn't make us spiritually healthy. Only when we are measured by God's standard of righteousness (Jesus) do we know the condition of our spiritual health.

None of us can achieve the righteousness of Christ, but thankfully we don't have to. He shares His righteousness with us (5:21). The good news is that the Great Physician can make us well.

Julie

September 24

READY FOR THE WEDDING

MATTHEW 25:1-13

"Therefore keep watch, because you do not know the day or the hour."

Matthew 25:13

"I'm hungry," said my eight-year-old daughter. "I'm sorry," I said, "I don't have anything for you." We had been waiting over an hour for the bride to arrive at the church. As I wondered how much longer it would be, I hoped I could occupy my daughter until the wedding started.

As we waited, I felt like we were enacting a parable. Although our house is close to the church, I knew if I went to fetch snacks, the bride might come and I would miss her entrance. I thought about Jesus's parable about the ten virgins (MATTHEW 25:1-13). Five came prepared with enough oil for their lamps to stay lit as they waited for the bridegroom, but five did not. Just as it was too late for me to dash back for food, so it was too late for the young women to go and buy more oil for their lamps.

Jesus told this parable to emphasize that we need to be prepared, for when He comes again we will give an account of the state of our hearts. Are we waiting and ready?

Amy

September 25

A BETTER SONG
GALATIANS 5:16–25

> Since we are living by the Spirit,
> let us follow the Spirit's leading
> in every part of our lives.
>
> Galatians 5:25 (NLT)

In Greek mythology, the island of Sirens was where beautiful temptresses ensnared passing sailors with their sweet songs. The music led the men to the shore where they were shipwrecked and destroyed. Jason of the Argonauts came up with a plan to thwart the Sirens' call. He hired a skilled musician to play a tune as his ship sailed within earshot of Sirens. His boat floated by with the crew unaffected by the alluring tunes.

They enjoyed a *better* song.

Although many of us make resolutions to "change our tune," it doesn't take long for old habits to return. Paul reminds us that freedom from one pleasure can come only as we pursue greater pleasures: "righteous living, faithfulness, love, and peace" (2 TIMOTHY 2:22 NLT).

Paul reminds us to "let the Holy Spirit guide [our] lives. Then [we] won't be doing what [our] sinful nature craves" (GALATIANS 5:16 NLT). The bad habits that held us back last year will continue to slow us down this year unless we follow the "better song" of the Holy Spirit (GALATIANS 5:22–23). By the Spirit's power, we can make beautiful music for Christ!

Ruth

September 26

OUR GUILT IS GONE

PSALM 32:1–11

> I said, "I will confess my transgressions to the Lord." And you forgave the guilt of my sin.
>
> Psalm 32:5

As a young girl, my friend and I were in a gift shop when she shoved a handful of colorful barrettes into my pocket and yanked me out the door of the shop without paying for them. Guilt gnawed at me for a week before I approached my mom—my confession pouring out as quickly as my tears.

Grieved over my bad choice, I returned the stolen items, apologized, and vowed never to steal again. The owner told me never to come back. But my mom forgave me, so I slept peacefully that night.

King David also rested in forgiveness through confession (PSALM 32:1–2). He had hidden his sins against Bathsheba and Uriah (2 SAMUEL 11–12) until his "strength was sapped" (PSALM 32:3–4). But once David refused to "cover up" his wrongs, the Lord erased his guilt (V. 5).

We can't choose the consequences of our sins or control people's responses when we confess and seek forgiveness. But the Lord can empower us to enjoy freedom from the bondage of sin and peace through confession as He confirms that our guilt is gone—forever.

Xochitl

September 27

A GRATITUDE VISIT
ROMANS 16:1-16

> I commend to you our sister Phoebe, a deacon of the church in Cenchreae. I ask you to receive her in the Lord in a way worthy of his people and to give her any help she may need from you, for she has been the benefactor of many people, including me.
>
> *Romans 16:1-2*

Counting your blessings promotes good physical health, according to a study by some US doctors. Volunteers who kept weekly gratitude journals reported fewer aches and pains than those who recorded daily hassles or neutral events.

A "gratitude visit" was developed by Dr. Martin E. P. Seligman to promote strong emotional health. He tells people to think of someone who has made an important difference in their lives, write the story of how that person has helped them, and then to visit that person and read the story aloud. Tests show that people who did so were happier and reported fewer episodes of depression.

Paul had a long list of people who had helped him and for whom he was grateful (ROMANS 16:1-16). He wrote that Phoebe had been a helper and Priscilla and Aquila had "risked their lives" for him. He wrote his thanks in a letter to the church at Rome.

Who has helped to shape your life? Could you make a gratitude visit—for their sake and yours?

Anne

LET YOUR CONVERSATION BE ALWAYS *full of grace,* SEASONED with SALT, SO THAT YOU MAY KNOW HOW TO ANSWER EVERYONE.

Colossians 4:6

September 28

GRACE IN OUR HEARTS

EPHESIANS 2:4–10

> Let your conversation be always full of grace, seasoned with salt, so that you may know how to answer everyone.
>
> Colossians 4:6

A few years ago, four-star general Peter Chiarelli (the second-highest-ranking general in the US Army at that time) was mistaken for a waiter by a senior presidential advisor at a formal Washington dinner. As the general stood behind her in his dress uniform, the senior advisor asked him to get her a beverage. She then realized her mistake, and the general graciously eased her embarrassment by refilling her glass as they both laughed about the faux pas.

The word *gracious* comes from the word *grace*, and it can mean an act of kindness or courtesy, like the general's. But it has an even deeper meaning to followers of Christ. We are recipients of the incredible free and unmerited favor—grace—that God has provided through His Son, Jesus (EPHESIANS 2:8).

Because we have received grace, we are to show it in the way we treat others. Grace in our hearts pours out in our words and deeds (COLOSSIANS 3:16–17).

Learning to extend the grace in our hearts toward others is a by-product of the life of a Spirit-filled follower of Christ Jesus—the greatest of grace givers.

Cindy

September 29

RULES OF DISENGAGEMENT

GENESIS 50:15–21; JOHN 8:31–36

"So if the Son sets you free, you will be free indeed."

John 8:36

In her book *Throw Out Fifty Things*, Gail Blanke outlines four "Rules of Disengagement" to help people clear the clutter from their lives. The first rule states: "If it . . . weighs you down, clogs you up, or just plain makes you feel bad about yourself . . . let it go [and] move on."

I think this rule of disengagement has a spiritual application too: We don't have to stay connected to past sin. Joseph's brothers struggled with this. Years after they sold Joseph into slavery, they recalled their cruelty and feared revenge (GENESIS 50:15). So they sent a message to Joseph, begging for forgiveness (vv. 16–17). They did this despite previous merciful actions and reassurances from their brother (45:4–15).

Many of us remain connected to age-old offenses despite mercy and forgiveness from those we may have hurt. However, true freedom comes when we confess our wrongdoing to God. He forgives it (1 JOHN 1:9) and separates us from it (PSALM 103:12). Because of this, we can remind ourselves that the Son has made us free, and we are free indeed (JOHN 8:36).

Jennifer

September 30

SACRIFICIAL LOVE
LUKE 9:21-27

"If any of you wants to be my follower, you must give up your own way, take up your cross daily, and follow me. If you try to hang on to your life, you will lose it. But if you give up your life for my sake, you will save it."

Luke 9:23-24 (NLT)

Charlie gave up everything to care for his wife, Sarah, who had early onset Alzheimer's. Charlie rearranged his schedule to more effectively care for her. He cherished her in sickness, health, disappointment, and frailty. Great love drove him to selflessly give up his life for her whether she knew it or not.

Charlie's sacrificial decision reminds me of what it means to "take up [our crosses] daily" (LUKE 9:23-24). When we're truly in love with Jesus, our hearts become devoted to Him. We want to spend every waking minute in His presence to become more like Him. We want to do whatever it takes to live like Jesus.

We have to turn from our selfish tendencies—our plans and our desires—to follow our Savior's example. In Romans 8:12–13, Paul wrote, "You have no obligation to do what your sinful nature urges you to do. . . . If through the power of the Spirit you put to death the deeds of your sinful nature, you will live" (NLT).

Like Jesus, may we carry our cross today and sacrifice our lives out of love.

Marlena

October 1

LOOKING GOOD
MATTHEW 23:23-31

"Blind Pharisee! First clean the inside of the cup and dish, and then the outside also will be clean."

Matthew 23:26

"Your hair is really healthy," said my hairdresser after giving me a haircut. "I hope it's because you use our products." "No. I'm sorry," I said. "I just use whatever product is cheap and smells good." But then I added, "I also try to eat well. I think that makes a big difference."

We work hard to make ourselves look good. Do we do that with spiritual matters? Jesus addressed this issue with the religious leaders in Jerusalem (MATTHEW 23). They followed an elaborate set of religious rules that went well beyond the ones God had given them. They worked hard to look good to their peers—to prove that they were better than others. But their hard work didn't impress God. Jesus said to them, "You clean the outside of the cup and dish, but inside [you] are full of greed and self-indulgence" (V. 25).

Every culture values various religious behaviors and traditions, but God's values transcend cultures. And what He values isn't measured by what others see. God values a clean heart and pure motives. Spiritual health is expressed from the inside out.

Julie

THE LORD IS MY
LIGHT
AND MY
SALVATION—
WHOM SHALL I FEAR?
THE LORD IS THE
STRONGHOLD
OF MY LIFE—OF WHOM
SHALL I BE AFRAID?

PSALM 27:1

October 2

TAKING GOD AT HIS WORD
1 JOHN 5:1–13

I write these things to you who believe in the name of the Son of God so that you may know that you have eternal life.
1 John 5:13

Many true believers in Christ are plagued with doubt about their salvation. Even though they've come in repentance and faith to Jesus as their Savior, they still wonder, *Will I really go to heaven?*

My late husband Bill often told about something that happened to him when he was two years old. One day he wandered from home and got lost. When his parents realized he was missing, they went searching for him. Finally, to everyone's immense relief, they spotted their tearful boy and carried him safely home.

Later Billy overheard his mother retell the incident. When she reached the part where they went out searching for him, Billy began to relive the story. "Mommy!" he sobbed. "Did you ever find me?" Surprised and touched by his doubt, she embraced him and said, "Of course, my child! See, you're with us now, and we'll make sure you always are." That comforted Billy, because he took her at her word.

The New Testament letter of 1 John was written to give believers the assurance of salvation. That assurance can be yours as you take God at His word.

Joanie

October 3

THE GREENER GRASS MYTH

EPHESIANS 5:22-23

Each one of you also must love his wife as he loves himself, and the wife must respect her husband.

Ephesians 5:33

Nancy Anderson says she grew lukewarm in her faith and thus believed the world's lie: "I deserve to be happy." This led to an extramarital affair that nearly ended her marriage. She wrote her book *Avoiding the Greener Grass Syndrome* to help keep her painful story of infidelity from "becoming someone else's story."

In her book, Nancy offers six action suggestions on how to build "hedges" to protect your marriage:

- Hear—give a listening ear to your spouse.
- Encourage—build up your spouse by focusing on positive qualities.
- Date—celebrate your marriage by playing and laughing together.
- Guard—establish safeguards; set clear boundaries.
- Educate—study your mate to understand him or her.
- Satisfy—meet each other's needs.

The grass on the other side of the fence may look greener, but faithfulness to God and commitment to your spouse alone bring peace of mind and satisfaction.

When you dedicate yourself to loving and respecting your spouse, your marriage will be a picture of Christ and His church to those around you.

Anne

October 4

GOD'S EMBRACE

ROMANS 12:3-11

Be devoted to one another in love. Honor one another above yourselves.

Romans 12:10

After her family left for the evening, Carol started to think that her hospital room was the loneliest place in the world. Nighttime had fallen, her fears about her illness were back, and she felt overwhelming despair.

Closing her eyes, she talked to God: "O Lord, I know I am not really alone. You're here with me. Please calm my heart and give me peace. Let me feel your arms around me, holding me."

As she prayed, Carol felt her fears beginning to subside. And when she opened her eyes, she looked up to see the warm, sparkling eyes of her friend Marge, who reached out to encircle her in a big hug. Carol felt as if God himself were holding her tightly.

God often uses fellow believers to show us His love. "In Christ we, though many, form one body" (ROMANS 12:5). We serve others "with the strength God provides, so that in all things God may be praised through Jesus Christ" (1 PETER 4:11).

When we show love and compassion in simple, practical ways, we are a part of God's ministry to His people.

Cindy

October 5

THANKFUL IN ALL THINGS

1 THESSALONIANS 5:12–22

Give thanks in all circumstances; for this is God's will for you in Christ Jesus.

1 Thessalonians 5:18

My daughter is allergic to peanuts. Her sensitivity is so acute that eating even the tiniest fragment of a peanut threatens her life. As a result, we scrutinize food package labels. We carry a prefilled syringe of medicine (to treat allergic reactions) wherever we go. And before we eat out, we call ahead and quiz the wait staff about the restaurant's menu items.

Despite these precautions, I still feel concerned—both for her current safety and for her future safety. This situation is not something I would naturally be thankful about. Yet God's Word challenges, "Give thanks in all circumstances; for this is God's will for you in Christ Jesus" (1 THESSALONIANS 5:18). There's no getting around it. God wants us to pray with thanksgiving when the future is uncertain, when heartbreak hits, and when shortfalls come.

God's promise that He will work all things together for our good and His glory (ROMANS 8:28) can inspire us to be thankful in all things.

Jennifer

October 6

LOVE IN ACTION
1 JOHN 4:7–21

Do nothing out of selfish ambition or vain conceit. Rather, in humility value others above yourselves.

Philippians 2:3

"Do you have a few items you'd like me to wash?" I asked a visitor to our home in London. His face lit up, and as his daughter walked by, he said, "Get your dirty clothes—Amy's doing our laundry!" I smiled, realizing that my offer had been extended from a few items to a few loads.

Later as I hung clothes outside on the line, a phrase from my morning's Bible reading floated through my mind: "In humility value others above yourselves" (PHILIPPIANS 2:3). Paul exhorts us to live worthy of Christ's calling through service and unity with others. He knows that unity enables us to stay strong in faith.

We might claim to love others without selfish ambition or vain conceit, but the true state of our hearts isn't revealed until we put our love into action. Though I felt tempted to grumble, I knew that as a follower of Christ, my call was to put my love for my friends into practice—with a clean heart.

May we find ways to serve our family, friends, and neighbors for God's glory.

Amy

October 7

GIVING BACK
PHILEMON 1:1–20

Put into action the generosity that comes from your faith.
Philemon 1:6 (NLT)

Not long ago, two newlyweds kissed their honeymoon good-bye. They also purposely did not plan a wedding reception to celebrate their union. Instead, they used the money they would have spent on themselves to help people in each of the fifty US states. In Arkansas, they gave gifts to sick children. In Utah, they aided victims of domestic abuse. In New Jersey, they donated clothing to a homeless shelter—and so on.

Selflessness often means letting go of comforts so we can make life better for someone else. As a prisoner, Paul decided it would be better to set free his helper and fellow inmate, Onesimus, than to enjoy the pleasure of their Christian fellowship (PHILEMON 1:13). Paul denied his own desires and did what was best for his slave friend and for his owner, Philemon.

Paul led Onesimus to Jesus and called him his child in the faith (PHILEMON 1:10). His words encourage us to let go of treasured people and possessions when necessary. Our ability to "give back" comes from recognizing all that we have received in and through Jesus.

Jennifer

October 8

FROM BAD TO WORSE

EXODUS 5:1-14, 22-23

"Therefore, say to the Israelites: 'I am the Lord, and I will bring you out from under the yoke of the Egyptians. I will free you from being slaves to them, and I will redeem you with an outstretched arm and with mighty acts of judgment.'"

Exodus 6:6

It happened again. I got the urge to clean my office. Before I could resist, I had created an even bigger mess than I started with. One pile turned into many piles as I sorted books, papers, and magazines. As the mess mushroomed, I lamented that I had started. But there was no going back.

When God recruited Moses to rescue the Hebrews from slavery, their situation went from bad to worse as well. Clearly, the job needed to be done. The people had been petitioning God for help (EXODUS 2:23). Reluctantly, Moses agreed to appeal to Pharaoh on behalf of the Hebrews. The encounter did not go well. Instead of releasing the people, Pharaoh increased his demands. Moses questioned whether he should have started (5:22–23). Only after a lot more trouble for a lot of people did Pharaoh let the people leave.

Whenever we set out to do something good, the situation might get worse before it gets better. This doesn't mean we're doing the wrong thing; it just reminds us that we need God to accomplish everything.

Julie

October 9

PERSEVERE IN PRAYER
1 SAMUEL 12:16-25

"As for me, far be it from me that I should sin against the Lord by failing to pray for you. And I will teach you the way that is good and right."

1 Samuel 12:23

My friends' marriage is on the rocks. For months, as they received counseling, I thought they were going to make it. But now I'm full of doubt.

Things have turned so sour in their relationship that as I prayed recently, I had little hope. I wondered, *Why pray if there's no chance (or so it appears) they will reconcile?*

When I admitted to God that I'd grown weary of talking to Him about this couple, the Holy Spirit prompted me to turn to His Word. In doing so, I was reminded to . . .

- Continue to lift them up in prayer, asking "God to help them; intercede on their behalf, and give thanks for them" (1 TIMOTHY 2:1 NLT; SEE 1 SAMUEL 12:23).
- Remember that Jesus "is able to save completely those who come to God through him, because he always lives to intercede for them" (HEBREWS 7:25).

We have a God who understands that we grow weary, and He invites us to cast our burdens on Him. He alone can give us rest and the strength to carry on in prayer and good deeds (MATTHEW 11:28).

Roxanne

October 10

TREASURE IN TOMB 7
PSALM 119:161–168

I rejoice in your promise like one who finds great spoil.

Psalm 119:162

In 1932 Mexican archaeologist Antonio Caso discovered Tomb 7 at Monte Alban, Oaxaca. He found a huge cache of artifacts and pre-Hispanic jewelry he called "The Treasure of Monte Alban." One can only imagine Caso's excitement as he held a jade cup in its purest form.

Centuries earlier, the psalmist wrote of an even more valuable treasure. He said, "I rejoice in your promise like one who finds great spoil" (PSALM 119:162). In Psalm 119, the writer knew how valuable God's instructions and promises are to our lives, so he compared them to the treasure obtained by a conqueror.

Caso's discovery in Tomb 7 can be enjoyed today if we visit a museum in Oaxaca. The psalmist's treasure, on the other hand, is always at our fingertips. We can dig into the Scriptures and find diamonds of promises, rubies of hope, and emeralds of wisdom. And even better is the person to whom the book points: Jesus himself.

Let's seek diligently this treasure that will enrich us. As the psalmist said, "Your statutes are my heritage forever; they are the joy of my heart" (V. 111).

Keila

October 11

Big Cats and Confidence

DANIEL 6:1-28

> When Daniel learned that the law had been signed, he went home and ... prayed three times a day, just as he had always done, giving thanks to his God.
>
> Daniel 6:10 (NLT)

I was eight when our family visited South Africa's Kruger National Park. We saw many amazing animals but no lions. As we concluded our safari by car, I was disappointed. When we stopped at the exit gate, I took one last look down the road behind us, and there she was! Without thinking, I jumped out of the car and began running toward her shouting, "Lion, it's a lion!"

This story came to mind as I thought of Daniel in the lions' den. King Darius had made Daniel an administrator in his kingdom. This made other leaders jealous, and they plotted to take him down. They proposed a law, signed by the king, which outlawed praying to anyone except the king. The penalty? A trip to the lions' den. Daniel responded by going home and kneeling as usual in his upstairs room—by the windows. There "he prayed three times a day ... giving thanks to his God" (DANIEL 6:10).

Daniel was wise to trust God. We too can rest confidently in Him today, knowing that He actively intervenes in our lives.

Ruth

October 12

RECKLESS WORDS
1 PETER 2:13-15

When they hurled their insults at him, he did not retaliate; when he suffered, he made no threats. Instead, he entrusted himself to him who judges justly.

1 Peter 2:23

I was driving when my daughter suddenly wailed from the backseat. "What happened?" I asked. She said her brother had grabbed her arm. He claimed she had pinched him first. She said she pinched him because he had said something mean.

Unfortunately, this pattern, which is common between children, can show up in adult relationships too. One person offends another, and the hurt person shoots back a verbal blow. The original offender retaliates with another insult. Before long, anger and cruel words have damaged the relationship.

The Bible says that "a harsh word stirs up anger" but "a gentle answer turns away wrath" (PROVERBS 15:1 NASB). Sometimes not answering at all is the best way to deal with mean or cruel comments.

Before Jesus's crucifixion, the religious authorities tried to provoke Him with their words (MATTHEW 27:41-43). Yet "when they hurled their insults at him, he did not retaliate" (1 PETER 2:23).

Jesus's example and the Spirit's help offer us a way to respond to people who offend us. We don't need to use words as weapons.

Jennifer

October 13

UNOPENED TOMORROWS

MATTHEW 6:25–34

We live by faith, not by sight.
2 Corinthians 5:7

One day my ten-year-old granddaughter Emily and I were boiling eggs for breakfast. As we stared into the boiling water and wondered how long it would take to get the eggs just right, Emily said, "Pity we can't open them up to see how they're doing." I agreed. But that would have spoiled them, so we had to rely on guesswork, with no guarantee of results.

We began talking about other things we would like to see but can't—like tomorrow. Too bad we can't crack tomorrow open, we said, to see if it's the way we would like it. But meddling with tomorrow before its time, like opening a partly cooked egg, would spoil both today and tomorrow.

Because Jesus has promised to care for us every day—and that includes tomorrow—we can live by faith one day at a time (MATTHEW 6:33–34). A wise person has said, "Though we can't see around corners, God can."

Emily and I decided to leave tomorrow safely in God's hands. Have you?

Joanie

October 14

LESSONS FROM MOM
ROMANS 1:8-16

That is why I am so eager to preach the gospel also to you who are in Rome.

Romans 1:15

Dementia was slowly taking Mom Cetas from us. There was nothing my husband or I could do to keep her from slipping away.

In those difficult days, Mom taught us many lessons. She forgot how to do most things, but one thing she did not forget was how to pray. Occasionally, someone would mention a problem they were having, and she'd stop right there to pray.

She also continued to talk to others about Jesus. Those who took care of her at the nursing home said she often asked the other residents and workers if they knew Jesus as their Savior.

When I think of these qualities in Mom, I recall Romans 1. The apostle Paul remembered the people in the Roman church "always in [his] prayers" (V. 9 NKJV). And he was always "ready to preach the gospel" (V. 15 NKJV). He was "not ashamed of the gospel of Christ" (V. 16 NKJV).

As long as Mom Cetas was able, she kept praying and telling others about Jesus. We can learn from her example of boldness and trust in the Lord.

Anne

October 15

MIXED BAG
GALATIANS 5:16–24

The sinful nature wants to do evil, which is just the opposite of what the Spirit wants. And the Spirit gives us desires that are the opposite of what the sinful nature desires.
Galatians 5:17 (NLT)

My pastor told me about a parishioner he encountered years earlier at another church. The woman told him he did nothing right, and she didn't like his kind of preaching. But even with all of the venom he received from her, my pastor could say to me, "There were many wonderful things she did for the church. We're all mixed bags, Marlena."

I took his words to heart because he's right. I may not often struggle with constantly and publicly criticizing others, but I do grumble in my heart against people. As Galatians 5:17 says, "The Spirit gives us desires that are the opposite of what the sinful nature desires. These two forces are constantly fighting each other" (NLT).

When I'm tempted to point out the sins of others—to take specks out of their eyes (MATTHEW 7:3-5)—I need to remember that I too am a mixed bag. In fact, we're all much more sinner than saint sometimes.

Praise God that He helps me deal with my faulty, human ways—producing a mixed bag of "fruit" that can honor Him (GALATIANS 5:22)!

Marlena

October 16

MEDITATE
PSALM 119:89–105

They speak of the glorious splendor of your majesty—and I will meditate on your wonderful works.

Psalm 145:5

Some Christians get a little skeptical when you start talking about meditation—not recognizing the distinction between biblical meditation and some types of mystical meditation. In mystical meditation, according to one explanation, "the rational mind is shifted into neutral . . . so that the psyche can take over." The focus is inward, and the aim is to "become one with God."

In contrast, biblical meditation focuses on the things of the Lord, and its purpose is to renew our minds (ROMANS 12:2) so we think and act more like Christ. Its objective is to reflect on what God has said and done (PSALM 77:12; 119:15–16, 97) and on what He is like (48:9–14).

In Psalm 19:14, David wrote, "May these words of my mouth and this meditation of my heart be pleasing in your sight, Lord."

Fill your mind with Scripture and focus on the Lord's commands and promises and goodness. And remember: whatever is true, noble, just, pure, lovely, and of good report, "if anything is excellent or praiseworthy—think about such things" (PHILIPPIANS 4:8).

Cindy

October 17

KORAH'S REDEMPTION
NUMBERS 16:1-35

> However, the sons of Korah did not die that day.
>
> Numbers 26:11 (NLT)

In Numbers 16, although God had given the Levites special access to perform various roles within the sanctuary, Korah wasn't satisfied. He envied the leadership status of Moses and Aaron. In time he managed to incite several other tribal elders to rebel against them (NUMBERS 16:2).

God judged this rebellion with a spectacular show of force, wiping out fallen leaders and followers alike. But "the sons of Korah did not die" (NUMBERS 26:11 NLT). Although Korah instigated the uprising, his family wasn't destroyed.

Fast-forward a bit and Korah's name pops up again. His descendants were still stirring up the people. Only this time they were doing it in a good way—seeking God's glory. Humility and contentment replaced arrogance and envy. In a song, they declared, "I would rather be a gatekeeper in the house of my God than live the good life in the homes of the wicked" (PSALM 84:10 NLT).

God saw past an ancestor's pride and preserved generations of worshipers. No matter your past or that of relatives who have come before, He can redeem and restore those who have fallen.

Remi

October 18

CHOOSE LIFE
DEUTERONOMY 30:11–20

This day I call the heavens and the earth as witnesses against you that I have set before you life and death, blessings and curses. Now choose life, so that you and your children may live and that you may love the Lord your God, listen to his voice, and hold fast to him.

Deuteronomy 30:19-20

What is God's will for my life? This question haunted me when I was growing up. What if I couldn't find it? What if I didn't recognize it?

My view of God's will was wrong because my view of God was wrong. God wants us to know His will. He makes it clear, and He makes it simple. He doesn't even make it multiple-choice. He gives just two choices: "life and good" or "death and evil" (DEUTERONOMY 30:15 ESV). In case the best choice isn't obvious, He even says which one to choose: "Choose life" (V. 19). To choose life is to choose God himself and obey His Word.

When Moses addressed the Israelites for the last time before he died, he pleaded with them to make the right choice by observing "all the words of this law. . . . They are your life" (DEUTERONOMY 32:46–47). God's will for us is life. His Word is life. The right choice may not be easy, but when the Word is our guide and worship is our goal, God will grant us the wisdom to make life-affirming choices.

Julie

October 19

A SAFE PLACE
1 CORINTHIANS 6:9–11; 13:4–7

And that is what some of you were. But you were washed, you were sanctified, you were justified in the name of the Lord Jesus Christ and by the Spirit of our God.

1 Corinthians 6:11

A young Japanese man had a problem—he was afraid of leaving his house. He was a *hikikomori*, a modern-day hermit. The problem began when he stopped going to school because of poor grades. The longer he stayed home, the more he felt like a social misfit—and he soon was seeing no one. Eventually he got help toward recovery by visiting a youth club called an *ibasho*—a safe place where broken people start reintroducing themselves to society.

What if we thought of the church as an *ibasho*? Without a doubt, we are a community of broken people. When Paul wrote to the church in Corinth, he described their former way of life as antisocial, harmful, and dangerous to themselves and others (1 CORINTHIANS 6:9–10). But in Jesus they were being transformed. And Paul encouraged these rescued people to love one another, to be patient and kind, not to be jealous or proud or rude (13:4–7).

The church is to be an *ibasho* where we can find God's love. May the hurting world experience Christ's compassion from all who follow Him.

Poh Fang

October 20

PRAISE FROM PURE HEARTS

PSALM 51:7–17

My sacrifice, O God, is a broken spirit; a broken and contrite heart you, God, will not despise.

Psalm 51:17

During my friend Myrna's travels to another country, she visited a church for worship. She noticed that as people entered the sanctuary they immediately knelt and prayed, facing away from the front of the church. They were confessing their sin to God before they began the worship service.

This act of humility is a picture to me of what David said in Psalm 51: "My sacrifice, O God, is a broken spirit; a broken and contrite heart you, God, will not despise" (v. 17). David was describing his remorse and repentance for his sin of adultery with Bathsheba. Real sorrow for sin involves adopting God's view of what we've done—seeing it as clearly wrong, hating it, and not wanting it to continue.

When we are truly broken over our sin, God lovingly puts us back together (SEE 1 JOHN 1:9). This forgiveness produces a fresh sense of openness with Him and is the ideal starting point for praise. After David repented and was forgiven, he said, "Open my lips, Lord, and my mouth will declare your praise" (PSALM 51:15).

Praise is our heart's response to His forgiveness.

Jennifer

October 21

RELIGION OR CHRIST?
EPHESIANS 2:1-10

> For it is by grace you have been saved, through faith—and this is not from yourselves, it is the gift of God—not by works, so that no one can boast.
>
> *Ephesians 2:8-9*

Mary works hard because she wants her boss to recognize her accomplishments and reward her with a higher-paying position. Nancy loves her job and the product her company sells, and out of loyalty she works hard to make the product better.

Mary is like the person who hopes that good works or religion will be rewarded by God someday. Such people count on their good deeds to get them into heaven.

Nancy is a picture of those who have faith in God to get them into heaven. Such people do good works out of gratitude and love for Him.

Someone with religion may believe in God, attend church, say prayers, show kindness, and be seen as a good person. People with religion have many good qualities, but religion is not a substitute for faith in Jesus Christ.

The apostle Paul said that the way of salvation is by grace through faith. It's not of works but is the gift of God (EPHESIANS 2:8-9).

The only way to the Father in heaven is through faith in Jesus (JOHN 14:6).

Do you choose religion or Christ?

Anne

October 22

LIFE, LOVE, AND CHOCOLATE
1 JOHN 3:16–23

Follow God's example, therefore, as dearly loved children and walk in the way of love, just as Christ loved us and gave himself up for us as a fragrant offering and sacrifice to God.

Ephesians 5:1-2

An entry on a favorite blog caught my eye. It was the morning of the writer's ninth wedding anniversary. Not having a lot of money, he ran out (literally; no car) to get his wife their favorite French pastry—*pain au chocolat*. He arrived home, exhausted, to find her in the kitchen just pulling a chocolate-filled croissant out of the oven. It was *pain au chocolat*.

That husband compared his life with his wife to the lives of the people in O. Henry's short story "The Gift of the Magi." It tells of a man who sold his lone valuable possession—a pocket watch—to buy hair combs for his wife, who had sold her long, beautiful hair to buy a gold chain for his watch.

We sometimes need a reminder that acquiring "things" is not as important as appreciating the people God has placed in our lives. When we put others' interests before ours (PHILIPPIANS 2:3), we learn what it means to love, serve, and sacrifice—and how to pattern Christ in our relationships (EPHESIANS 5:1–2).

Life, love, and chocolate taste better when shared with others.

Cindy

October 23

A SHEPHERD FOR LIFE
GENESIS 48:8–16

"God ... has been my shepherd all my life to this day."
Genesis 48:15

When my son changed grades in school, he cried, "I want my teacher for life!" We had to help him realize that changing teachers is a part of life. We may wonder, *Is there any relationship that can last a lifetime?*

Jacob, the patriarch, found one. After living through many dramatic changes and losing loved ones along the way, he recognized one constant presence in his life. He prayed, "May the God . . . who has been my shepherd all my life to this day . . . bless these boys" (GENESIS 48:15–16).

Jacob compared his relationship to God with that of a shepherd and his sheep. From the time a sheep is born, the shepherd cares for it—guiding it during the day and protecting it during the night. Later David highlighted the eternal dimension in the divine-human connection when he said, "I will dwell in the house of the LORD forever" (PSALM 23:6).

The Shepherd has promised to be with us every day of our earthly existence (MATTHEW 28:20). And when life here ends, we will be closer to Him than ever.

Keila

October 24

HELD BY GOD

PSALM 131

I have calmed and quieted myself, I am like a weaned child with its mother; like a weaned child I am content.

Psalm 131:2

As I neared the end of lunch with my sister and her children one afternoon, my sister told my three-year-old niece, Annica, it was time to get ready for her nap. Her face filled with alarm. "But Aunt Monica did not hold me yet today!" she objected, tears filling her eyes. My sister smiled. "Okay, she may hold you first—how long do you need?" "Five minutes," she replied.

As I held my niece, I was grateful for how, without even trying, she constantly reminds me what it looks like to love and be loved. I think we forget that our faith journey is one of learning to experience love—God's love—more fully than we can imagine (EPHESIANS 3:18).

Psalm 131 can help us to "become like little children" (MATTHEW 18:3) and let go of the battle in our mind over what we don't understand (PSALM 131:1). Through time with Him we can return to a place of peace (V. 2), finding the hope we need (V. 3) in His love—as calm and quiet as if we were children again in our mother's arms (V. 2).

Monica

October 25

NO NEED IS TOO TRIVIAL

ISAIAH 49:13–18

As a father pities his children, so the Lord pities those who fear him.

Psalm 103:13 (NKJV)

Several mothers of small children were sharing encouraging answers to prayer. Yet one woman said she felt selfish about troubling God with her personal needs. "Compared with the huge global needs God faces," she explained, "my circumstances must seem trivial to Him."

Moments later, her little boy pinched his fingers in a door and ran screaming to his mother. She didn't say, "How selfish of you to bother me with your throbbing fingers when I'm busy!" Instead, she showed him great compassion and tenderness.

In Isaiah 49, God said that even though a mother may forget to have compassion on her child, the Lord never forgets His children (V. 15). God assured His people, "I have inscribed you on the palms of My hands" (V. 16 NASB).

Such intimacy with God belongs to those who fear Him and who rely on Him rather than on themselves. As that child with throbbing fingers ran freely to his mother, so may we run to God with our daily problems.

Our compassionate God has limitless time and love for each of His children. No need is too trivial for Him.

Joanie

October 26

THE WAY TO AN "EASY" LIFE

1 THESSALONIANS 3

We sent Timothy . . . so that no one would be unsettled by these trials. For you know quite well that we are destined for them.

1 Thessalonians 3:2-3

Do parents try too hard to make their kids happy? And does this have the opposite effect? These questions introduce an interview with Lori Gottlieb, author of an article on the subject of unhappy young adults. Her conclusion: Yes. Parents who refuse to let their children experience failure or sadness give them a false view of the world and do not prepare them for the harsh realities of adult life. They're left feeling empty and anxious.

Some Christians expect God to protect them from all sorrow and disappointment. But that's not the kind of Father He is. He lovingly allows His children to go through suffering (ISAIAH 43:2; 1 THESSALONIANS 3:3).

When we start with the mistaken belief that only an easy life will make us truly happy, we will soon grow weary. But when we face the truth that life is difficult, we can invest in what strengthens us for the times when life is difficult.

God's goal is to make us holy, not just happy (1 THESSALONIANS 3:13). And when we are holy, we are more likely to be truly happy and content.

Julie

October 27

HE UNDERSTANDS
PSALM 27:1-8

The LORD is my light and my salvation—whom shall I fear? The LORD is the stronghold of my life—of whom shall I be afraid?

Psalm 27:1

Some young children have trouble falling asleep at night. My daughter explained one reason for that one evening as I turned to leave her bedroom. "I'm afraid of the dark," she said. I tried to relieve her fear, but I left a night-light on just the same.

I didn't think much more about my daughter's fear until a few weeks later when my husband went on an overnight business trip. After I settled into bed, the dark seemed to press in around me. I heard a tiny noise and jumped up to investigate. It turned out to be nothing, but I understood my daughter's fear when I experienced it myself.

Jesus understands our fears and problems. He lived on the earth as a human and endured the same types of trouble we face. "He was despised and rejected by mankind, a man of suffering, and familiar with pain" (ISAIAH 53:3). When we describe our struggles to Him, He relates to our distress. Somehow, knowing that He understands can dispel the loneliness that often accompanies suffering. In our darkest times, He is our light and our salvation.

Jennifer

October 28

DON'T STOP CARING
MICAH 6:6-8

He has shown you, O mortal, what is good. And what does the Lord require of you? To act justly and to love mercy and to walk humbly with your God.
Micah 6:8

In the midst of an icy winter, more than eight hundred illegal shack-dwelling families were evicted from their homes in South Africa. The eviction caused a public outcry because the leaders involved appeared to show a lack of compassion.

Old Testament prophet Micah lived at a time when great emphasis was placed on acquiring wealth and when unjust leaders habitually showed no compassion for the poor and vulnerable (MICAH 2:1). Testing the Lord's patience, the rich and powerful would steal from those who trusted them, seize their land by fraud or violence, and cut short their inheritance (VV. 2, 7-9).

False prophets ignored this wickedness (VV. 6, 11). Micah, however, put a stop to Israel's self-deception and delivered a strong message from the Lord, charting the consequences for their selfish ambition (VV. 1:10-16; 2:1-5). God brought the full weight of His presence to bear on those in charge (1:2-4), holding them responsible for violating the Mosiac covenant. He wanted them to love mercy and to walk humbly with Him (6:8).

Lord, help us submit to you and your compassionate heart today.

Ruth

October 29

"BREAD!"

JOHN 6:34–51

"I am the bread of life."
John 6:48

Until recently, I lived in a small Mexican city where every morning and evening you can hear a distinctive cry: "Bread!" A man with a huge basket on his bike offers a great variety of fresh sweet and salty breads for sale. I enjoyed having fresh bread brought to my door.

Moving from the thought of feeding physical hunger to spiritual hunger, I think of Jesus's words: "I am the living bread that came down from heaven. Whoever eats this bread will live forever" (JOHN 6:51).

Someone has said that evangelism is one beggar telling another beggar where he found bread. Many of us can say, "Once I was spiritually hungry, spiritually starving because of my sins. Then someone told me where to find bread: in Jesus. And my life changed!"

We have the privilege and responsibility of pointing others to this Bread of Life. We can share Jesus in our neighborhood, our workplace, our school, our places of recreation. We can take the good news to others through doors of friendship.

Jesus is the Bread of Life. Let's tell everybody the great news.

Keila

October 30

KEEPING BUSY?

MATTHEW 11:25–30

"Come to me, all you who are weary and burdened, and I will give you rest."

Matthew 11:28

People who know I'm a freelance writer who works from home ask, "Are you keeping busy?" That may seem harmless, but I think it carries a subtle message about personal value. If I can't rattle off a list of things I have to do, I feel as if I'm admitting that I'm not worth much.

One of the first verses I learned as a child was Matthew 11:28, "Come to me, all you who are weary and are burdened, and I will give you rest." It didn't mean much to me at the time because I didn't understand weariness. But now that I'm older, I feel the temptation to keep pace with the world so I won't be left behind.

But followers of Jesus don't have to live like that. He released us not only from slavery to sin but also from the bondage of having to prove our worth.

Accomplishing a lot for God may make us feel important, but what makes us important to God is what we allow Him to accomplish in us—conforming us into the image of His Son (ROMANS 8:28–30).

Julie

October 31

FAKE FAMILY

MATTHEW 15:1–19

"These people honor me with their lips, but their hearts are far from me."

Matthew 15:8

A builder in California has come up with an innovative idea to sell his houses. He thinks a good way to make a house more appealing is to have a family there when showing the house. So he hires actors to play happy families in his company's model homes. Would-be buyers can ask them questions about the house. Each fake family cooks, watches television, and plays games while house hunters wander through.

That type of faking may not do any harm, but think about the sham of the religious leaders in Jesus's day (MATTHEW 15:1–9). They pretended to love God and piously made up a long list of rules that they and others were to obey. Jesus called them "hypocrites" (V. 7). He said their words sounded as if they honored God, but their hearts told another story—they were far from Him (V. 8).

That kind of pretending goes on in people today as well. We say we love Jesus, but our hearts may be far from Him. God wants us to be real.

Anne

November 1

THE ROMANCE
RUTH 3:1-14

> The women living there said, "Naomi has a son!" And they named him Obed. He was the father of Jesse, the father of David.
>
> *Ruth 4:17*

Ruth and her mother-in-law, Naomi, faced poverty after each lost her husband. But God had a plan for them.

Boaz, a wealthy landowner and a relative of the women, knew of and admired Ruth (RUTH 2:5-12). Yet he was surprised when he awoke one night to see her lying at his feet (3:8). She asked him to "spread the corner" of his garment over her to indicate that as a close relative he was willing to be her "guardian-redeemer" (V. 9). This was more than a request for protection; she was requesting marriage. Boaz agreed to marry her (VV. 11-13; 4:13).

Ruth's choice to follow Naomi's instructions (3:3-6) placed her in God's plan of redemption! From Ruth's marriage to Boaz came a son (Obed), the eventual grandfather of King David (4:17). Generations later, Joseph was born to the family, and he became the "legal father" of Mary's child (MATTHEW 1:16-17; LUKE 2:4-5)—our Guardian-Redeemer, Jesus.

Ruth trusted God and followed Naomi's instructions even though the ending was uncertain. We too can count on God to provide for us when life is unsure.

Cindy

In Him we have
REDEMPTION
through His blood,
the forgiveness of sins,
in accordance with the riches of
God's grace.
EPHESIANS 1:7

November 2

DARTBOARD OR PIPELINE?

COLOSSIANS 1:24–29

To this end I strenuously contend with all the energy Christ so powerfully works in me.

Colossians 1:29

One day during my devotional time, this thought came to my mind: *Don't let life happen to you. Let life happen through you.*

The first phrase described me to a T, for I tended to see life as something coming at me. I felt like a worn-out dartboard. I was using all my energies to shield myself from the darts of life's trials.

But the second phrase, "Let life happen through you," presented a different approach. Instead of dodging life's fiery darts, I was to let God's life and love be channeled through me, blessing me on its way to blessing others.

I chose that day to become God's pipeline instead of life's dartboard. Then I could begin living more effectively for Him.

In his letter to the Colossians, Paul mentioned the many troubles he was facing. Yet he was determined to be a channel of blessing by allowing God to work through him.

What about you? Are you a dartboard or a pipeline? It's a challenge and a choice for every believer.

Joanie

November 3

JUST THE TICKET
EPHESIANS 1:1–10

In him we have redemption through his blood, the forgiveness of sins, in accordance with the riches of God's grace.

Ephesians 1:7

When a police officer stopped a woman because her young daughter was riding in a car without the required booster seat, he could have written her a ticket. Instead, he asked to meet the mother and daughter at a nearby store where he bought them the needed car seat. It was something the struggling mother couldn't have purchased on her own.

Although the woman should have received a fine, she walked away with a gift instead. Anyone who knows Christ has experienced something similar. All of us deserve a penalty for breaking God's laws (ECCLESIASTES 7:20). Yet because of Jesus, we experience undeserved favor from God. This favor excuses us from the ultimate consequence for our sin. "In [Jesus] we have . . . the forgiveness of sins, in accordance with the riches of God's grace" (EPHESIANS 1:7).

When the young mother experienced this, she later remarked, "I will be forever grateful!" This response to the officer's gift is an inspiring example for those of us who have received the gift of God's grace!

Jennifer

November 4

WHERE WE ARE
MATTHEW 6:25–34

"Seek first his kingdom and his righteousness, and all these things will be given to you as well."

Matthew 6:33

I took the day off from work to experience some much-needed silence and solitude. I had much to be thankful for, but internally I was struggling with something I wanted to talk to God about.

While sitting on a park bench overlooking a pond, I noticed a robin searching for food. As I watched it yank at a worm, I was reminded of Matthew 6:26: "Look at the birds of the air; they do not sow or reap or store away in barns, and yet your heavenly Father feeds them. Are you not much more valuable than they?"

I sensed God telling me He would provide what I need as I seek His kingdom each day (v. 33). I don't need to worry or work in order to bring it about. I'm to faithfully obey Him, trust Him, and rest in His power to bring about what I cannot.

Worry won't add to my life; it will only take away from it (v. 27). After all, my heavenly Father knows exactly what I need.

Marlena

November 5

LOVE LETTER
PSALM 119:97–104

Oh, how I love your law! I meditate on it all day long.
Psalm 119:97

Each morning when I reach my office, I check my emails. Most of the time, I'll work through them in a perfunctory fashion. There are some emails, however, that I'm eager to open. You guessed it—those from loved ones.

Someone has said that the Bible is God's love letter to us. But perhaps on some days, like me, you just don't feel like opening it and your heart doesn't resonate with the words of the psalmist: "Oh, how I love your law!" (PSALM 119:97). The Scriptures are "your commands" (V. 98), "your statutes" (V. 99), "your precepts" (V. 100), "your word" (V. 101).

It is said of some people that the more you know them the less you admire them; but the reverse is true of God. Familiarity with the Word of God, or rather the God of the Word, breeds affection, and affection seeks yet greater familiarity.

As you open your Bible, remember that God—the One who loves you the most—has a message for you.

Poh Fang

November 6

SACRIFICIAL FAITH

ACTS 6:8–15; 7:59–60

> "Blessed are those who are persecuted because of righteousness, for theirs is the kingdom of heaven."
>
> Matthew 5:10

Our church in London hosts a vibrant Iranian congregation. We feel humbled by their passion for Christ as they share their stories of persecution and tell of those, such as the pastor's brother, who have been martyred for their faith. These faithful believers are following in the footsteps of the first Christian martyr, Stephen.

Stephen, one of the first appointed leaders in the early church, garnered attention in Jerusalem when he performed "great wonders and signs" (ACTS 6:8) and was brought before the Jewish authorities. He gave an impassioned defense of the faith before describing the hard-heartedness of his accusers. They were "furious and gnashed their teeth at him" (7:54). They dragged him from the city and stoned him to death—even as he prayed for their forgiveness.

The stories of Stephen and modern martyrs remind us that the message of Christ can be met with brutality. If we have never faced persecution for our faith, let's pray for the persecuted church around the world. And may we, if tested, find grace to be found faithful to the One who suffered so much more for us.

Amy

November 7

LOVING THE LONELY
RUTH 1:1–22

> I went away full, but the LORD has brought me back empty. Why call me Naomi? The LORD has afflicted me; the Almighty has brought misfortune upon me.
>
> *Ruth 1:21*

Finishing up a long day's work, I pressed the touch screen on my computer one last time and saw a familiar date. After a moment, I realized, *Today is my dad's birthday.* Quickly my thoughts went to my mom. Widowed twenty years earlier, my mother was a living testimony of God's provision and strength for those who come face-to-face with life's hard unpredictability.

As our society becomes more transitory, many widows and widowers must learn to navigate this drastic change in life without family members nearby. But regardless of our busy lives, the Bible reveals that the care of the widow rests first with family and then with the church (1 TIMOTHY 5:3–16).

In the Old Testament, Ruth's commitment to Naomi became a source of God's blessing for both women, one that extended into subsequent generations (RUTH 1:16; 4:13–20).

"God sets the lonely in families" (PSALM 68:6) to remind them that they're still needed and—most of all—*loved.* Loved by Him and by those who live out His love.

Regina

November 8

LOOPHOLES

JOHN 10:1–9

I have hidden your word in my heart that I might not sin against you.

Psalm 119:11

Five-year-old Jenna was not having a good start to her day. Every attempt to arrange the world according to her liking was having the opposite result. Arguing didn't work. Pouting didn't work. Crying didn't work. Finally, her mother reminded her of the Bible verse she had been learning: "I have hidden your word in my heart that I might not sin against you" (PSALM 119:11).

Apparently Jenna had been thinking about this verse, because she was quick to answer, "But, Mom, it doesn't say that I won't sin; it says that I 'might not' sin."

Her words are all too familiar. I often make similar arguments. There's something very appealing about loopholes, and we look for them whenever there's a command we don't want to obey.

Jesus addressed this with religious leaders who thought they had found a loophole in their religious laws (MARK 7:1-13). Instead of supporting their parents, they dedicated all their possessions to God, thereby limiting their use. Although their disobedience was not blatant, Jesus said their behavior was unacceptable.

Whenever we start looking for loopholes, we stop being obedient.

Julie

November 9

HOPE FOR THE BLUES
PSALM 62

Trust in him at all times, you people; pour out your hearts to him, for God is our refuge.

Psalm 62:8

Ever have the blues—times of discouragement? Family counselor Lynette Hoy, in an online article, tells how those dark times can be changed by Jesus, the Light of the World:

- Light up your heart through prayer. Pour out your heart to God when you're feeling overwhelmed (PSALM 62:8). Take your anxieties to Him in prayer (PHILIPPIANS 4:6–7). Journal your prayers so you can look back later to see how the Lord has answered you.
- Light up your mind with truth. Read the Word of God every day. Let His truth challenge, permeate, and transform your incorrect thinking that life is hopeless (PSALM 46:1; ROMANS 12:2).
- Light up your life by doing God's will. His will for you is to worship and serve Him. Stay involved in your church; worship and fellowship with others and serve Him (HEBREWS 10:25). This will help you grow in your trust of God.

When we feel darkness begin to close in on us, we need to turn to Jesus, the Light. He will be a refuge (PSALM 62:7–8) and will give us the strength to keep going.

Anne

November 10

TAKE NOTICE
RUTH 2:13–20

[Ruth's] mother-in-law asked her, "Where did you glean today? Where did you work? Blessed be the man who took notice of you!" Then Ruth told her mother-in-law about the one at whose place she had been working. "The name of the man I worked with today is Boaz," she said.

Ruth 2:19

While standing in a checkout line, I was estimating my bill and trying to keep my son from wandering away. I wasn't paying attention when the woman ahead of me shuffled toward the exit, leaving her items behind. The clerk confided that the woman didn't have enough money to pay her bill. I felt terrible; if only I had noticed her situation earlier, I would have helped her.

In the book of Ruth, Boaz became aware of Ruth's plight when he saw her gleaning in his fields (2:5). He learned that she was recently widowed and was the breadwinner for herself and her mother-in-law. Boaz saw her need for protection and warned his harvesters to leave her alone (v. 9). He supplied her with extra food by instructing his workers to let grain fall purposely (v. 16). When Naomi heard about this, she said, "Blessed be the man who took notice of you!" (v. 19).

Are you aware of the needs of the people around you? Today, consider how you might help bear someone's burden. Then you will be fulfilling God's plan for you (GALATIANS 6:2; EPHESIANS 2:10).

Jennifer

November 11

BABY STEPS
PSALM 18:31-36

He makes my feet like the feet of a deer; he causes me to stand on the heights.

Psalm 18:33

My baby is learning to walk. I have to hold her, and she clings to my fingers because she's unsteady on her feet. She is afraid of slipping, but I'm there to steady her. As she walks with my help, her eyes sparkle with joy. Sometimes she cries when I don't let her take dangerous paths—not realizing that I am protecting her.

Like my baby girl, we often need someone to watch over us, to guide and steady us in our spiritual walk. And we have that someone—God our Father—who keeps us on the right path.

King David knew all about the need for God's watchful care. In Psalm 18 he describes how God gives us guidance when we are lost or confused (v. 32). He keeps our feet steady, like the feet of the deer that can climb high places without slipping (v. 33). And if we do slip, His hand is there for us (v. 35).

All of us need God's guiding, steadying hand.

Keila

HE MAKES MY FEET LIKE THE FEET OF A DEER; HE CAUSES ME TO *stand* ON THE *heights.*

PSALM 18:33

November 12

BUYER'S REMORSE
GENESIS 3:1–8

> I delight greatly in the Lord; my soul rejoices in my God. For he has clothed me with garments of salvation and arrayed me in a robe of his righteousness, as a bridegroom adorns his head like a priest, and as a bride adorns herself with her jewels.
>
> *Isaiah 61:10*

Have you ever experienced buyer's remorse? I have. Sometimes, just after buying an item I was sure I needed, a wave of remorse crashes over me. Did I really have to have this?

In Genesis 3, we find the first record of buyer's remorse. The whole thing began with the crafty serpent and his sales pitch. He persuaded Eve to doubt God's Word (v. 1). He then capitalized on her uncertainty by casting doubt on God's character (vv. 4–5). He promised that her eyes would "be opened" and she would become "like God" (v. 5).

So Eve ate. Adam ate. And sin entered the world. But the first man and woman got more than they bargained for. Their eyes were opened all right, but they didn't become like God. In fact, their next act was to hide from God (vv. 7–8).

Sin has dire consequences. But God in His mercy and grace sent Jesus Christ to die on the cross as a sacrifice for our sins. Have you trusted Jesus for your salvation? That's one transaction with no remorse!

Poh Fang

November 13

BE SPECIFIC
JAMES 5:13–18

"What do you want me to do for you?" Jesus asked him. The blind man said, "Rabbi, I want to see."

Mark 10:51

On the day before major surgery, I shared with a friend that I was scared about the procedure. "What part scares you?" she inquired. "I'm afraid I won't wake up from the anesthesia," I replied. Immediately, Anne prayed: "Father, you know all about Cindy's fear. Please calm her heart and fill her with your peace. And, Lord, please wake her up after surgery."

I think God likes that kind of specificity when we talk to Him. When Bartimaeus, the blind beggar, called out to Jesus for help, Jesus said, "What do you want me to do for you?" The blind man said, "Rabbi, I want to see!" Jesus said, "Go, your faith has healed you" (MARK 10:51–52).

We don't need to beat around the bush with God. We can say bluntly, "God, I'm so sorry for what I said," or simply, "Jesus, I love you because . . ." Being specific with God is a sign of faith; we are acknowledging that we know we're talking to Someone real.

God is not impressed by a flurry of fanciful words. Speak from your heart.

Cindy

November 14

All Welcome!

LUKE 5:27–32

"I have not come to call the righteous, but sinners to repentance."

Luke 5:32

The much-prayed-for film night at the church youth club had arrived. Posters had been displayed around the village, and Steve, the youth pastor, hoped the film—about gang members in New York who were brought face-to-face with the gospel—would bring new young people into the church.

Steve was about to begin the film when five leather-clad members of the local motorcycle club came in. Steve went pale.

The leader of the group, who was known as TDog, nodded in Steve's direction. "It's free and for everyone, right?" he said. Steve started to say, "Youth club members only" when TDog picked up a bracelet with the letters WWJD (What Would Jesus Do) stamped on it. "This yours, mate?" he asked. Steve nodded, hot with embarrassment, and waited while the new guests found a seat.

Have you ever been in Steve's situation? You long to share the good news about Jesus, but you have a mental list of the "right" people who would be acceptable? Jesus welcomed those everyone else avoided, because He knew they needed Him most (LUKE 5:31–32). Maybe we should too.

Marion

November 15

Come Alongside
EXODUS 17:8–16

When Moses' hands grew tired, they took a stone and put it under him and he sat on it. Aaron and Hur held his hands up—one on one side, one on the other—so that his hands remained steady till sunset.

Exodus 17:12

Her thirty classmates and their parents watched as Mi'Asya nervously walked to the podium to speak at her fifth-grade graduation. When the principal adjusted the microphone to Mi'Asya's height, she turned her back to the microphone and the audience. The crowd whispered words of encouragement, but she didn't budge. Then a classmate walked to the front and stood by her side. With the principal on one side of Mi'Asya and her friend on the other, the three read her speech together. What a beautiful example of support!

Moses needed support in Israel's battle with the Amalekites (EXODUS 17:10–16). "As long as Moses held up his hands [with the staff of God in his hands], the Israelites were winning, but whenever he lowered his hands, the Amalekites were winning" (V. 11). When Aaron and Hur saw what was happening, they stood beside Moses and supported his arms when he grew tired. With their support, victory came by sunset.

Let's step up and encourage one another on our shared faith journey. God is right here in our midst, giving us His grace to do that.

Anne

November 16

HAPPY AT YOU
ISAIAH 49:8–23

"See, I have written your name on the palms of my hands."

Isaiah 49:16 (NLT)

My three-year-old daughter caught me staring at her. "Mommy, why are you looking at me like that?" "Because I love you and delight in you," I said. "God looks at you that way too." "You mean, God looks happy at me?" she earnestly inquired. "Yes!" I said. "God always looks happy at you," I emphasized.

When we're going through extreme difficulties—things that threaten to overwhelm us—we may wonder if God cares. *If God loves me, why is He letting this happen?* we wonder. While I have no satisfying answers, I'm convinced God loves us and delights in us.

In Isaiah 49:15–16, God reveals His loving heart toward His children: "Can a mother forget her nursing child? Can she feel no love for the child she has borne? But even if that were possible, I would not forget you!" He promised, "Those who trust in me will never be put to shame" (ISAIAH 49:23 NLT).

Knowing God's character and that we're His beloved sons and daughters elicits trust from us even during the darkest of nights.

Marlena

November 17

PRESENCE IN THE SEASONS
1 KINGS 19:1–21

> After the earthquake there was a fire, but the Lord was not in the fire. And after the fire there was the sound of a gentle whisper.
>
> **1 Kings 19:12**

For seven years, I was at home with our kids. I enjoyed the flexibility and routine of that season, and when I returned to full-time work, I had to shift my expectations.

Psalm 1:1–3 tells us, "Oh, the joys of those who . . . delight in the law of the Lord. . . . They are like trees planted along the riverbank, bearing fruit each season" (NLT). In reality, not every season feels or looks the same—even for those who "delight in the law of the Lord" (v. 2). And while it's true that we can learn to be content in various circumstances (PHILIPPIANS 4:11–12), some seasons require greater adjustment than others.

In 1 Kings 18:1–46, we find God doing amazing things through Elijah, even physically. A short time later, however, the prophet found himself fearing for his life and struggling to understand the plan of God.

We can feel the same way. The season suddenly changes, and we can't seem to find our bearings. In times of change, God invites us to wrap ourselves in His presence and trust in His purposes.

Regina

November 18

THINGS ABOVE
COLOSSIANS 3:1–13

Since, then, you have been raised with Christ, set your hearts on things above, where Christ is, seated at the right hand of God.
Colossians 3:1

Stepping outside and gazing heavenward on a star-studded evening always helps to soothe my soul after a trouble-filled day. When I peer into the night sky, I forget, at least for a moment, the cares of life on earth.

Ancient Israel's prolific songwriter wrote a poem thousands of years ago that still rings true: "When I consider your heavens, the work of your fingers, the moon and the stars, which you have set in place, what is mankind that you are mindful of them, and human beings that you care for them?" (PSALM 8:3–4).

When we try to imagine the immensity of God's heavens, our problems indeed seem trivial. Yet God doesn't think so! With all the galaxies He has to attend to, God is mindful of us. Not only are we on His mind, but He also cares for us.

"The heavens declare the glory of God" (PSALM 19:1). Let's join creation in praise to the One great enough to create the world yet care for you and me.

Julie

November 19

Common Ground
1 CORINTHIANS 9:19-23

> I try to find common ground with everyone, doing everything I can to save some. I do everything to spread the Good News and share in its blessings.
>
> *1 Corinthians 9:22-23* (NLT)

The apostle Paul altered the way he communicated to different people so they would clearly understand the good news. Although he himself was "free," he became "a slave" to all people, becoming like them and communicating in a way that would resonate—so that many would come to know and believe in Jesus (1 CORINTHIANS 9:19). When he was with the Jews, Paul lived like a Jew so he could bring them to Jesus. When he was with those who followed the Jewish law, he lived under the law. Even though he wasn't subject to the law, he did this so he could point others to Christ.

He said, "When I am with those who are weak, I share their weakness, for I want to bring the weak to Christ. Yes, I try to find common ground with everyone, doing everything I can to save some. I do everything to spread the Good News and share in its blessings" (1 CORINTHIANS 9:22–23 NLT).

May we also meet people where they are today, sharing the good news of Jesus with respect and relevancy as He leads us!

Ruth

November 20

RUN TO ME
PROVERBS 18:4–12

The name of the Lord is a fortified tower; the righteous run to it and are safe.
Proverbs 18:10

During a walk at a local park, my children and I encountered a couple of unleashed dogs. Their owner didn't seem to notice that one of them had begun to intimidate my son. My son tried to shoo the dog away, but the animal only became more intent on bothering him.

Eventually, my son panicked. He bolted several yards into the distance, but the dog pursued him. The chase continued until I yelled, "Run to me!" My son doubled back, calmed down, and the dog finally decided to make mischief somewhere else.

There are moments in our lives when God calls to us and says, "Run to Me!" Something troubling is on our heels. We can't shake it. We're too afraid to turn and confront the trouble on our own. But the reality is that we aren't on our own. God is there, ready to help and comfort us. We need to turn away from whatever scares us and move in His direction. His Word says, "The name of the Lord is a fortified tower; the righteous run to it and are safe" (PROVERBS 18:10).

Jennifer

November 21

EMPTY ME
EPHESIANS 4:17-32

"A good man brings good things out of the good stored up in his heart, and an evil man brings evil things out of the evil stored up in his heart. For the mouth speaks what the heart is full of."

Luke 6:45

"What a rotten design," I grumbled as I emptied our paper shredder. I couldn't empty the container without spilling debris all over the carpet! One day as I was gathering trash, I slipped a plastic bag over the half-filled container and flipped it upside down. Not a bit of paper fell on the floor.

The error had been mine. Earlier, I had been waiting until the container was full before emptying it!

When we allow sin to fill up our hearts, it too will overflow into our life. Luke 6:45 says that "an evil man brings evil things out of the evil stored up in his heart." Luke then concludes, "The mouth speaks what the heart is full of."

What if we were to empty our hearts of the rubbish of sin before it started spilling into our interactions with others? First John 1:9 reminds us that "if we confess our sins, [God] . . . will forgive us our sins and purify us from all unrighteousness."

A paper shredder is designed to be a rubbish receptacle. We are not!

Cindy

November 22

HEARING AID
1 SAMUEL 3:1–14

So Eli told Samuel, "Go and lie down, and if he calls you, say, 'Speak, Lord, for your servant is listening.'" So Samuel went and lay down in his place.

1 Samuel 3:9

Joshua, a precocious two-year-old, watched his mother baking cookies. "Please, may I have one?" he asked hopefully. "Not before supper," his mother replied. Joshua ran tearfully to his room, then reappeared with this message: "Jesus just told me it's okay to have a cookie now." "Jesus didn't tell me," his mother retorted, to which Joshua replied, "You must not have been listening!"

Joshua's motivation was wrong, but he was absolutely right about two things: God longs to speak to us, and we need to listen.

In 1 Samuel 3, another young boy learned those same ageless principles. When Samuel followed Eli's counsel and prayed, "Speak, Lord, for your servant is listening," he was open to receiving God's powerful message (v. 9). Like Samuel, we long to hear God speaking to us but often fail to discern His voice.

Today God speaks to us by His Spirit through the Scriptures, other people, and our circumstances. But some of us need a "spiritual hearing aid" like the one in Samuel's prayer: "Speak, for your servant is listening" (v. 10). Are we listening?

Joanie

November 23

BARRIERS AND BLESSINGS

JOHN 4:27–39

Many of the Samaritans from that town believed in him because of the woman's testimony, "He told me everything I ever did."

John 4:39

What did Jesus see when He looked at the woman at the well in John 4? He saw someone who wanted acceptance and desperately needed to know she was loved. Most of all, He saw someone who needed what only He could give—a new heart.

Jesus used this encounter to bless her with the truth of "living water" (JOHN 4:10). In just one conversation, He broke down barriers of old hostilities, of gender bias, of ethnic and racial divides. And this woman became the first of many Samaritans to confess that Jesus was the Messiah (VV. 39–42).

When she told others of her encounter with a man who knew "everything I ever did," she was already practicing the principle of "sowing and reaping" that Jesus was teaching His followers (JOHN 4:35–38). Many believed that day, and later Philip, Peter, John, and others would preach in Samaria and lead many more to Christ (ACTS 8:5–14; 15:3).

When we tell others of our own "encounter" with Jesus, we bless them with living water.

Cindy

November 24

MUSIC INSIDE
PSALM 98

> Shout for joy to the Lord, all the earth,
> burst into jubilant song with music.
>
> Psalm 98:4

Singing comes naturally to the four von Trapp children. They are the great-grandchildren of Captain Georg von Trapp, whose romance with his second wife, Maria, inspired the 1965 blockbuster *The Sound of Music*.

After their grandfather Werner von Trapp (portrayed as Kurt in the movie) had a stroke, the Montana-based siblings recorded their first CD in order to cheer him up. Soon the children were performing around the world. Stefan, the children's father, says, "The music is inside them."

The writer of Psalm 98 also had a song in his heart. The psalmist's heart was so overflowing with praise that he called on others to join him in singing "to the Lord a new song!" (v. 1). He praised God for His salvation, His righteousness, His mercy, and His faithfulness (vv. 2–3).

We have much to be thankful for as well. He faithfully cares for us, His children.

We may not be able to sing well. But when we recall all that God is to us and all that He has done for us, we can't help but "burst into jubilant song" (v. 4).

Anne

November 25

TRUE BEAUTY
COLOSSIANS 1:15–23

The Son is the image of the invisible God, the firstborn over all creation.
Colossians 1:15

A movement to see beauty in women of all shapes and sizes and to reject the false standards of the media continues to grow. From marketing campaigns using larger-sized models to local groups teaching young girls to be confident, the message is clear: You are beautiful and you are powerful—simply by being you.

I understand the appeal of these messages. Self-esteem campaigns, however, are not the answer. Beauty isn't skin deep.

Our true beauty and value come as a result of Jesus's death for us on the cross.

When we believe Jesus gave everything for us in a sacrificial act of love, we become a direct threat to the kingdom of darkness (LUKE 10:19; COLOSSIANS 2:13–15). People who know that their worth comes from Christ become spiritually powerful as they look for ways to love Jesus with their whole lives even as they reflect His beautiful image (1:15).

In Christ we are loved and adored by our perfect, loving God (V. 22). That's a truth far greater than anything skin-deep (PHILIPPIANS 3:3; 1 JOHN 4:17).

Regina

NO ONE HAS EVER SEEN GOD; BUT IF WE *love* *one another,* GOD LIVES IN US & HIS LOVE IS MADE COMPLETE IN US.

1 John 4:12

November 26

LET US LOVE
1 JOHN 4:7–21

> No one has ever seen God; but if we love one another, God lives in us and his love is made complete in us.
> 1 John 4:12

It was a great tragedy for our whole community. My daughter's first-grade teacher died in childbirth, along with her baby. It broke my heart to see her in a casket with the baby in her arms.

Something that inspired all of us who grieved was that this teacher was characterized by the love and joy she showered on everyone she met. She loved children, parents, and community members whether they were believers in Jesus or not, and God's love was "made complete" in her (1 JOHN 4:7, 12).

Her jam-packed funeral was a real celebration. Her own family testified that she was the same person in private as she was in public. She lived out God's love—something we're all called to do (v. 19). Like her, love can be our legacy as we reflect God, for He *is* love (v. 16). Kind and compassionate, caring and serving—those qualities mark the heart of a person who "[lives] like Jesus" (v. 17). May we "lay down our lives" for others as He works in and through us (3:16).

Marlena

November 27

OUT OF THE BLUE
LUKE 2:8-14

Suddenly, an angel of the Lord appeared among them, and the radiance of the Lord's glory surrounded them.
Luke 2:9 (NLT)

Occasionally I receive unexpected Facebook messages from people I don't know well. Sometimes it's a word of encouragement; sometimes it is someone asking about being a writer. Someone thought of me, appreciated me, and simply wanted to tell me! It's good news right out of the blue—totally unexpected.

My favorite type of good news is the kind that's "more than we might ask or think" (EPHESIANS 3:20 NLT). It's a surprising gift that comes from God, often through others. It's God's idea and His special way of blessing us.

As we move toward December and Christmas, I'm reminded of the night the shepherds were watching their flocks—simply going about business as usual (LUKE 2:8). They didn't expect a choir of angels to appear to them or to be the first to hear that the Messiah was born (LUKE 2:9-10)! On what started out as a most ordinary night, God quite unexpectedly—and in a most spectacular way—intervened in their lives (LUKE 2:11-12).

May we see the "good gift" surprises He has for us today!

Marlena

November 28

SPOONFUL OF SUGAR
PSALM 19:7-14

The fear of the Lord is pure, enduring forever. The decrees of the Lord are firm, and all of them are righteous. They are more precious than gold, than much pure gold, they are sweeter than honey, than honey from the honeycomb.

Psalm 19:9-10

Where is Mary Poppins when you need her?

I know this sounds as if I'm longing for the good old days when cheerfully unrealistic movies featured characters like this fictional nanny, but what I'm really longing for are people with a vision for the future that is realistically optimistic. I yearn for joyful, creative people who can show us the positive side of what we consider negative, who can remind us that "just a spoonful of sugar makes the medicine go down."

David wrote a song that expressed a similar truth. In his words, "the decrees of the Lord" are "sweeter than honey" (PSALM 19:9-10). Often we hear that truth is bitter or hard to swallow. But truth is a gourmet meal that should be presented as a culinary delight, enticing the hungry to "taste and see that the Lord is good" (34:8).

"Jesus is the sweetest name I know," says the song. Pure truth, untainted by pride, is the sweetest, most refreshing taste of all to those who hunger for spiritual sustenance. We have the privilege of serving it to a starving world.

Julie

November 29

CHINESE PROVERBS
2 TIMOTHY 3:14-17

Therefore, my dear brothers and sisters, stand firm. Let nothing move you. Always give yourselves fully to the work of the Lord, because you know that your labor in the Lord is not in vain.

1 Corinthians 15:58

Chinese proverbs are common and often have stories behind them. The proverb "pulling up a crop to help it grow" is about an impatient man in the Song Dynasty. He was eager to see his rice seedlings grow quickly, so he would pull up each plant a few inches. After a day of tedious work, the man surveyed his paddy field. He was happy that his crop seemed to have "grown" taller. But his joy was short-lived. The next day, the plants had begun to wither because their roots were no longer deep.

In 2 Timothy 2:6, the apostle Paul compares the work of being a minister of the gospel to that of a farmer. He wrote to encourage Timothy that, like farming, making disciples can be continuous, hard labor. You plow, you sow, you wait, you pray. You desire to see the fruits of your labor quickly, but growth takes time. And as the Chinese proverb so aptly illustrates, any effort to hurry the process won't be helpful.

As we labor faithfully, we wait patiently on the Lord, who makes all things grow (1 CORINTHIANS 3:7).

Poh Fang

November 30

PLAYING YOUR PART
ROMANS 12:1-8

Each of us has one body with many members, and these members do not all have the same function.

Romans 12:4

For the past several years, my daughter Rosie has been the director of drama at a local middle school. A few students are selected to play the lead roles. But there are many other important supporting roles that must be cast—roles that are vital to the production.

Other young people want to be a part of the show but don't relish the spotlight. They change scenery, open and close the curtains, run the lights, and assist with makeup and costume changes. The successful performances are the culmination of an intense four- to five-month process that is dependent on the hard work of a wide range of dedicated people.

Similarly, for the body of Christ to function fully, each of us must play a part. Every believer is uniquely gifted for service. When these gifts are combined in a cooperative relationship, "each part does its share" (EPHESIANS 4:16), and the separate parts make up the whole (ROMANS 12:5).

We need each other. What part are you playing in the life of the church?

Cindy

December 1

LOST TREASURE
MARK 10:17-27

Jesus looked at him and loved him. "One thing you lack," he said. "Go, sell everything you have and give to the poor, and you will have treasure in heaven. Then come, follow me."

Mark 10:21

Don takes walks on the city's railroad tracks and searches under freeway overpasses. He's not looking for lost treasure; he's looking for homeless people. Don met Jake, who lives in a makeshift underground shack and is mentally ill. He stops by to see Jake occasionally, making sure he's warm and has food. He tells Jake about Jesus because he wants him to find "treasure in heaven."

Jesus talked about this treasure with a rich young man who asked Him how to inherit eternal life. Jesus said, "Sell everything you have and give to the poor, and you will have treasure in heaven. Then come, follow me" (MARK 10:21).

Jesus wasn't teaching that we must give up our wealth to be acceptable to Him. We can never earn eternal life by our works. He was showing this man he was spiritually bankrupt. We all are, unless we have Jesus.

No good deed can earn eternal life—not helping the homeless or giving away all our money. Jesus wants us to give Him our heart. Then we'll have real treasure—treasure in heaven—and we'll seek to help others.

Anne

EVERY
good & perfect gift
IS FROM ABOVE,
COMING DOWN from the FATHER of the
heavenly lights,
WHO DOES NOT CHANGE
like SHIFTING SHADOWS

James 1:17

December 2

THE SENSUOUS CHRISTIAN

EXODUS 37:1-9

Every good and perfect gift is from above, coming down from the Father of the heavenly lights, who does not change like shifting shadows.

James 1:17

The gratification of our senses has gotten a bad reputation, perhaps because we live in a world obsessed with pleasure. But God approves of the proper experience of pleasure through our five senses.

First, God created our senses—sight, hearing, smell, taste, touch—and all that He created is good.

Second, God made sensuousness a part of worship. Consider God's first formal worship setting: the tabernacle. It housed an ornate, gold-covered ark to hold the stone tablets God gave to Moses on Mount Sinai. God approves of beauty. Around the tabernacle were curtains made from colorful yarn and finely twisted linen. God approves of beautiful colors and textures. Music was also a component of worship, as we learn from reading 2 Chronicles 29:28. God approves of pleasing sounds.

Yes, God values things that look, sound, smell, taste, and feel good. But He doesn't want us to worship them; He wants our enjoyment and gratitude to prompt us to worship Him, the Creator and giver of all good things.

Julie

December 3

ABIGAIL'S REMINDER
1 SAMUEL 25:14-33

> When the Lord takes pleasure in anyone's way, he causes their enemies to make peace with them.
>
> *Proverbs 16:7*

David and four hundred of his warriors thundered through the countryside in search of Nabal, a prosperous brute who had harshly refused to lend them help. David would have murdered him if he hadn't first encountered Abigail, Nabal's wife. She had packed up enough food to feed an army and traveled out to meet the troops, hoping to head off disaster. She respectfully reminded David that guilt would haunt him if he followed through with his vengeful plan (1 SAMUEL 25:31).

David realized she was right and blessed her for her good judgment.

David's anger was legitimate—he had protected Nabal's shepherds in the wilderness (VV. 14-17) and had been repaid evil for good. However, his anger was leading him into sin.

When we've been offended, it's good to compare our instincts with God's intent for human behavior. Choosing a gracious response will help us avoid regret, and most important, it will please God. When our desire is to honor God in our relationships, He is able to make even our enemies be at peace with us (SEE PROVERBS 16:7).

Jennifer

December 4

Living Differently

DANIEL 9:1-22

"We have sinned and done wrong. We have been wicked and have rebelled; we have turned away from your commands and laws."

Daniel 9:5

Trapped in a foreign culture, Daniel knew firsthand the challenges of life in a society steeped in sin. While his story teaches us how to remain pure and prayerful regardless of what others around us are doing, the events that took him to Babylon hold lessons as well.

Although they had been warned by God's prophets for years, the people of Israel chose idolatry above their love for Him. They knew how to perform their rituals, ask for His intervention, and speak the right words, but their hearts remained in love with the secular culture (ISAIAH 29:13).

Daniel was different. He saw not only the sin of the pagan society to which he had been transported but, more important, he also recognized the compromise that had infiltrated God's people. Because Daniel cared about God's standards more than his own need for comfort, God not only spoke to Daniel but also gave him "insight and understanding" (DANIEL 9:22).

With God's help and for His glory, the same opportunity to rise above an unholy culture is available to us today.

Regina

December 5

NO LONGER LOST

JOEL 2:1–25

> "I will give you back what you lost to the swarming locusts, the hopping locusts, the stripping locusts, and the cutting locusts."
>
> *Joel 2:25* (NLT)

I knew someone who had a difficult time believing she could ever experience God's goodness and faithfulness (JOEL 2:23). She grew up with an emotionally and physically abusive mother and an absent father. She thought she'd overcome the tragedy of early life, but although she was faithful to Jesus and did her best to serve others, she couldn't shake some of the dark influences that shadowed her.

Thankfully, God is more powerful than our circumstances and sin. And His grace is much bigger than any of our past hardships. I reassured her that God "forgives all [our] sins and heals all [our] diseases. He redeems [us] from death and crowns [us] with love and tender mercies. He fills [our] [lives] with good things" (PSALM 103:3–5).

We all suffer the consequences of our own sin or sins committed against us by others. But when we begin to rely on God, we find that sin doesn't have the last word. *He* does. He starts righting the wrongs in our lives and giving us back what one day will be fully restored in Jesus (JOEL 2:25; ACTS 3:21)!

Marlena

December 6

SIGNET RING
HAGGAI 2:15–23

"'On that day,' declares the Lord Almighty, 'I will take you, my servant Zerubbabel son of Shealtiel,' declares the Lord, 'and I will make you like my signet ring, for I have chosen you,' declares the Lord Almighty."

Haggai 2:23

I once met a man who wore a ring on his little finger that bore his family crest. It was a bit like a signet ring—perhaps like the one in Haggai 2.

In this short Old Testament book, the prophet Haggai calls for the people of God to restart rebuilding the temple. They had been exiled and had returned to their homeland and begun rebuilding, but enemy opposition to their project had stalled them. Haggai's message includes God's promise to Zerubbabel, Judah's leader, that he had been chosen and set apart as their leader, like a signet ring.

A signet ring was used for identification. Instead of signing their name, people would press their ring into soft clay to make their mark. As God's children, we too make a mark on the world as we spread the gospel, share His grace through loving our neighbors, and work to end oppression.

Each of us has our own unique stamp that expresses our particular mix of gifts, passions, and wisdom. It's our privilege to act as this signet ring in God's world.

Amy

December 7

START AFRESH
PSALM 86:5–15

> Because of the LORD's great love we are not consumed, for his compassions never fail. They are new every morning; great is your faithfulness.
>
> Lamentations 3:22-23

One of my favorite books as a girl was *Anne of Green Gables* by Lucy Maud Montgomery. In one amusing passage, young Anne, by mistake, adds a skin medication instead of vanilla to the cake she's making. Afterward, she exclaims hopefully to her stern-faced guardian, Marilla, "Isn't it nice to think that tomorrow is a new day with no mistakes in it yet?"

I like that thought: tomorrow is a new day—a new day when we can start afresh. We all make mistakes. But when it comes to sin, God's forgiveness is what enables us to start each morning with a clean slate. When we repent, He chooses to remember our sins no more (JEREMIAH 31:34; HEBREWS 8:12).

Some of us have made wrong choices, but our past words and deeds need not define our future in God's eyes. There's always a fresh start. When we ask for His forgiveness, we take a first step toward restoring our relationship with Him and with others (SEE 1 JOHN 1:9).

God's compassion and faithfulness are new every morning (LAMENTATIONS 3:23), so we can start afresh each day.

Cindy

December 8

A WAY OF LIFE
COLOSSIANS 3:5–9

"In your anger do not sin": Do not let the sun go down while you are still angry.

Ephesians 4:26

How did everything get so dirty so fast?" I grumbled as I dusted the glass tabletop. "I had the whole house clean a month ago."

"Cleaning is a way of life, not an event," my husband responded.

I know he's right, but I hate to admit it. I want to clean the house once and have it stay that way. But dirt doesn't surrender that easily. Speck by speck, the dust returns. Piece by piece, the clutter piles up.

Sin is like the dust and clutter in my house. I want to eliminate all of it with one prayer of confession. But sin doesn't surrender that easily. Thought by thought, bad attitudes return. Choice by choice, unpleasant consequences pile up.

Paul said believers should get rid of "anger, rage, malice, slander, and filthy language" (COLOSSIANS 3:8). And he also said, "In your anger do not sin" (EPHESIANS 4:26).

Christ's death and resurrection eliminated the need for daily sacrifice. But confession and repentance are still essential. Getting rid of such things as anger, rage, and malice is a way of life, not a one-time event.

Julie

December 9

REMINDERS OF LOVE
JOHN 19:1-7, 16-18

> Whoever does not love does not know God, because God is love.
> 1 John 4:8

After the United States entered World War II in 1941, Estelle tried to talk her boyfriend, Sidney, out of joining the army. But he enlisted and began his training the following April. For the next three years, he wrote her love letters—525 in all. Then in March 1945, she learned that her beloved fiancé had been killed in combat.

Although Estelle did eventually marry, the memories of her first love lived in her heart. To honor that love, she published a book of Sidney's wartime correspondence more than sixty years later.

Like those letters, the Lord has left us with reminders of His love—the Scriptures. He says, "I have loved you with an everlasting love; I have drawn you with unfailing kindness" (JEREMIAH 31:3).

The Bible also tells us that "Christ loved the church and gave himself up for her" (EPHESIANS 5:25).

"[Jesus] gave himself for us to redeem us" (TITUS 2:14).

"God is love" (1 JOHN 4:8).

Read God's Word often and be reminded that Jesus loves you and died for you.

Anne

December 10

GOD'S WILL AND OUR HOPES
GENESIS 1:1-31

Now the earth was formless and empty, darkness was over the surface of the deep, and the Spirit of God was hovering over the waters.
Genesis 1:2

Just a few inches long, the sonogram image looked like something from a science fiction movie. With distinctive little nubs for hands and a clearly defined head, I could see the promise of our firstborn. Those pictures were treasures for my husband and me. What we couldn't see with our naked eye was indeed real, though hidden.

The capacity to produce and bring forth something seen from the unseen is inherent in all living things (GENESIS 1:12, 24). Humans are unique, however, in our ability to hope. We live in hope because—though marred by sin—we carry the DNA of our Creator (GENESIS 1:27).

For the believer, hope is based on this truth: *God fulfills what He designs* (PSALM 139:13, 15–16). The fulfillment of a hoped-for outcome takes place in stages, though—many of them imperceptible to the natural eye.

Waiting can be difficult, so we choose to settle ourselves on the "strong and trustworthy anchor for our souls" (HEBREWS 6:19 NLT). Whether a hope is realized or not is based in God's perfect plans. Our role? Stay focused, be patient, and accept His loving will.

Regina

December 11

LOTTIE'S LEGACY

HEBREWS 10:23-29

> Patient endurance is what you need now, so that you will continue to do God's will. Then you will receive all that he has promised.
>
> Hebrews 10:36 (NLT)

More than a hundred years after her death, the legacy of Lottie Moon lives on. Originally from the United States, she traveled to China as a missionary and later established the Lottie Moon Christmas Offering, which has raised more than $1.5 billion for missions since 1888. Many received salvation in Jesus during her years of ministry, but she endured difficult circumstances—including illness, famine, war, and discrimination as a single woman.

God provided what Lottie Moon needed as she served Him. It wasn't easy, but she persevered by His power and strength.

When many of us first came to Christ, we were eager to do His will—even ready to endure suffering for His sake (HEBREWS 10:32-34). Over the years, however, it's easy to grow weary as difficult circumstances leave us disillusioned.

Like Lottie, though, we can be encouraged to hold tightly without wavering, for God can be trusted to keep His promises to care for us!

Lord, help us to patiently endure all things, remaining true to God's call in our lives.

Ruth

December 12

TRUDGING ON

PSALM 84:1–12

What joy for those whose strength comes from the Lord.

Psalm 84:5 (NLT)

Kellie Haddock is a courageous woman. In 2004 I first read the blog she penned following a tragic car accident that took the life of her husband and left her baby, Eli, with permanent injuries.

Kellie's writings convey hope in God and deep trust in His faithfulness. On her website, Kellie writes, "Psalm 84:5–7 says, 'Blessed are those whose strength is in you, whose hearts are set on pilgrimage.' This word *pilgrimage* means that one is moving, that you aren't paralyzed and stuck in fear, but rather that you are painstakingly putting one blistered foot in front of the other. This is what I've aimed to do, to keep trudging onward. Not to let the grief hold me down and make me stop living my life. For 'when they walk through the Valley of Weeping'—not around, there are no shortcuts on this way—'it will become a place of refreshing' where pools of blessing collects after the rain" (PSALM 84:6 NLT).

When hard times come, may we, like Kellie, rest in the arms of our loving God, who can always be trusted!

Roxanne

December 13

INSPIRATION TO PERSPIRATION

TITUS 3:1–8

Do not merely listen to the word, and so deceive yourselves. Do what it says.

James 1:22

I love visiting beautiful gardens—they inspire me. They make me want to create something equally beautiful in my own yard. But I have trouble moving from the inspiration to the perspiration part of gardening. My great ideas don't become reality because I don't spend the time and energy to make them happen.

This can be true in our spiritual lives as well. We can listen to the testimonies of other people and marvel at the work God is doing in their lives. But we have trouble finding the time or making the effort to follow through.

James described such Christians as being like those who look in a mirror, see themselves, but do nothing to fix what is wrong (JAMES 1:23–24). They hear the Word, but it doesn't lead to action. James says we need to do—not just hear.

When we move from the inspiration of simply "hearing" about the good being done by others to the perspiration of actually "doing" good works ourselves, the implanted Word of God (1:21) will bloom into a beautiful garden of spiritual fruit.

Julie

December 14

FAME AND HUMILITY
PHILIPPIANS 2:1–11

And being found in appearance as a man, he humbled himself by becoming obedient to death—even death on a cross!

Philippians 2:8

Many of us are obsessed with fame—either with being famous ourselves or with following every detail of famous people's lives.

In a recent study in the United States, researchers ranked the names of famous individuals using a specially developed algorithm that scoured the Internet. Jesus topped the list as the most famous person in history.

Yet Jesus was never concerned about obtaining celebrity status. When He was here on earth, He didn't seek fame (MATTHEW 9:30; JOHN 6:15)—although fame found Him as news about Him traveled throughout the region of Galilee (MARK 1:28; LUKE 4:37).

Wherever Jesus went, crowds gathered. The miracles He performed drew people to Him. But when they tried to make Him a king by force, He slipped away by himself (JOHN 6:15). United in purpose with His Father, He repeatedly deferred to God's will and timing (4:34; 8:29; 12:23). "He humbled himself by becoming obedient to death—even death on a cross!" (PHILIPPIANS 2:8).

Fame was never Jesus's goal. His purpose was simple: He humbly, obediently, and voluntarily offered himself as the sacrifice for our sins.

Cindy

December 15

MEGAN'S HEART

JAMES 1:19-27

> Do not merely listen to the word, and so deceive yourselves. Do what it says.
>
> *James 1:22*

When Megan was in third grade, she kept coming home from school without her winter gloves. It drove her mom crazy because she had to keep buying new ones, which the family couldn't afford. One day Mom got angry and said, "Megan, you've got to be more responsible! This can't go on!"

Megan began to cry. Through her tears she told her mom that because she kept getting new gloves, she gave hers away to kids who didn't have any.

Now that she is eighteen years old, Megan's hobbies include volunteering in the community and mentoring inner-city kids. Referring to her desire to help people, she said that it "felt like that was the kind of thing I was supposed to be doing."

As Christians, we are to have a heart of giving. James gives us a practical way for us to give of ourselves: "Look after orphans and widows in their distress" (v. 27).

Ask God for a heart like Megan's. Out of love for God, obey what He tells you to do. It's what we're "supposed to be doing."

Anne

December 16

STAIRWAY TO HEAVEN

JOHN 1:35–51

"The Son of Man . . . is the stairway between heaven and earth."

John 1:51 (NLT)

While in Paris, my husband and I visited the famous Arc de Triomphe on the Champs-Elysees. We climbed the 284 stairs to reach the top, and when we emerged, we relished the panoramic view of the city.

In the Old Testament, Jacob dreamed of a stairway that reached from earth to heaven (GENESIS 28:12–15). Angels ascended and descended on the structure. God stood at the top (V. 13).

Centuries later, Jesus referenced a staircase like the one in Jacob's dream. He told His listeners, "You will see greater things than this. . . . You will . . . see . . . angels of God going up and down on the Son of Man, the one who is the stairway between heaven and earth" (JOHN 1:50–51 NLT). Jesus was teaching the disciples that He was (and is) the way to get to heaven (JOHN 14:6). We can't reach God on our own.

Jesus takes away our sin when we believe in Him. If you know Jesus, you can look forward to spending eternity with Him. If you don't know Him, consider the One who died for you—your personal "stairway to heaven."

Jennifer

December 17

THE GIFT OF SLEEP
PSALM 127:1–5

> In vain you rise early and stay up late, toiling for food to eat—for he grants sleep to those he loves.
>
> *Psalm 127:2*

She told me she was depressed—extremely depressed.

It's hard to know what to say in such situations, so we talked about several things—medication, relationships with others and with God, and her habits. We agreed that if she could begin to sleep well, it would help her feel better emotionally and physically.

A lack of rest can make handling the challenges of life difficult. When it comes to sleep, I'm always fascinated that Jesus slept on a boat in the midst of a raging storm (MARK 4:38). *How could He do that?* The disciples didn't get it either. But the psalmist points to an answer: "[God] grants sleep to those he loves" (PSALM 127:2). Even in our struggle to rest, God is with us. We can rest in Him even when our eyes refuse to stay shut.

During those times, may we learn to "cast [our] cares on the LORD" (PSALM 55:22). As we do, we *can* choose to wait confidently for the gift of rest He alone can provide (PSALM 127:2).

Marlena

December 18

DOERS OF THE WORD

JAMES 1:19-27

Do not merely listen to the word, and so deceive yourselves. Do what it says.

James 1:22

Just after we moved to a new neighborhood, we invited my sister-in-law and her husband over for Sunday dinner. As we greeted Sue and Ted at the door, an odd noise directed their eyes toward the kitchen. As I followed their gaze, I froze in horror. An errant hose of our old portable dishwasher had disengaged—spewing water everywhere!

Sue went into action mode. Dropping her purse, she was in the kitchen before me, shutting off the water and calling for towels and a mop. We spent the first fifteen minutes of their visit on our knees mopping the floor.

Sue is a doer—someone always ready to pitch in, be involved, and even lead if necessary.

Many of the doers of the world are also doers of the Word. These are followers of Jesus who have taken the challenge of James to heart: "Do not merely listen to the word. . . . Do what it says" (1:22).

As you read God's Word, think about what it means to put what you've learned into practice. It's another way to enjoy the blessings of God (v. 25).

Cindy

December 19

STAGECOACH PRAYER
JOHN 15:7-14

"I will do whatever you ask in my name, so that the Father may be glorified in the Son."

John 14:13

Five-year-old Randy wanted a toy stagecoach for Christmas. While shopping with Mom, he found the one he wanted. About six inches long, it had cool wheels and nifty plastic horses. "Mommy, I want this one. Pleeeease!" he begged. He insisted she get that stagecoach. Mom said, "We'll see," and took him home.

On Christmas morning, he opened the package confidently. Sure enough, it was the stagecoach he had begged for. He was so pleased—until his older brother said, "You did a dumb thing when you insisted on getting that one. Mom already bought you a much bigger one, but when you begged for that one, she exchanged it!" Suddenly the small stagecoach didn't seem so appealing.

Sometimes we're like that with God. We pray about a specific need and tell Him how He ought to answer. We beg and plead—and God may even give us what we ask for. But He may have had something better in mind.

Phillips Brooks once said, "Pray the largest prayers. You cannot think a prayer so large that God, in answering it, will not wish you had made it larger."

Anne

December 20

DOOR OF HUMILITY
PHILIPPIANS 2:5–11

At the name of Jesus every knee should bow, in heaven & on earth and under the earth.
— Philippians 2:10

> Therefore God exalted him to the highest place and gave him the name that is above every name, that at the name of Jesus every knee should bow, in heaven and on earth and under the earth.
>
> *Philippians 2:9-10*

Over the centuries, the entrance to Bethlehem's Church of the Nativity has twice been made smaller. It's now referred to as the Door of Humility because visitors must bend down to enter.

As we age, bending our knees becomes more and more difficult and painful. In the physical realm, some people courageously undergo knee replacement surgery. To avoid years of increasingly painful joint damage, they endure several weeks of agony.

Like physical knees, spiritual knees can grow stiff over time. Years of stubborn pride and selfishness make us inflexible, and it becomes increasingly difficult and painful for us to humble ourselves. Seduced by false feelings of importance when others submit to us, we never learn that true importance comes from submitting ourselves to God and to others (EPHESIANS 5:21; 1 PETER 5:5).

It's good to remember the Door of Humility. The only way to enter the presence of God is with humility.

That's how we honor the One who bent so low to be with us.

Julie

December 21

A GIFT OF SHELTER
LUKE 2:1-7

She gave birth to her firstborn, a son. She wrapped him in cloths and placed him in a manger, because there was no guest room available for them.

Luke 2:7

Life was tough for Datha and her family. She had coronary artery disease, and her teen daughter Heather became paralyzed in a car accident. Datha quit her job to care for Heather, and the bills piled up. Eviction threatened them. Datha was so angry with God that she stopped praying.

But on Christmas Eve, a young girl knocked on Datha's door, wished her a "Merry Christmas," gave her an envelope, and left. Inside was a gift that would cover Datha's housing needs for the next year. A note read, "Please accept this gift in honor of the Man whose birthday we celebrate on this holy night. His family also had a shelter problem."

Luke 2 tells the story of Joseph and Mary as they searched for a shelter for Mary to deliver her baby, and it ended up being a stable. Later Jesus had "no place to lay his head" (MATTHEW 8:20).

Jesus understood Datha's troubles. He brought her hope and met her needs through others.

We can cast all our cares on God (1 PETER 5:7). In Him, we find shelter (PSALM 61:3-4).

Anne

December 22

JOY TO THE WORLD
PSALM 98:1-9

Shout to the Lord, all the earth; break out in praise and sing for joy!
Psalm 98:4 (NLT)

Sometimes it's hard to feel joyous during Christmas. For those who have lost loved ones during this period, the festive season reminds them of the painful absence.

How can we sing "Joy to the World" when our heart is grieving in pain? Isaac Watts penned the song not as a Christmas carol but as a reinterpretation of Psalm 98—a psalm that calls the earth to praise God in view of His coming reign. The lyrics contain rich themes of Jesus's coming to dwell among us as a human being, so most hymnals list the song as an Advent carol.

The fact that Christ came in the flesh is grounds for true joy.

He came to save (PSALM 98:1), announce His victory, and reveal His righteousness (V. 2).

When we think about Christmas and face it with tears, we still have hope: *Jesus is coming again.* The baby who was placed in a manger will wipe every tear from our eyes, and we will enjoy His blessings forever (REVELATION 21:4).

Yes, joy to the world—for our Savior *has* come!

Poh Fang

December 23

NOW IS THE TIME
LUKE 2:8–20

"Glory to God in the highest heaven, and on earth peace to those on whom his favor rests."

Luke 2:14

During our church's Christmas celebration, I watched the choir members assemble in front of the congregation while the music director riffled through papers on a slim black stand. The instruments began, and the singers launched into a well-known song that started with the suggestion that it was time to begin worshiping.

Although I expected to hear a time-honored Christmas carol, I smiled at the appropriate choice of music. While reading Luke's account of Jesus's birth, I noticed that the first Christmas lacked our modern-day parties, gifts, and feasting—but it did include worship.

After the angel announced Jesus's birth to some wide-eyed shepherds, a chorus of angels began "praising God and saying: 'Glory to God in the highest!'" (LUKE 2:13–14). The shepherds responded by running to Bethlehem where they found the newborn King. They returned to their fields "glorifying and praising God for all the things they had heard and seen" (V. 20). Coming face-to-face with the Son inspired the shepherds to worship the Father.

Today, as you think of Jesus's birth, is there room in your heart for worship?

Jennifer

December 24

WORSHIP AND CHRISTMAS
LUKE 2:1-20

"The Savior—yes, the Messiah, the Lord—has been born today in Bethlehem, the city of David!"

Luke 2:11 (NLT)

Last year, as we were headed to my sister's house on Christmas Eve, my husband and I picked up a few last-minute items at a large grocery store. My yuletide excitement turned to dismay when I headed past an aisle that had contained Christmas items only days earlier. In their place was a Valentine's Day display.

Christmas had not yet arrived, but it was already gone.

This retail makeover revealed to me the human desire for *more*—whether it's more money or the drive to make holidays bigger and better. How quickly secondary things can steal our attention! And we lose the ability to be in awe of something—or better yet, *Someone* (LUKE 2:11).

The record of Jesus's birth (VV. 1-16) reveals to us a central truth: *We're called to worship Jesus—the Messiah who came to save us.* May we follow the shepherds' example this Christmas: "The shepherds went back to their flocks, glorifying and praising God" (V. 20 NLT).

In this most precious time of year, we should let the Holy Spirit lead our celebrations. The Savior of all humankind is worthy of our full worship.

Regina

December 25

THE "MOM BOX"
2 TIMOTHY 3:14-17

From infancy you have known the Holy Scriptures, which are able to make you wise for salvation through faith in Christ Jesus.
2 Timothy 3:15

Each Christmas I give both of my daughters a "Mom box." Each contains items to encourage them to be the best mothers they can be. It might have craft books or special projects, devotional books or tapes geared toward young moms, first-aid kits, recipes for cooking with kids—and often something personal like bubble bath for a little pampering after a tough day of mothering! It's become a tradition that Rosemary and Tanya have looked forward to every year for the last decade.

Encouraging our children to be good parents can begin even earlier. The best way is to start equipping them with the Word of God while they are still young. Nothing is more essential than "the Holy Scriptures" to equip them for all of life's challenges.

There is nothing better than the Bible for making the next generation "wise for salvation through faith in Christ Jesus" (2 TIMOTHY 3:15).

Cindy

December 26

LEANING INTO THE LIGHT

1 PETER 2:4–10

But you are a chosen people, a royal priesthood, a holy nation, God's special possession, that you may declare the praises of him who called you out of darkness into his wonderful light.

1 Peter 2:9

One day I received a bouquet of pink tulips. I placed them in water in a vase at the center of our kitchen table. The next day, the flowers were facing a different direction and leaning to the side as if reaching toward sunlight that streamed in through a nearby window.

In one sense, we all were made to be like those flowers. God has called us to turn to the light of His love. Peter writes of the wonder of being called "out of darkness into [God's] wonderful light" (1 PETER 2:9). Because of God's mercy and love, He made a way for us to escape spiritual darkness through the death and resurrection of His Son (COLOSSIANS 1:13–14).

Jesus is the Light of the world. Only as we turn to Him will we increasingly reflect His goodness and truth (EPHESIANS 5:8–9).

May we never forget to lean into the Light.

Jennifer

December 27

FEEDING OURSELVES
HEBREWS 5:12–6:2

> In fact, though by this time you ought to be teachers, you need someone to teach you the elementary truths of God's word all over again. You need milk, not solid food!
>
> *Hebrews 5:12*

The eaglets were hungry, and Mom and Dad seemed to be ignoring them. The oldest of the three decided to solve his hunger problem by gnawing on a twig. Apparently it wasn't too tasty, because he soon abandoned it.

As I watched this webcam drama, I noticed that a big fish lay just behind the eaglets. But they had not yet learned to feed themselves. Within a few weeks, however, the parents will teach the eaglets how to do that—one of their first survival lessons. If the eaglets don't learn this skill, they'll never be able to survive on their own.

The author of Hebrews spoke of a similar problem in the spiritual realm. Certain people in the church were not growing up spiritually (HEBREWS 5:14). Like the eaglet, they hadn't learned the difference between a twig and a fish. They still needed to be fed by someone else when they should have been feeding not only themselves but others as well (V. 12).

While receiving spiritual food from preachers and teachers is good, spiritual growth and survival also depend on knowing how to feed ourselves.

Julie

December 28

ALL ALONE
1 KINGS 19:1-8

> "I will preserve 7,000 others in Israel who have never bowed down to Baal or kissed him!"
>
> *1 Kings 19:18* (NLT)

Depression rolled over Leigh, a wife and mother, as she sat on the edge of the bed holding a revolver—tormenting voices urging her to pull the trigger. The consuming illness had clouded her mind. Fortunately, Leigh slowly put the gun down, walked out of the room, and chose to reach out to others.

Following Elijah's stunning victory over the prophets of Baal, Queen Jezebel threatened to kill him (1 KINGS 19:1-2). Fearful, he fled alone into the wilderness where he begged the Lord to take his life. Elijah fell asleep, but an angel of God woke him, telling him to eat and drink. Later God met with Elijah and told him to return through the wilderness. The prophet felt alone in his convictions, but God showed him that there were seven thousand others who had also remained faithful to Him (1 KINGS 19:18).

When you're at your wit's end, spend time with God. Courageously tell Him and others how you truly feel. Find others with whom you can pray, be accountable, and remind yourselves of God's presence and promises. God doesn't leave us alone.

Ruth

December 29

LOVE COMES FIRST
1 JOHN 4:7-19

We love because he first loved us.
1 John 4:19

One evening my friend showed me one of the three decorative plaques for a wall arrangement in her living room. "See, I've already got Love," she said, holding up the plaque with the word written on it. "Faith and Hope are on order."

So Love comes first, I thought. *Faith and Hope soon follow!*

Love did come first. In fact, it originated with God. First John 4:19 reminds us that "we love [God] because he first loved us." God's love, described in 1 Corinthians 13 (known as the "love chapter"), explains a characteristic of real love when it says, "Love never fails" (V. 8).

Faith and hope are essential to the believer. It is only because we are justified by faith that "we have peace with God through our Lord Jesus Christ" (ROMANS 5:1). And hope is described in Hebrews 6 as "an anchor for the soul, firm and secure" (V. 19).

"Now these three remain: faith, hope and love. But the greatest of these is love"—it's first and last (1 CORINTHIANS 13:13).

Cindy

December 30

START THE PARTY!
PSALM 84

My soul yearns, even faints, for the courts of the Lord; my heart and my flesh cry out for the living God.

Psalm 84:2

Three-year-old Tobias loves to go to church. He cries when he isn't able to attend. Each week when he arrives for the children's program of Bible stories, games, singing, and dinner, he runs into the building and enthusiastically announces to the leaders and other children: "Let's get this party started!" The Lord must smile at this child's excitement!

The author of Psalm 84, one of the sons of Korah, also had a love for God's house. Some commentators have speculated that for a time he, a temple singer, was unable to go to the temple—either because of sickness or circumstances. So as he wrote this psalm, his soul was especially longing and crying out to be in "the courts of the Lord" (v. 2). He believed that one day of worship in God's house gave more satisfaction than a thousand days spent anywhere else (v. 10).

There's something special about praising God together with His people, and we should take every opportunity to do so. The Lord is pleased and we'll be blessed when our heart's desire is to be with Him and His people.

Anne

December 31

NEVER TOO OLD

GENESIS 18:1–15

"Is anything too hard for the Lord? I will return to you at the appointed time next year, and Sarah will have a son."

Genesis 18:14

The women of Brown Manor had raised their families and retired from their careers. Now they could no longer live on their own, so they came to Brown Manor as a sort of "last stop before heaven." They enjoyed each other's company but struggled with feelings of uselessness.

One of the women, who had spent years playing the piano, often played hymns on the manor's piano. Other women joined her, and together they lifted their voices in praise to God.

One day a government auditor was conducting an inspection during one of their spontaneous worship services. When he heard them sing "What Will You Do with Jesus?" he recalled the song from his childhood. That day, God spoke to him again, and this time he trusted Jesus.

Like the women of Brown Manor, Sarah thought she was too old to be used by God (GENESIS 18:11). But God gave her a child in her old age who was the ancestor of Jesus (21:1–3; MATTHEW 1:2, 17). Like Sarah and the women of Brown Manor, we're never too old for God to use us.

Julie

The Writers

Alyson Kieda has been an editor for Our Daily Bread Ministries for over a decade and has more than thirtyfive years of editing experience. Alyson has loved writing since she was a child and is thrilled to be writing for *Our Daily Bread*. She is married with three adult children and a growing number of grandchildren. Alyson loves reading, walking in the woods, and being with family. She feels blessed to be following in her mother's footsteps—she wrote articles many years ago for another devotional.

Amy Boucher Pye is a writer, editor, and speaker. The author of *Finding Myself in Britain: Our Search for Faith, Home, and True Identity*, she runs the Woman Alive book club in the United Kingdom and enjoys life with her family in their English vicarage.

Anne Cetas became a believer in Jesus in her late teens. At nineteen, she was given a copy of *Our Daily Bread* by a friend to help her read the Bible consistently. She also devoured Discovery Series topical study booklets. Several years later, she joined the editorial staff of *Our Daily Bread* as a proofreader. Anne began writing for the devotional booklet in September 2004 and at her retirement in 2020 was senior content editor for the publication. Anne and her husband, Carl, enjoy walking and bicycling together, and working as mentors in an urban ministry.

Cindy Hess Kasper served for more than forty years at Our Daily Bread Ministries—thirty of those in publishing where she was senior content editor for *Our Daily Journey*. She is a daughter of longtime senior editor Clair Hess, from whom she learned a love for singing and working with words. Cindy and her husband, Tom, have three grown children and seven grandchildren, in whom they take great delight.

Elisa Morgan has authored more than twenty-five books on mothering, spiritual formation, and evangelism, including *The NIV Mom's Devotional Bible, She Did What She Could, The Beauty of Broken,* and *Hello, Beauty Full.* She speaks widely and writes a blog under the title *Really* (elisamorgan.com). For twenty years, Elisa served as CEO of MOPS International. She is married to Evan, and they have two grown children and two grandchildren who live near them in Denver, Colorado.

Jennifer Benson Schuldt has been writing professionally since 1997 when she graduated from Cedarville University and began her career as a technical writer. Jennifer lives in the Chicago suburbs with her husband, Bob, and their two children. When she isn't writing or serving at home and church, she enjoys painting, reading poetry and fiction, and taking walks with her family.

Joanie Yoder, a favorite among *Our Daily Bread* readers, went home to be with her Savior in 2004. She and her husband established a Christian rehabilitation center for drug addicts in England many years ago. Widowed in 1982, she learned to rely on the Lord's help and strength. She wrote with hope about true dependence on God and His life-changing power. Joanie authored the book *Finding the God-Dependent Life*.

Julie Ackerman Link, after a lengthy battle with cancer, went to be with the Lord on April 10, 2015. Julie began writing articles each month for *Our Daily Bread in 2000*. She is a popular author with *Our Daily Bread* readers, and her insightful and inspiring articles have touched millions of lives around the world. Julie also wrote the books *Above All, Love* and *100 Prayers Inspired by the Psalms*.

Karen Wolfe is a native of Jamaica who now lives in the United States. She became a follower of Christ at age twenty-six, and one of the first devotionals she read was *Our Daily Bread*. Karen enjoys teaching and writing so she can share the truths she learns from Scripture. Her desire is to see men and women walk in the freedom that Christ has given and to see lives transformed by the Word of God. She completed her biblical studies degree at New Orleans Baptist Theological Seminary. In addition to writing, Karen loves to cook, especially when she can use locally sourced ingredients in her dishes. She and her husband, Joey, live in Georgia. Karen currently writes at thekarenwolfe.com.

Keila Ochoa and her husband have two young children. She helps Media Associates International with their training ministry for writers around the world and has written several books in Spanish for children, teens, and women. She serves in her church in the areas of youth, missions, and women's ministry.

Marion Stroud went to be with her Savior on August 8, 2015, after a battle with cancer. In 2014 Marion began writing *Our Daily Bread* devotional articles that touched the lives of readers around the world. Two of her popular books of prayers are *Dear God, It's Me and It's Urgent* and *It's Just You and Me, Lord*. As an international author and writing mentor, Marion worked as a cross-cultural trainer for Media Associates International, helping writers produce books for their own culture. Marion is survived by her husband, Gordon, and their five children and sixteen grandchildren.

Marlena Graves is a bylined contributor for *Hermeneutics*, *Gifted for Leadership*, and *Missio Alliance*. She is married to her favorite person in existence, Shawn Graves. Together they have three little girls. They enjoy their life together and always desire to welcome others into it. She's on staff at her church—offering and coordinating pastoral care. Her first book, *A Beautiful Disaster: Finding Hope in the Midst of Brokenness* released in June 2014.

Monica Brands is from Edgerton, Minnesota, where she grew up on a farm with seven siblings. She studied English and Theology at Trinity Christian College in Palos Heights, Illinois, and worked with children with special needs at Elim Christian Services before completing a Master of Theological Studies degree at Calvin Seminary in Grand Rapids. She treasures time with friends, family, and her awesome nieces and nephews.

Poh Fang Chia never dreamed of being in a language-related profession; chemistry was her first love. The turning point came when she received Jesus as her Savior as a fifteen-year-old and expressed to Jesus that she would like to create books that touch lives. She serves with Our Daily Bread Ministries at the Singapore office as an editor and is also a member of the Chinese editorial review committee.

Regina Franklin is a mom at heart, and she teaches God's Word with passion. She loves being in the trenches with people. Regina teaches full-time at

Westminster Schools of Augusta, Georgia, serves alongside her husband in ministry, and also freelances in writing. Married since 1995, Scott and Regina believe the greatest calling on their lives is that of pastoring their two children, Charis and Micah. After more than twenty years of youth ministry at New Hope Worship Center, Scott and Regina felt the Lord directing them to step out into church planting—a dream they had carried in their hearts since their dating years. With the support of their home church and many others, they launched inMotion Church in September 2013.

Remi Oyedele is a finance professional and freelance writer with twin passions for God's Word and children's books. Her ultimate life goal is to shape scriptural truths into stories for children and children at heart. C. S. Lewis is a major inspiration for her. Remi has an MA in Writing for Children and has completed correspondence courses with the Christian Writer's Guild and the Institute of Children's Literature. A native of Nigeria, she currently resides in Central Florida where she spends her spare time reading and blogging at www.wordzpread.com. Remi is married to David, her number one blog fan.

Roxanne Robbins, a former sports reporter, public relations specialist, and Olympic chaplain, spent a majority of her career around professional athletes and celebrities. After working with the influential and famous in Washington, DC, for several years, she left it all behind to move to East Africa.

Now based in Florida, Roxanne directs Tukutana—a Kampala, Uganda, non-profit organization she founded to provide resources and opportunities for orphaned and vulnerable children and the people who care for them. Among the poor, Roxanne says she has experienced the most fulfilling chapter of her life thus far.

Ruth O'Reilly-Smith is a qualified secondary school teacher with very little teaching experience and twenty years of radio broadcasting experience. Her brief stint on university radio got her hooked to what has become her vocation. Ruth has worked in community radio in South Africa and on FM and shortwave radio across Central and Southern Africa from the United Kingdom. She hosts a weekend radio show, broadcasting across the United Kingdom on UCB Inspirational. Ruth is married to an Englishman, and they have been blessed with twins.

Xochitl (soh-cheel) **Dixon** equips and encourages readers to embrace God's grace and grow deeper in their personal relationships with Christ and others. Serving as an author, blogger at xedixon.com, and speaker, she enjoys singing, reading, photography, motherhood, and being married to her best friend, Dr. W. Alan Dixon Sr. Her devotional book, *Waiting for God*, released in 2019.

MORE FROM
GOD HEARS HER

DEVOTIONALS TO MEET YOUR NEEDS

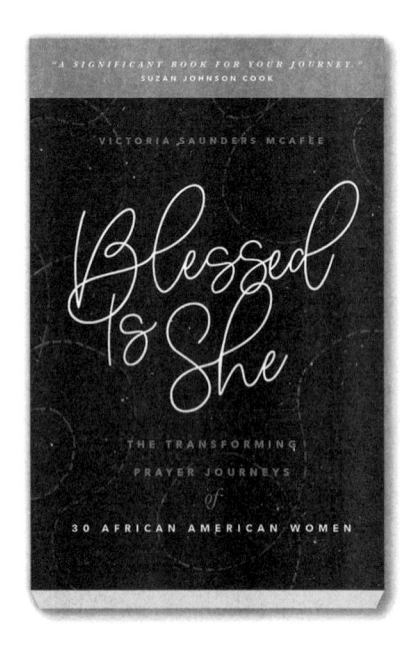

Moments of Peace for Moms
365 Daily Devotions from Our Daily Bread

Blessed Is She
The Transforming Prayer Journeys of 30 African American Women
Victoria Saunders McAfee

"A SIGNIFICANT BOOK FOR YOUR JOURNEY."
— SUZAN JOHNSON COOK

What Really Matters
Faith, Hope, Love
Our Daily Bread

If you appreciated *God Hears Her Creative Journaling Edition*, please let others know.

- Pick up another copy to give as a gift.
- Share a link to the book or mention it on social media.
- Write a review on your blog, on a bookseller's website, or at our own site (ourdailybreadpublishing.org).
- Recommend this book for your church, book club, or small group.

Contact us to share your thoughts.

godhearsher.org

@godhearsher

@godhearsher

@godhearsher

Our Daily Bread Publishing
PO Box 3566
Grand Rapids, Michigan 49501 USA

books@odb.org